My Theory of
Everything

Part 3: Life with Meaning

William Coakley

NEWMAN SPRINGS PUBLISHING
320 Broad Street
Red Bank, NJ 07701

First originally published by Newman Springs Publishing 2024

ISBN 979-8-89308-092-6 (Paperback)
ISBN 979-8-89308-093-3 (Digital)

Printed in the United States of America

This is how it was, has, and will be executed:

- 10 percent skills or smarts
- 10 percent minds or fun
- 10 percent animals or kids
- 10 percent sports
- 10 percent music
- 10 percent entertainment
- 10 percent endless connections or signs
- 10 percent intruding into the "stars" of the world
- 20 percent concentrated power of Will Coakley

10 Percent Skills or Smarts

This can include reading books, including textbooks; playing video games; working on business plans; athletes training for their games; performing in front of an audience; teaching students at all levels; and listening to people's conversations to learn how to turn that into productivity in their own lives. When reading as an adult, you learn and relearn words that might have been forgotten since your student days, and you also learn concepts that are applicable in our lives. When I read books from various fields, I often think about people suffering from brain disorders, diseases, etc. that, as a human race, we hope can be cured one day.

As I was writing about the *Supernatural* script, I also wanted to discuss this subject that I read about in a books. There are two different types of people in the world: outliers and the rest of the population. The outliers stand out from the rest and are considered the best. This group includes most famous people, and since I consider myself among the best in the world, it includes me, as well as book writers and pretty much anyone who stands out. Many people in this world are satisfied with attending grade school, going to college, working, retiring, and then dying. This is not how I view the world. I see life as an opportunity for us to become immortal beings who can achieve perfection, seeking the "full potential" theory. I believe we can make heaven and earth combine into one magical force. We also need productive demons to have a big impact on our lives because this gives us the driving force to be limitless, to have the sex drives we need, and to have the extra adrenaline rush that gives us advantages in sports, working out, and even when we're sitting in our cubicles.

Outliers are very important because they're not built like the rest of us. Everyone is not created equal, but everything will be equalized in this world. One man's pain is another man's gain, so every time someone dies, it ends up benefiting someone else in the world. As I mentioned before, if the Illuminati didn't give me proper credit, then I just walked away when I was at COMTEK. I thought it was my fraternity that was testing me, but it was actually them. They knew that Hollywood had laid the groundwork in me, so they kept track of everything that was happening in my life, including the songs I was listening to and how I was feeling, and observed who was dying and who was living depending on how my life was going. They also kept track of who it was benefiting and who was suffering because of the gains and pains people were dealing with ever since I was born.

We need outliers to help the less fortunate because they are more fortunate than other people in this world. Don't get me wrong; they work hard every single day to maintain that progress, to make sure they are doing things by the book, and to make the world a better place. But outliers feel like they need to be mentors to those who are less fortunate, especially to the kids who look up to them every single day.

I wanted to talk about this, and I think it is important to include in my book. I have been trying to become really rich for a long time, and nowadays, it's been a struggle because of the hard path that was given to me by people. The first part I want to mention is that Ray and I are selling umbrellas because of Rihanna's song called "Umbrella" and because of the one time when Busta Rhymes and his company targeted me. I was dating Ava and walking with her to dinner on her birthday night, holding the umbrella for both of us, and acting like my cousin Chris. Katy Perry said that every move I make is magic, and Miley Cyrus said that all that matters are the steps I take. After a lot of time to recollect my thoughts and with all these pictures running through my mind, I realized that we are actually selling umbrellas because of that one time I was holding the umbrella for Ava as we walked to her birthday dinner. I started realizing that I wanted to be an entrepreneur after I took a trip to Pennsylvania and was hospitalized twice, feeling like I was God, Jesus, and the devil all within the span of six months. Then I was talking to my friend Aaron, who said we should start a company from the ground up. All these positive vibes started running through my mind, and we tried to build a PowerPoint presentation for our friend Andrew Ke and his cousin. It was pretty amateur and funny for people to watch. This actually reminds me of the scene in *Pain and Gain* with Mark Wahlberg, Dwayne Johnson, and Anthony Mackie when they presented their business in front of an investor, who said that they looked like a bunch of amateurs. This is how they got this part, similar to how Aaron and I were acting when we showed a shitty but funny presentation to our friends to try to get them to join us. It was so stupid and immature.

Next, I started trying to get more people to join up with Aaron and me to start a sports agency. The way I was doing it was a lot more mature and professional than the way Aaron was doing it, and many of our friends wanted to join in. My old friend Tim Cogswell, whom I haven't talked to in a long time, was going to be a big part of it, along with other friends, such as Chris Lewis and Josh Zastudil. However, this fell through because it was really hard to keep everyone together, and Ray thought it was simpler if we did exactly what we are doing now and didn't involve so many people.

Next, Rory approached me at a party and wanted to start a company with me. He talked big business ideas with me. Then I talked to Ray on the phone, and he was like, "Yeah, everything you guys are telling me sounds great, and we should do this." I was talking to Rory about so many different ideas, but Rory was just giving me ideas. We never moved past the fact that we were just discussing ideas and not putting anything on paper. I still want to work with Rory in the future, but for the time being, I think it would be just easier if I worked with Ray.

Ray is my cousin and one of the people who have had my back since we were very young. Ray and I have been trying hard to make it big for a long time, and now we are trying to add more items to our catalog by selling baseball cards. I started taking really good care of my baseball cards and hope to get them appraised so we can make some good money off them. This is still a work in progress, but since I control my own destiny, I will get rich. And I hope that this baseball card venture can help make me some money. Ray and I did some research, and I understand the baseball card business pretty well. I am a smart person, so just a little bit of research made me understand how we can become successful by selling baseball cards. This is all I want to talk about—the business and how everything I do is special. They said that within the last year or two, baseball cards started gaining popularity again. Rory was actually the first person who brought up selling baseball cards with me. Rory is busy, and it's hard to get him motivated enough to actually start up the business. So I brought this idea up to Ray. He loved it.

This thought crossed my mind, so I wanted to get it down on paper. In one O.A.R. song, he said that he knew the future of the world was right here the entire time. As I've said in other parts of my book, I have probably been in control since 1996, not 2006. I was talking to Aaron and Ethan Stewart one day about God. Aaron was loving God back then, but I am not sure how he feels about him now. Aaron said, "God is funny, right?" and I was agreeing to all the positive things about God. I went outside to smoke a cigarette with Ethan Stewart, and I was telling him about some of the negative things I have been through in my past and said, "But I don't think that God saved my life."

Ethan Stewart then laughed and said, "After all that?"

The main reason I am bringing this up is that there was a guy in the media who went through some bullshit with his life and said that God saved his life. When I told Ethan Stewart, "But I don't think that God saved me," I was able to connect the dots and figured out that I actually saved that guy's life. I just started figuring these things out recently, and this is how I am about to get these things down on paper. I think that guy was actually watching me that day from the outside, just like how Hollywood likes to show people my positive influence and highlights to the world. I think this is one example of me not realizing that I might be a god and that I can't believe I actually saved his life. Everything I do is very powerful, and when I told Dr. O'Connor about the one guy whom Hollywood actually made a character about that I ran into at Silver Diner when I said, "I don't fuck with gay shit" (meaning that I am Jesus, which means "I can't fuck with you now"), he wanted to talk to me about God and all

4

that. I know the meaning of life since the world's been returning, but I don't know the Bible that well. I could explain all these things to people. I am bringing this up about the guy I ran into at Silver Diner because Jack told me that I don't fuck with two things, and one of those things is the devil. I thought I was an atheist until I realized I was a god, just like what Watsky said in his song, but that guy was watching me when I was walking to Giant one day.

Jack and all the other people in my life who disrespect me walk into traps, and people from the outside world start dying. It just makes me a stronger person. Hollywood and the CIA purposely do these things for me because they want me to connect to everyone in the world with my personality traits and all the great things I am doing for the world, so they put me in the spotlight for my positive highlights. If people don't believe in me, then they can live without knowing that a higher power named Will Coakley (me) is on call 24-7 to help solve their problems. We are looking for a solution to every single person's problems in the world. I had to conquer everything so that we can solve every single person's problems in the world, no matter what your problems are. This will all take place once karma catches up.

I know that back when I was twenty-four or twenty-five years old, I was going on all these false missions looking for answers, and it was part of the devilish games that were being played with me. Hollywood was pretty convinced that Jack had to pay the ultimate price because Jesus ended up dying because of Judas's sins. My mom said that Jesus ended up forgiving everyone, including Judas, when he was alive the first time. I know that I said I am not a forgiving god, but I actually can forgive people pretty easily. So once I am fixed up, I will forgive Jack. When I make my billions and can help people with monetary ways instead of with my powers, I can make an impact on the world in those ways.

I thought this was a good topic to discuss in my book as well. Eric Sanchez once told me there would never be another Albert Einstein in the world. Well, I have news for Sanchez: I am the Albert Einstein of the new world. I know they talked about how important it is that we manage our time wisely, and Albert Einstein spoke extensively about time during his lifetime. I have connected the whole world to the clocks on our walls since I was going through all those crazy tests in survival mode back two or three years ago. I was also reciting Bible verses while undergoing these tests. I mentioned that if the clock stops at a certain point during athletic games, then it's connected to a Bible verse. When it comes to the time on the clocks, we will "kill time" and be forever young, thanks to my powers. Also, I can assist people throughout the day by using time as a value in other people's worlds. For example, when the clock hits forty-seven, every single time, it helps Mark Wahlberg because he is the forty-seventh best person in the world. When the clock hits forty, every single time, it aids Ronda Rousey because she is the fortieth best person in the world. Another example is when the clock hits twenty-five because, if God were alive right now, he wouldn't age past the age of twenty-five, and that could assist as many as a million people in the world who are around that age every time the clock hits twenty-five. I come alive at nighttime ever since those tests, and I have to wake up every night around two or three because of the adrenaline rush from all the positive things I do for people every day. When the clock hits thirty-six, every single time, it helps manage our time throughout the day and for the rest of our lives. I know we are going to be here forever, but it helps people within our generation and our parents' generation because they can regain their youthful bodies. We can also use this as a solution for the human race for age management.

I thought this was also cool to include in my book. Jesus, when he was alive the first time, died at the age of thirty-three. Nas mentioned this in one of his songs back in 2001, and I read about it in a book. The book mentioned that God said Jesus had accomplished all the things he needed to by the time he was thirty-three, so then he was supposed to sacrifice himself for the greater good. I talked to my real creator about it, and he said Jesus was a carpenter until he was thirty and then started saving lives when God gave him permission to. Then he was supposed to sacrifice himself. When I read about that in the book, I was scared I wouldn't make it to my thirty-fourth birthday unless people saved me. The girl knew exactly what she was doing when she told me about that in her book, and Hollywood knew exactly what they were doing when they wanted me to listen to that part in Nas's song. It is pretty ironic because my thirtieth birthday was a turning point for my lonely nights when everyone started buying into my products about me being the devil. However, the turning point was actually because I was a religious figure and not the devil. I didn't know too much about the world when I was dating Ava and before professional athletes and Hollywood made my life too hard so that I could work with this box full of tricks and save the world. Before my thirtieth birthday, I was useless, but I actually wasn't completely useless because I was still helping people out. I was more successful at helping people out, though, after my thirtieth birthday.

People were praying for me, and I was helping out every single one of those people. People were fixing me all across the world, and I was returning the favor for every single one of those people. They released a lot of songs suggesting I was either God or Jesus. Atmosphere mentioned in his last album that he had to keep his songs simple, stating he is thanking God, alive only if I am God. If my real creator is God, then he is still thanking Jesus. He said this because he was like, "Fuck the devil's progress" when all the athletes were embracing sin. Then he had to keep the songs simple. Back in 2008 or 2010, he said, "Nobody befriends the beast" when I was going through all those hellish things back then. However, Atmosphere was the first artist I could relate to who wrote an apocalyptic song and mentioned my name in that song. He wrote that song in 2012 after I took a trip to Pennsylvania.

On that trip, I learned there is a big difference between heaven and hell. Jack is the one who is going to fall further than I am. However, Avery was the guy who tried to beat me back in the day and then started facing karma and eventually stopped. His fake-ass empire stopped too once they all started facing karma in bad ways when I started breaking free from the curses they put on me. Anyway, I wanted to talk about this, and the main reason was that my transgression was when I found Christ, not because I was the devil. The timeline of my life in the real world is similar to when Jesus was alive for the first time, except this time we are going to make this life ever-

7

lasting so that we can all become one big family and finish exactly what Mr. Drewer and company wanted to accomplish back when I first moved to Virginia from New York.

Fort Minor played an essential role in my future and past and in how I was able to create this new world and how so many people were buying into my products. He was pissed that he couldn't produce a second album because of the politics in Hollywood, and when he produced his second song, he made it clear that we never really knew how it would all unfold and that if you disrespect me, then "fuck them."

Anyway, I wanted to talk about how important his songs are. In one song, he mentioned that I was on the wrong plane and how the devil's got a new place to play, and you can hear my voice in your head when nobody is around. This part in this song is how they came out with the singing show called *The Voice*. It doesn't sound too complicated to me in understanding how they came up with this title. Many people became famous, and the show earned a lot of respect worldwide because of the troubles I was going through and all the hardships and how I was able to overcome these obstacles. They came out with this show with the superstars of the world and singers who would choose who would win every single year.

Another part of this Fort Minor song I wanted to mention was when he said that every day was the same shade of grey. Anyway, this is how they came up with the title Grey's Anatomy. It might have been a way for Hollywood to shut him down, but he was still with his band and set many new standards in this world, leading to the creation of this fantastic show *Grey's Anatomy*, which is on its seventeenth season now.

I know that people think this show doesn't accurately depict 100 percent of what's going on in the real world. Those would be the asshole critics, but so many people like this show. Every single time they showed a life being saved on this show was when I was able to help those people out in the real world because of this show. Unfortunately, not everyone can be saved because this is just how life works. However, at some point, there will be no more sick children in this world, and this will be the major move we are all looking forward to in the future, which is why Lady Gaga put that part in one of her songs. I actually want to download that song in the future, but in the meantime, I can listen to it on Pandora. The name Pandora in *Avatar* was based on all the problems and military issues that were going on in this world and the military lives I was going to save every time I listened to songs on Pandora Radio.

I wanted to add this part to this section because I think it's funny, and people in Hollywood think it's funny. When I work out, I am on another level with the anxiety meds I take in the morning, my pre-workout, and the water I am drinking. I sometimes go into character mode and become kind of a tough guy and a thug, so sometimes when I work out, I act like those two gay guys from *Shameless*. And I know that Emmy Rossum and other people from Hollywood were laughing when I went into those mindsets. The other script was *Supernatural*'s, which I talk a lot about in the section below and, I am pretty sure, in my second book, but I act like one brother, who is supposed to be Avery. He gets really animated when he is killing demons and the enemy in this world. I love working out in my home and in my basement, where nobody is judging me, and I obviously can't work out like that in a gym. But I have the time and space to act the way I am in the basement. I know that at some point, I will step back between the lines and won't have to worry about people judging me anymore, but I want to mention this part in my book.

This is actually something really important that I should probably write about. If Jesus were alive right now, he could punish anyone who played him and even put them on their deathbeds if they played him. When I was going through all those tests in 2012 and 2013, Kid Cudi came out with this song that goes, "You all were playing him, and now you know." There was also another artist, Gnash, who came out with a song that goes, "You wish you hadn't played me now." I was going through hell and went through the apocalypse twice, and this didn't go without punishment for those who thought they were Jesus when I was the one going through all this bullshit. I didn't get mad at all when people thought they were Jesus, but they were definitely paying a price afterward. Actually, when I was in the movie theaters and Rebel Wilson was in a movie, one of the lines in the movie was "You guys wish you hadn't played me," and two guys coughed right after she said that line. These two guys are good with me, but they shouldn't have acted like they were Jesus. Hollywood wanted to make examples out of these two guys, and I guess they figured out it was because of me.

There were other people in the world who started dying because they thought they were Jesus. Priena, Cogswell's wife, showed him, me, and another girl I saw for, like, three weeks, Soraya, a video of a guy who got murdered because he thought he was Jesus. A homeless guy saw the guy get killed and spoke humorously about the incident to the media. Although the video was shown on YouTube, I don't think it was shown on the actual news. Another example is Kanye West, who claimed he was Jesus in his songs and didn't care what people thought. He actually had a near-death experience, and I pretended as if I wasn't the promised-land dude and that his near-death experience wasn't because of me. I think it was actually because of Avery and the Jesus karma that nobody wants to face. At least, I don't care if I am the promised-land dude. I tell people that if they are going through fear, they should not always assume it's demons. It could also be statues or Jesus, and they might be facing Jesus karma. This Jesus karma isn't coming from me; it is coming from Avery. It is pretty clear that when I was younger, and then again around twenty-four or twenty-five, Avery tried to beat me, and I started taking control. He was facing a lot of God karma for the things he did to me and for trying to beat me twice. Honestly, Kid Cudi said that Jack is mean, but I think Avery is equally mean with his Jesus bullshit and needs to cut the bullshit. Hollywood should never have respected him for all the crap that he did to try to beat me.

Thankfully, Hollywood, the CIA, and the 1 percent had my best interests at heart, and every time Avery and the Mafia attacked me, they helped me out. Avery is not welcome in Hollywood, and they even released a Flobots song, which I talk about in this book or my previous book, as an early warning for him to stay the fuck away from Hollywood. I was listening to this song back in school when I was hanging out with my friends Julian, Eric Sanchez, and Alex Shalak. Avery was not welcomed in Hollywood, yet he still tried to go. He forgot about all the shit he did to me when we started hanging out, but I don't trust him to be a good friend. I have better friends in this world than him, and I don't think my sister likes him; he is kind of like a virus that entered my life. I don't want anybody else in Hollywood to accept him as part of my group because it is really clear to me that he tried to beat me twice and faced serious karma for it both times. He might or might not die when this is all over, but Hollywood said it was a betrayal of trust with Jack. However, it was also a betrayal of trust with Avery because we cannot wait until I am thirty-eight for this to all be over. We must put ourselves before Jesus. This has to end by the time I am thirty-six at the latest because we are all getting older, and honestly, I shouldn't be as old as I am right now.

I was hanging out with Rory one day, and people were watching the highlights of my life. He asked me, "Were you and Ava dealing with bipolar disorder?"

I replied that neither of us was bipolar because I had talked to people who actually know me in this world, and nobody thought I was crazy. I didn't think too much about his comment at the time, but it actually ended up as a worldwide issue that superstars and Hollywood started to talk about. People such as Katy Perry, Lady Gaga, Halsey, and Kevin Love started talking about their issues. Athletes like Dontrelle Willis and Rick Ankiel started publicizing their struggles with anxiety and depression while playing sports. I thought this was all interesting because I fell into this rut by mistake, and I have been through so fucking much and regret every day that this bullshit ever happened to me.

I don't blame Rory for saying this to me; I think it was actually a blessing in disguise, and these kids, and even adults, can relate to the superstars of the world who are going through similar things. These superstars are just people who are outliers and better at certain things than the rest of the population. I have kind of risen above people in the middle class, so I am pretty much an outlier as well. Lady Gaga even starred in a movie, *A Star Is Born*, where the male protagonist deals with mental issues the entire time and ends up killing himself because he couldn't deal with the disrespect he was given. I have thought about suicide so much because of all this crap and fear that I have been going through; and I need to rely on outside help because nobody in my life, except for maybe one person, can help me get through this. Anyways, this was something I wanted to write about in my book.

I wanted to add this part to my book: the Hollywood awards for TV shows. I wanted to talk about Jimmy Kimmel and the ideas they got for the award show. Before the awards were announced, they got the idea of burning fire and then the words they said after that from the *Supernatural* script. They would do that to all the vengeful and bad spirits to make sure that people's lives were saved. Another part of the *Supernatural* script they incorporated into the award show was Jimmy Kimmel walking down the aisle with cabinets on both sides to announce the winners. They got this idea because, in the *Supernatural* show, this is what death looked like. The character Death would have cabinets full of every single person in this world, and when their time was up. It was crazy how they performed in Hollywood and got all these ideas from *Supernatural*.

Another thing I wanted to mention about Jimmy Kimmel was that he was making examples out of haters with his speeches, including Patrick Mahomes. When Tony Dungy was talking about Mahomes and said that his play had a lot more to do with the money he was making and that money didn't matter to him at all, I said to my real creator after Dungy commented that it had a lot to do with money because he just got fucking $500 million in the offseason. I guess Hollywood agreed with my comment, and Jimmy Kimmel made an example out of Mahomes in the award show. Another example he made was of someone who played Candy Crush too much, and he said, "Stop playing that Goddamn game because you are screwing with people with your game, and it is very obnoxious." Jimmy Kimmel wasn't shy about his comment, and the person he was talking about knew exactly who Jimmy was talking about. And he cut the bullshit. I made notes of all the shows that were nominated and the shows that won so that I can watch those shows and make more notes in my document and my book about how they relate to my life.

I wanted to write about this competition and the full potential theory that everyone used to talk about. It started when Karmin wrote her song "You Can Kiss My Oh My God" because I was paying a price for being God. I was running fast in my court and in my basement, and I was on some kind of drug and on another level. Unfortunately, Hollywood knew I was going to be sent to the hospital against my will, and some of the people who sent me to the hospital paid the ultimate price and died because of it. The competition has two sides: one is the sinners, which is Jack's team, and the heathen team, which is also Jack's team. The good side is heaven, and this is my side. I made a list of about sixty thousand people and stopped making that list about a year ago because I was sick of other people having a say and power in this world when they didn't deserve it and when their opinions on matters were wrong. I was getting bad advice from people and didn't want to hear people talk because most people are built with greed and don't understand or know the ins and outs of life the way I do. Maybe it is because I got smarter with all these tests that I was taking, but if people disrespect me or if people are wrong, then they or someone who made them say it will face karma. Anyway, I always win in the end, and Jack will lose every bit of say he ever had in this world because I am so sick of that Goddamn asshole interfering in my everyday life activities. Like it or not, he is fucking mean, and I am sick of him getting in my way. I made the list as even as possible, and every single person on that list gives more to society, has had it tougher, and has a bigger heart than the rest of the people in the world.

10 Percent Minds or Fun

I like to solve other people's problems during my free time, and I thought I should write about this. When I started the Forever Young movement, many people wanted to jump on ship, but I wasn't really active on Facebook and wasn't really hanging out with people, although I was seeing my therapist often. She once told me, "As long as you have room for two more," referring to her daughter and herself. I then came back to another therapy session and expressed my frustration to Dr. O'Connor, saying, "Nobody is on board with me. You know, this world is so unpredictable, and everyone is going against the positive vibes that I am sending out to the world."

She was very serious and adamant, responding, "Will, I'm on board with you!"

Her daughter ended up getting sick one day, and while I was working with my tricks inside my bedroom, her daughter got better.

I went back to therapy another time, and Dr. O'Connor was like, "Thank God that my daughter is okay now."

I said to her I was sick of people thanking God and didn't want anyone doing so in my presence anymore. I wanted to tell her it was my doing, but I didn't know how.

I look at all the signs in my world and what people are still telling me, and maybe everything wrong in my life really had nothing to do with anything up there. Perhaps it was people's faults that I was stuck as deep as I was, and karma will catch up with me. And we will all be forever young. Of course, everyone has their choices, but I still think that many people want to be here forever. We all turn to dust in the afterlife, which I don't think is cool. I really appreciate everyone's help, but maybe I shouldn't have been stuck as deep as I was to begin with.

I started seeing my therapist once a week after 2012 and was sent to the hospital twice, nearly a third time, because of the spaceman. You can kiss my oh my god. Those incidents happened quickly, and Avery was living here when both those things happened. I think many people heard funny noises in their heads when I was sent to the hospital those times, and this is when outsiders started to join in with everything I was doing. For instance, there was a time Aaron was acting sketchy with one of our other friends, Skinner. He looked me in the eyes, thanked God, then started showing off. I thought he was mocking me, but he was actually saying that in appreciation for my existence on this planet. A switch inside me turned on, and my feet were healed, allowing me to run to the basket and make a layup pretty much as fast as I have ever done in my entire life.

When I started missing my baskets, Aaron was like, "It's because Will's not trying. He would usually make those shots." He was saying that because the Almighty is the best of the best in this world and should be perfect at everything. Aaron was saying this as a compliment for me being God and missing my basketball shots.

Afterward, I ran into our friend Skinner, who was working at Red Robin. He was talking about Lou Ferrigno, the Hulk, and referred to him as the ageless one. He said it with a serious face because we are all getting older, and he is a little bit older than Aaron and me. He also suggested that I could make time stop so that we could be forever young. Again, he was assuming that I was God and that everything is possible with the power of God.

I also wanted to talk about this. Sanchez is my *Star Wars* buddy. During the CIA and KGB conspiracy on St. Patrick's Day in 2010, when all my friends went to the bar and I was home by myself in Fair Lakes watching *Star Wars*, I was so fucking scared. That was the craziest shit you could possibly imagine. They were reflecting into the lights in the police car I was in, and Aaron and Niket got busted for marijuana. I ended up apologizing to Aaron and felt bad for Niket. However, I was scared out of my fucking mind. I didn't know what the fuck was going on and ended up working at COMTEK for two and a half years, during most of which I was so paranoid and scared of what these evil assholes were doing to me. Nevertheless, when it comes to Sanchez, I guided him to move to Boston and followed his journey through his time on Facebook. Afterward, I ended up hanging out with him, and he was like, "Maybe God was guiding me not to watch the Boston teams when they weren't playing good throughout, like, a two-year span."

We kept on talking, touching on topics like gravity and how it affects all of our lives, when he was like, "We will see evidence of God in our lifetime."

I thought he was talking about my real creator or somebody above, but he was actually talking about me.

I was like, "Why can't you just do it on your own?"

He didn't respond after that. This is really biblical and important because these are just some stories I can tell about the people I have helped throughout my time of self-reflection.

Selena Gomez then came out with a song called "It Ain't Me." In this song, she talks about how my soulmate and I start seeing eye to eye and that I am going to leave behind the worst of us. She was talking about my real creator, and they even covered this in the movie *Deliver Us from Evil*, which is a scary movie. In one particular reality show, they kept on saying, "Deliver us from Evil" and "Thank you, Lord Jesus." My high school friend Lindsay Alexander posted on Facebook that it's God's creation and that God would provide. She was wrong and they were right because they saw what was going on with me and knew something was wrong. They sort of work with Hollywood, so they were thanking me for their existence on this planet, not God.

I haven't talked about this person much, but I want to now. His name is Jacob Stewart, and he has been my closest friend from New York since we were three years old. My family, his family, and other families would do everything together during our time in New York. We would play roller hockey outside our houses with our other friends, but nobody was closer to me than Jacob was. He has always been my best friend and is still one of my closest friends. I would do anything for him. Unfortunately, his real creator passed away from cancer, and he was like a second real creator to me. To add to it, he passed away on my birthday, which was terrible. We would visit each other all the time when we were growing up in other states. I was so pissed that my real creator took a job in Virginia because I was one of the most popular kids in East Meadow and had so many fucking friends. It took me a while, but I realized there was a reason I moved to Virginia. It was because this is where the CIA headquarters are. Whenever Hollywood incorporates positive aspects about the CIA in their scripts and there is someone in the world helping them out, they are talking about me. It doesn't matter if the actor is Tom Cruise in the *Mission: Impossible* movies or somebody else in other movies; they are talking about the positive relationship I have developed with the CIA. They are the reason I am living in Virginia, and I have formed so many positive relationships with so many people here.

I don't miss New York at all. Now that I am more mature, I realize I was supposed to meet every single person I have met in Virginia. However, Jacob has always been my closest friend, and we will be close to each other forever. I think about him all the time and how much he means to me, as do his family and especially his younger brother Dean, who means the world to me. I have grown really close to Dean; we go to sporting events together and keep in touch throughout the year to make sure everything is good with everybody in our lives and that all our families are healthy. However, like I said, their real creator died of cancer, and there is no cure for the type of cancer he had. I am actually conquering everything so that certain people in the world can come up with a solution for the human race. I sort of became a science experiment, developing symptoms similar to what Max was dealing with, but I was able to overcome them. I probably shouldn't know these things or have gone through them because it was hell. But then people saved me from the devil's wrath, and I am getting back to normal now. I can start living my life again like I used to. However, now that I am older and more mature, I realize that I don't need alcohol to be happy. I am all about living healthier. I know I am addicted to nicotine, but alcohol isn't all that healthy for you either; it kills your brain cells and destroys your liver. This is all I am going to write about for the time being.

I thought this was good to put in my book. When everyone was saying that we are delivered from evil and thanking Lord Jesus, my high school friend Lindsay Alexander posted on Facebook, "God's creation." She said, "God will provide, praying works." I figured out why she said this. When I was in my home, back when I was dating Ava, I was exercising my concentrated power of Will, and Lindsay's name popped into my memory. I can't remember what else I was doing that day, but I was pretty much controlling Mother Nature and thought Lindsay was watching me. However, she believed her prayers were being answered by God. I don't know if I am God, but her prayers were being answered by me. I followed up on her birthdays and tried to wish her a happy birthday every time I saw it on Facebook, making sure she was doing okay. Once, I saw on her feed that her back was hurting, but I hope her back is doing better now.

They came out with the script for *Deliver Us from Evil*, and the Black community on TV was saying, "Thank you, Lord Jesus," and "Deliver us from evil" because of the events happening when I was hanging out with Cogswell and Priena, and I was about to start dating their friend Soraya. I was smoking a bowl with their friend Rafael, who is named after a figure from the Bible, and then I had all these thoughts running through my head. I pretty much turned into Charles Xavier every time I smoked weed after my mind started getting really corrupted, and people everywhere could hear my thoughts, whether they were positive or negative. This one time was really fucking scary. I was smoking this bowl with Cogswell and Priena's friend Rafael and thought I was going to fucking die because of these thoughts running through my head: *This is what evil people do, but we don't hurt anybody.* Some serious bad things were going through my mind. I was happy when the high wore off, and I was going back to normal. It took me a long time to finally stop smoking pot, but every time I did, I would start living in this type of fear that almost nobody in the world ever experiences. After I grew up and figured out that I could be happy without smoking weed, I never smoked again. I also stopped drinking alcohol and using dip because I figured out that I could be happy without these two things as well. The main reason I wanted to write about this was that Lindsay was convinced that praying worked and that it was God's creation, even though it was me answering her prayers. Maybe I am God, or maybe

I am not. But I have helped out billions of people all over the place because of my concentrated power of Will.

I also thought this would be good to add to my book. My grandma is convinced that my grandpa's spirits are helping her and guiding her to live as long as she is expected to and that God is guiding her in that direction. I put these thoughts in my grandma's head, knowing she would be very happy because I know how to please anyone in this world, whether they are old people, young people, my future soulmate, my friends, or people abroad who need my help. When I wished my grandma a happy birthday this year, in 2020, she said on the phone that the noises from the people around her were making her happier, and she was happy that God led her to talk to me on the phone. What she does or does not realize is that I implanted these voices inside her head with my supernatural abilities so that she can live with happiness, knowing that my grandpa is helping her out from the afterlife, even when she sees him in her dreams. My grandma has always been there for me on my birthday, so I figured I would call her, just like I did the last two years, and wish her a happy birthday. I thought my grandpa was immortal when I was younger and more naive, and I thought my mom was playing tricks on me when he passed away.

I was still going through the side effects of a trip I took to Pennsylvania and was distinguishing the difference between heaven and hell. Let me tell you, there is a big difference. The demons that I have experienced in my life, and continue to experience, are very mean and disturbing. I also don't know who keeps making my life a living hell, but I wouldn't wish this on my worst enemy. I don't know how I started developing enemies, but most of the positive work I do is from my house. I can still help people when I leave my house. I am looking forward to the day when I don't deal with any more demon problems and when I can completely break free from the wrath of society and eventually make it to Hollywood. Then people won't be searching for a God anymore because he is talking to everyone on TV. This all, obviously, has to be done with perfect timing and when the world is in the shape it needs to be so that everyone who made me the perfect person that I am going to be and am starting to be can be ready for these changes to be made. I have this vision, and I can bring all these things to life because I am working with this solution pit. In the matter of a day, I can solve as many as a million people's problems in the world. I think big picture a lot, and the examples I have given in the first three books I have written show the world that God is great all the time. And if I am Jesus, then the resurrection from the dead has been a successful one because everyone who believes in him has received the benefits of being a believer. He has even turned nonbelievers into believing in him because of all of his positive supernatural abilities. Those who saw the past videos of him suffering with demon problems and when he was breaking free from the wrath of society have even started to believe that a higher power exists because he can help out those who pray and those who don't pray. This is what our supernatural God does, and he is always there to help people, having pretty much quit his day job to help out those in need and in times of struggle so that he can help out the greedy and the poor at the same time. He doesn't judge people, no matter what their situation is on this planet, and he can provide the weak with goods, just like they did in *The Hunger Games*. He can also provide the wealthy with goods so that they can continue to be happy.

This came to my mind, so I wanted to talk about it. I have made some serious lifestyle changes. One of them is fitness, another is quitting alcohol, and the last is quitting dip. Let me talk about my fitness. I listen to people when they talk and heed the advice they give me. I am currently working out about six days a week, engaging in a lot of cardio and strength training. I am in the best shape of my life at the age of thirty-four. I know that age is still just a number, but I am trying to say that it is never too late to try to be a better person and make positive changes that can impact you and the people around you in a better manner. I work out with four different workouts, rotating through four days in a row. The first day I do chest and triceps. I use this machine that my real creator bought me for both muscles and then I go do dumbbells and free weights. I used to lift heavier weights but now understand that overworking can lead your body to self-destruct at an earlier age, so I've lowered the weight but still work out really hard. With the free weights, I do a regular bench press, an incline, and alternating arms on the floor. When I go do triceps, I do the one where I'm lying down on the bench doing something like skull crushers, and I also do the one where I am sitting on the bench and lifting the weight over my shoulders. These two exercises, I do with the bar. For the last workout with triceps, I lie on the bench and do triceps extensions with the dumbbells.

Every single time I work out, I use *Men's Journal* magazine and do exercises from there. The first one I do is for my core muscles. I do five exercises that I find in that magazine to strengthen my core. The next three exercises involve me using the medicine ball; and these strengthen my core, my agility, and my lower body. The next few exercises I do, I use the bar that people use for bench presses; and these exercises strengthen my back, my shoulders, and my lower body. I also add push-ups every single time I work out. I do five different pushups. I do three sets of ten for five different exercises. The first one is a regular pushup, the second one is a negative pushup, the third one is a decline pushup, and the fourth and fifth ones strengthen my chest. I feel tired but also very strong every time I finish my workouts. I also do a shitload of core exercises every single time I work out. I do planks for a minute for my main core muscles and for my sides. I also do like ten other ones to strengthen my core.

The next day, I'll work on back and biceps. I use the machine my real creator bought me for these two muscle groups and also add two core exercises on the machine. I do the one exercise where the bar is over your head, and you lift it to your upper back to strengthen it. I also do the exercise where you lift handles to your middle back and the one where you lift from the bottom to your middle back. With these three exercises, I figure I cover most of, if not all, my back muscles. For my biceps, I do curls with the bar and another exercise where you have the chair on an incline and lift with your arms. I feel really strong after I am done with my machine workout for the day. After this, I go to my free weights and start with my back. I also add one shoulder exercise because my back has already been worked enough. I start with the free-weight exercise where you bend over and lift the free weights up to target your middle back. Next, I use the bar and lift it the same exact way, but this one makes my back really strong. The next one I do is the full shoulder exercise. I forget what it's called, but I lift the bar to my shoulders and then over my head. I do it with a light weight of sixty-five pounds so that I am not overworking my muscles, and I do each of these exercises three times.

For my biceps, I start off with regular biceps curls, and I only do forty-five pounds even though I could do more. To avoid overworking my muscles, I stick to forty-five pounds. Next, I do an incline biceps curl and follow that up with a hammer curl. For the hammer curl, I use twenty-five pounds. After I complete all these exercises, I figure that's enough for the day. Then I do the workouts from *Men's Journal* and all the core-muscle-group exercises.

On the third day, I work my legs and shoulders. For my legs, I start on the machine and do squats, calf raises, and lunges. These three exercises get me off to a solid start for the day. After this, I do three exercises for my shoulders: shoulder raises, the one where you lift the bar over your head, and the one where you lift the bar from the ground to just below your head. After I am done with this, I've covered enough for the machine part of this day's workout. Then I move to free weights. I do three shoulder exercises: shrugs, lateral raises, and the one where you lift the bar over your head. These three exercises give me enough strength to cover all my shoulders for the day. For legs, I do squats, lunges, and the exercise where you strengthen your hamstrings. This one is the hardest, but it's so effective because my legs have gotten really strong as I keep pushing myself to workout as hard as I am in these workouts. I follow all this up with the workouts from *Men's Journal* and the workouts for my core muscles.

On the fourth day (and I know a lot of people don't do these exercises, but I find them very effective), I use the rope and the kettlebell and follow this up with my core and the workouts I find in *Men's Journal*. With the kettlebell and the rope, it is more of a full–body-workout day. I get tired doing these exercises, but they work my muscles real nice, and I am very satisfied.

For my cardio, I once talked to my therapist, and she said that she does a sixty-minute walk every day. This equates to about three miles. Ever since she told me this, I started doing sixty-minute walks on my treadmill, and it is exactly 2.99 miles, which is pretty much three miles. I like to look at the treadmill and see what signs connect when I am doing these workouts. For instance, forty-four connects with thirty-three, and eighty-eight connects with sixty-six. These are mile markers I like to use. When the treadmill hits twenty-five, every single time, people think the Lord moves in mysterious ways because it is important that I hit these marks every single time to achieve my purpose and my destiny on this planet and help others lose weight and get their own personal bodies into better shape. I also add two other cardio workouts throughout my day. I don't do these every single time, but I try to add them to my workouts. The first one is a walking cardio. I use this video that came into my inbox one day, and it helps me lose fat. It is a twenty-five-minute workout, and now that faith has solved my feet problems, I don't have problems moving around. The other one is a bit harder, and it's a faster-paced cardio. The girl who made this video said that if you do this for four weeks straight, you can lose so much body fat. Well, I have been doing this workout for a long time now, and you can tell by looking at my muscle mass in comparison to my body fat that these workouts and cardio exercises are really working out very well for me. This is all I want to talk about for my workouts for the time being, but I thought it was important to put into my book.

10 Percent Animals or Kids

10 Percent Sports

This is the first time I am adding to the sports section in this book because of the coronavirus, but I wanted to talk about the extension that Christian McCaffrey got. I put my TV channel on in my upstairs bedroom at volume 16, and a lot of guys in the NFL are getting $16 million contracts because *we own the technology now*. He received a four-year, $64 million contract extension. The Carolina Panthers have agreed to a four-year, $64 million extension with star running back Christian McCaffrey, according to ESPN's Adam Schefter and NFL Network's Ian Rapoport. McCaffrey ran for 1,387 yards and 15 touchdowns while catching 116 passes for 1,005 yards and four scores in 2019. He was on my fantasy football team last year and led my team into the playoffs until Dalvin Cook got hurt. Those two running backs carried my team, and it is important to remember that injuries are not inevitable. He will live at least two of these years injury-free with the rest of the NFL players. Hollywood knows there is nothing left to fix in the world because of me, so they won't worry about injuries anymore. And the replacement players can probably create another league if they need to. Ever since this player was in college, I always thought he was a superstar and would be an impact player in the NFL. There are so many people in this world trying to take the credit away from what I am doing for the world, and frankly, I am fucking sick of it. I have this vision, and I am ahead of my time.

I don't see anyone else doing these positive things in the world, and when Avery entered my life and the people thought Avery was a good person (he was also saying certain things about my life, as if he was the same person as me), I looked at it as stolen paradise. Next, he comes into my house and says that he has these superhuman abilities. *He does not.* I am the only one that was going through apocalyptic things, and he deserves the punishment he is getting. When a voice came into my house and it said nobody befriends the beast to pay rent and make ends meet because of that artist Atmosphere, Avery said, "Well, I am still going to be friends with you." The motherfucker didn't have any friends at the time, and now I am the only way he will ever have a life ever again. It is so stupid because everything in my life was going fine until Avery entered it in 2012, and then all this crazy, fucked-up shit started happening to me. It must have been the people he was working with and those evil empires.

As I was talking about the evil empires, Hank Steinbrenner, the heir to the Yankees, has died at sixty-three. After the death of their father, George, in 2010, he and his brother, Hal, took over one of the richest and most storied franchises in sports history. Hank Steinbrenner, who, along with his brother Hal, inherited the Yankees—one of the most storied and lucrative franchises in sports history—after the death of their father, George, in 2010, died on Tuesday at his home in Clearwater, Florida, at the age of sixty-three. A co-owner and the eldest of the two Steinbrenner sons, Hank Steinbrenner had been in poor health in recent years. His death was confirmed in a statement from the Yankees. Hal Steinbrenner is the Yankees' managing general partner and the final authority on the team's decisions. However, Hank was also a general partner and shared in the responsibilities of overseeing and directing the strategies of the Yankees both on and off the field. He served on the board of the YES Network, which broadcasts Yankees games, and sponsored a summer youth baseball program called Hank's Yanks that has sent dozens of players to college or professional baseball. "He was introduced to the Yankees organization at a very young age, and his love for sports and competition continued to burn brightly throughout his life," the Steinbrenner family said in a statement. Hank was fifteen years old when his father bought the Yankees in 1973. He briefly worked in the team's front office in the mid-1980s as an apprentice, of sorts, to the team's general managers. However, he found his passion in breeding, raising, and racing horses at the family farm in Florida and was a longtime member of the board of the Ocala Breeders' Sales Company. More recently, Mr. Steinbrenner became deeply involved in auto racing with his son, George Michael Steinbrenner IV. His team, Harding Steinbrenner Racing, competed on the IndyCar circuit last year with George Michael, then 22, as the youngest team owner in IndyCar history.

I wanted to talk about this because it ran through my mind. When I was doing my fantasy football draft a few years ago (and they came out with some of this in the script written for *Mr. Robot*), I was controlling who everyone was picking in two of my leagues. In one league, I ended up picking two guys with the last name Elliott, mirroring the last name in the script for *Mr. Robot*. The script, which I had already written about, involved individuals acting as gods without anyone's permission and centered around hacking and technology. I know how to control things with my mind and technology, especially when I am trying to make things right in this world. Consequently, I ended up winning in one of the leagues, and Andy won in the other league. I kept telling Andy to rely on me, and he kept winning every single week. Sometimes I like to think about myself when I am not trying to solve other people's issues in the world. Thinking about *Mr. Robot* and how they named the character Elliott in this script, I ended up drafting two guys with the last name Elliott. One of the guys I drafted was Ezekiel Elliott. The other was a kicker with the last name Elliott. Actually, when one of the Wayans brothers from Hollywood was on ESPN, he said that I deserved to win that award because I am dealing with this shit in real life. I asked my therapist if it was dumb to blame everything on the CIA, so the way they were able to connect with fans with their first advertisements was by portraying an average-day motherfucker who thought he blamed everything on guys who acted like they were God without anyone's permission. I thought this was important to write about in the sports section, mentioning the drafts I do with fantasy.

I wanted to talk about this story because I told my therapist that these six Colorado Avalanche players said they would help me overcome my fears of the coronavirus after I helped them out. The headline reads, "Avalanche Players with Coronavirus Are Feeling Better, Says Coach."

C oach Jared Bednar says the three Colorado Avalanche players who tested positive for the coronavirus are feeling better. In a teleconference call Thursday, Bednar said the players adhered to the guidelines and self-isolated. "As far as I know, they're all doing good and back with their families," Bednar said. "Those guys are lucky and were lucky there wasn't anything too serious with their symptoms. They were able to come through it without any major complications."

Jim Edmonds Gets Stitches After Losing "Fight" with His Shower Door

Accidents happen! Jim Edmonds received stitches on his face after mistakenly banging his head into his glass shower door.

Edmonds, 49, shared a photo on his Instagram Stories on Wednesday, April 8, that featured a bloody scar surrounding his eye. "Hasn't been a great 2020 yet! Got in a fight with a glass shower door," the retired MLB player wrote, sharing a zoomed-in version of the scar in a post that followed. "It was open when it wasn't supposed to be. In the dark." Edmonds then shared a third snap of the scar, which appeared to be improved after he paid a visit to the hospital and received stitches for it. "Ouch. I'm already ugly enough," he joked. "Just 12 more stiches for this body." The former St. Louis Cardinals athlete's injury comes days after he confirmed that he tested positive for the novel coronavirus. He first revealed his condition in an Instagram Stories update on April 1, noting that he "appreciated everyone who has said well wishes" as he worked towards recovery. "I did test positive for pneumonia and I did get a test back positive for the virus," he said in the video post. "I am completely symptom-free now and doing really well. So, I must've had it for a while before I got tested." Edmonds continued, "Thank God I quarantined myself and listened to what everyone said and kept our curve at our house flattened. My daughter has been tested. She's waiting for her results, but she is symptom-free. We're all doing really well here. I'm happy to be symptom-free and feeling great." Not all responses to Edmonds' diagnosis were supportive. On April 4, his estranged wife, Meghan King Edmonds, seemingly mocked him in a TikTok video. The former Real Housewives of Orange County star lipsynched to an individual who said, "Got a text from my ex the other day, he said he missed me. I said, 'I'm sorry I can't talk right now, I'm at a funeral.' He said, 'Oh, my god. Who died?' I said, 'My feelings for you did. Bye, fucker.'" Meanwhile, Jim appeared to be in good spirits on Tuesday, April 7, when he gave fans a tour of his home, during which he even made a coronavirus-related joke. He panned over a mess that surrounded his dining room table, and said: "Looks like some aliens or the virus is joining us for dinner."

I wanted to discuss this story. We were all told that 666 isn't actually the devil's code but a code of a God in this world. Throughout the day, I have people support me, and this report reads, "Laremy Tunsil, Texans Agree to Record-Setting 3-Year $66M Contract."

Laremy Tunsil has signed a massive three-year contract extension with the Houston Texans, per NFL Network's Ian Rapoport and Steve

Wyche. The 25-year-old tackle was traded from the Miami Dolphins, who drafted him 13th overall in 2016, to Houston last August along with wide receiver Kenny Stills. Prior to the trade's completion, Adam H. Beasley of the Miami Herald reported that Dolphins players "would revolt" if the team dealt Tunsil, "one of their best and most-liked players." Texas brass must agree with those Dolphins assessment of Tunsil if they were willing to invest in him beyond his four-year, 12.46 million rookie contract that ran through the 2020 season.

As a rookie, Tunsil excelled as a left guard. The dolphins shifted him to left tackle in 2017, and the transition was initially rocky as he allowed six sacks and was penalized eight times for false starts and holding, as the Miami Herald's Omar Kelly noted in 2018. In Houston, Tunsil has been tasked with protecting franchise quarterback Deshaun Watson and did so well enough to earn a Pro Bowl bid in 2019. According to ESPN's Field Yates, Tunsil is now the NFL's highest-paid offensive lineman on a per-year basis with an average annual salary of $22 million. Philadelphia Eagles right tackle Lane Johnson ranks second at $18 million.

I wanted to write about this article because I was able to help out Kyle Shanahan, the 49ers head coach. He received a new six-year contract through the 2025 season. This is significant because six represents me; and if God were alive right now, he wouldn't age past the age of twenty-five, which is why his contract is set to expire at the end of 2025. Age is still just a number, and people are working on a solution for the human race through me every single day. The article goes like this.

The San Francisco 49ers and head coach Kyle Shanahan reached an agreement Monday on a six-year contract extension, according to ESPN's Adam Schefter. Per Schefter, the deal adds three years to his previous contract, keeping him in the Bay Area through 2025. The move comes after the Niners reached Super Bowl LIV, where they lost 31020 to the Kansas City Chiefs. Shanahan entered 2019 under the Microscope. The Niners had compiled a 10–22 record over his first two years, which extended the storied franchise's playoff drought to five years. The struggles followed a stretch starting in 2011 in which they reached at least the NFC Championship Game three straight times.

Rather than landing on the hot seat. However, the 40-year-old Minnesota native led a massive turnaround by going against the grain offensively. In an era dominated by high-powered passing attacks, San Francisco leaned on a multifaceted rushing attack to complement its elite defense. The result was a 13–3 record to earn the top seed in the NFC and a trip to the Super Bowl thanks to dominant wins over the Minnesota Vikings and Green Bay Packers. Shanahan, the son of former NFL head coach Mike Shanahan, drew praise for his play-calling throughout the campaign. It allowed the 49ers to rank second in rushing yards per game despite not featuring a 1,000-yard rusher. Raheem Mostert led the way the 772 yards, but Matt Breida and Tevin Coleman also topped 500. The success continued in the postseason and was on full display in their triumph over the Packers in the NFC title game. The Niners ran the ball 42 times and averaged 6.8 yards per attempt, leaving quarterback

Jimmy Garoppolo to throw just eight passes in a 37–20 blowouts. "I think its demoralizing for an opponent," fullback Kyle Juszczyk told reporters. "But for us, it's so much fun. I love being so involved and playing with teammates who appreciate the outcome and don't care so much about individual numbers." Right tackle Mike McGlinchey added," Our coach is a genius."

Shanahan did receive criticism followed the Super Bowl for his play-calling while the Niners were in the lead, including drives of five and three plays that led to punts with the team up in the fourth quarter. It marked a disappointing end to a year of marked improvement for the offense. His breakout year as a head coach came at the perfect time. He proved his track record as one of the NFL's most promising assistants, highlighted by winning Assistant Coach of the Year with the Atlanta Falcons in 2016, could translate to leading a staff. In turn the 49ers, who will head into next season as a top-tier title contender thanks to their limited numbers of high-impact losses in free agency, have rewarded their head coach with a new contract.

I was all about breaking curses with teams in America and then started branching out to foreign leagues as well, particularly the international soccer leagues. I started following the players and teams of European soccer leagues. Liverpool, for the first time in their history, won England's league. Hollywood knows that there is nothing left to fix because of me, and this was one of the steps to move in that direction, along with other things and the things I have mentioned in this book. The players on Liverpool were well-deserving of their win this year, and it was time for a new champion in England instead of the usual teams that kept on winning every single year.

I was watching the golf tournament this past weekend, and Bryson DeChambeau won. I noticed a lot of their scores throughout the four days were around 65 and 66, while the par score was 72, a number that stands for Ava, my ex-girlfriend. She has been through a lot, and whenever she feels bad, the CIA gives her a screen to watch what I am doing in my life to make her happy again. Moreover, every second of my life is a highlight, which is part of what Jessie J was talking about because they really appreciate my help, especially Bryson on this particular weekend. He is very powerful not in terms of powers like me but on the golf course. He destroyed his competitors with a final score of around −22. He knows that Willpower will come through for him, maybe not in the next tournament because there will be probably somebody else who will take his place. He can be just as irreplaceable as me, but in terms of winning back-to-back tournaments, that might be unlikely. For the time being, he is happy with his victory, and so are all his fans watching from home. They were part of making my life harder so that we can understand the meaning of life a little bit better and fix the world the right way this time around. There's no need to make it too hard, though, because we are all getting older; and when karma catches up with me, we will figure out the rest after that. It is important that we get this shit done the right way because there's no more fucking around and no more stupid-ass games.

I wanted to add two more things to this section. In the Offspring's song, it says, "Show me how to lie" and with a "good disguise." I was the only reason George Mason made it to the Final Four in 2006. Jack is the only thing in my way, and Calvin Harris touched on this subject in his song called "My Way." I started playing in a fantasy baseball league with Ray his friends, his sister Kristen, and my real creator, in the first two days, I was losing 143–85, which is straight-up because of Jack. Nobody else is responsible for the people who die because of how badly I am losing, even when everything in this world is supposed to be equal; but for some reason, that demon Jack keeps getting in my Goddamn way every single day. I named my team the Equalizer in one of my fantasy basketball leagues and also in this fantasy baseball league, based on the Denzel Washington movie *Equalizer*. I am serious, though. I am going to save people's lives so that everything can become more equal in this world and people like Jack and Avery lose their say in this world because their opinions mean jack shit compared to all the progress and everything I am doing for other people in this world. Macklemore even said in his song that everything in this world is equal because of me, and this means that other people, including Aaron, need to lose their say in this world because they can't see the big picture like I can. If I lose at anything, I know it's because I was outplayed by my opponents. I am not going to let Jack get in my fucking way anymore, though. I don't want to keep losing because he's been getting in my way throughout my entire life.

Another topic I wanted to mention involves Alex Smith. I was just talking about him with my cousin Ray about how the head coach, Gruden, was too busy trying to fuck the cheerleaders rather than trying to fix Smith's injury. Well, I made a promise to Alex Smith a while ago that I would help him out despite what the trainers and coaching staff said about his injury. He was told by people that I was born to save and fix the world, and in a press conference interview, he was like, "Well, I wouldn't want that responsibility." To me, that expressed nothing but respect for everything I am trying to do for the world. Everything I do is special, and now, Alex Smith is making a comeback from a career-ending injury to play for the Redskins again.

Another thing I wanted to mention was that Aaron Judge, Giancarlo Stanton, and other major leaguers are healthy this year because of them putting me back into this devilish game for the second time. This time around, I know what I am doing a lot better and know how to solve other people's problems more easily. Somebody in the major leagues was dealing with a calf injury, and I was able to heal that based on my own experience healing my calf with an exercise my younger sister told me to do every day, based on a video a woman made on YouTube.

Another thing I wanted to mention was that I was watching the Mets game when Cespedes was up, and he was like, "Will is God, and he is always working with me." Everybody who has had my back and is buying into my products are way ahead of the people who used to doubt me and disrespect me, including the people who would choose Jack over me. Anyway, Cespedes, for the Mets, ended up hitting a home run at bat, and the Mets ended up winning the game 1–0 because of his power and having the concentrated power of Will on their side in this game. Like I've said, though, I am sick and tired of Jack always getting in my fucking way *every single fucking day.*

I was watching the Islanders playoff game and also working out that day. The Islanders were down 1–0 after I completed one of my cardio workouts downstairs, and with my magic, I was trying to help them win. I guess, at that point in time, the magic was working for other people around the globe. However, I then went upstairs to watch *Supernatural,* and Hollywood usually guides me in the right direction with what I need to do with myself at that given point in time. They mentioned "Bullocks" in the show; and then I went downstairs and learned Reggie Bennett, the defender on the Islanders, was the biggest contributor to their 4–2 victory. I thought they were also talking about Reggie Bennett, who has been my friend since I was in sixth grade.

I also want to talk more about *Supernatural* in this section. The two brothers in the show are facing karma for disrespecting Jack really badly, and I hear this voice that says anyone who helps Will will bring them down, especially the two brothers in *Supernatural.* That voice is coming from Jack. Tove Lo said in one of her songs that I am better off now, and I am glad that he is gone. He wanted me dead for a long time, and now I am better off and glad that he will die along the way. He is my biggest enemy in this world and is Satan, so he is the main reason for the apocalypse happening twice. He is Lucifer in the show *Supernatural,* and Jack doesn't understand anything about the world and is definitely my biggest enemy. It even happens when I am watching sports games, when I am doing my fantasy, or when I used to bet on games. He is the only person who would always get in my way. When I went through the apocalypse the first time, people had to save me from that demon that was destroying me and ripping me apart.

Anyway, I wanted to mention this particular game because the *Supernatural* writers, producers, and actors are guiding me in the right direction, and I could actually write a lot more about this script in the section below but just didn't get the motivation to keep on writing about the mixed messages in the *Supernatural* script. They guided the Islanders and myself to help the Islanders win in this particular playoff matchup 4–2.

I wanted to add to the sports section and talk about the NBA playoffs a little bit. The NBA playoffs started in July 2020 after the coronavirus was getting better in the world. The first game I wanted to talk about was the game between the Portland Blazers and the Los Angeles Clippers. I was thinking about Damian Lillard earlier in the day, and then I saw a report that the Trail Blazers were up by five with less than six minutes left in the game. I know it's pretty cool that I have this sixth sense, and I think the sixth sense is intuition. Lillard and company were trying to turn their back on me earlier in the day, before the game started, and this is why I was thinking about him. However, the Clippers ended up winning the game, and this was because they hit a game-winning shot with twenty-six seconds left in the game. Anything that people see with the number twenty-six is because of me, and it has a lot to do with karma catching up with me. It's also because if God were alive right now, he wouldn't age past the age of twenty-five. The number twenty-six also resembles the God creature that I am in this world because it's just one up the number twenty-five and has the same impact on people. The Clippers shouldn't rub this victory in the faces of the Trail Blazers. They also lost because of Jack and his satanic impact on this world. I am happy that I was able to help out the Clippers and guide them to a victory.

The other thing I wanted to mention was the injuries I was able to help out before the NBA started. Zion Williamson was severely injured at some point before the coronavirus happened, and he was able to come back to full strength before the first games started. Unfortunately, at Jack's own depth, he doesn't know jack shit about the world or himself. When I see people not responding to what I tell them and when people are acting weird around me, I always know it's because of Jack. When people pick fights with me and when things go wrong in my life, I always know it's because of Jack. Anyway, he said he was rooting for the Pelicans this season because Zion Williamson joined their squad. When my real creator mentioned something about Zion when we were watching their first game and I responded, my real creator just sat there with a blank smile. This was strictly because of Jack, and I got mad because I can't stand when people do that. So I started rooting against Zion. I can't remember exactly what team he was playing in his first game back from the coronavirus pandemic, but they ended up losing in a two-point game. I think the final score was 106–104. Jack was on the losing (Pelicans) side, and I was on the winning side. I can't deal with this satanic bullshit, and I am so fucking sick of it. I can always take matters into my own hands and make Jack lose in every battle since I am a god and he is the devil.

The next thing I wanted to talk about was the Lakers. Anthony Davis has dealt with his share of injuries, and I am so happy that I was able to help him out with his eye issues before the first game started. The Lakers won that close game by two points as well. I know that LeBron and company are very happy when they can rely on me and win their games. My eye issues are getting fixed every day. When my eyes got fixed on this particular day, Anthony Davis came back from his injury, and the Lakers won this game. The Lakers were the first team in this NBA format to make it to the playoffs, even though LeBron was dealing with his personal injury problems with his groin. I think, with his trainers and the 15 percent concentrated power of Will, he was able to heal up and will be ready for the playoffs. I am not picking any sides in the playoffs, but I do wish the best for the Lakers. The team that is most deserving will win because Hollywood knows there is nothing left to fix in the entire world because of me. LeBron already knew that with the Heat and then again with the Cavaliers. If he can win with the Lakers, that would be insane. However, there might be teams that deserve to win more than the Lakers do. We will all see how it turns out.

I talked about golf in the above paragraph, but I wanted to mention it again because it is pretty special what I am doing. The Asian golfer with the first name of Collin won the golf tournament this past weekend. He won the tournament with a final score of −13. As I mentioned above and wanted to reiterate here, the final scores on the final day of the four-day tournament, which happens to be on Sunday with all the best golfers of the tournament, were 66s. It is really crazy because I do so much for the world, especially for the sports world, and for all their scores to be exactly a 66? There was one golfer who finished with the final score of 65, which is the same as 66. The best golfers in the world look forward to *me* helping them out all the time, even every weekend; and for all of them to score a 66 on the final day, at least the best golfers of the tournament, is pretty cool. It completely speaks to me. I know that we learn about numbers, math, and accounting in school and at work, but in the real world, the numbers that I can influence with people are amazing. In the script written for *A Beautiful Mind*, the character played by Russell Crowe was obsessed with numbers. Those were more like science numbers, but in the real world, I can relate the names of every single person in the world and the numbers that correlate with each person. It can even be the credit card that the person owns. For instance, my real creator read the credit card numbers to one of my sisters, and each number on his card had a purpose behind it. I can make sense of each number on his card.

Anyway, I thought it was really cool that I was able to help out each individual in the golf tournament. I am so sick of people only worrying about Tiger Woods. He is one person, and he is not *God*. There are other golfers who are equally as talented as he is, and nowadays, there are sixty-five golfers who are better than he is. Tiger Woods is the best golfer of our era, but you have to think about other people. You can't just focus on one Goddamn person when so many of these guys are so fucking talented. It's like saying that your sports team is superior to other teams. Each team has value, and each team should be considered for a title every single year before the year starts. The most deserving team will win each year for a reason, but don't think that your team is better than the team that just beat you, that they were lucky, or that you didn't have God working for you on that particular evening. You have to give the other guys credit and appreciate their hard work. I know that I am viewing everything as being more equal in this world and that I have more purpose than everyone else viewing these games, but c'mon. Don't think the way you do. Open your eyes to view the world the way that I do. I do think the guy—I think his name is Dustin Johnson or something like that—is the best golfer on record for the time being, but I knew that he and the Bryson guy weren't going to win this tournament and that it was going to be someone new. The winner of this golf tournament happened to be the guy with the first name of Collin. Both those guys gave their best effort and were there throughout the entire time at the top of the winning scoreboard. However, Collin just outplayed them and won with the final score of −13.

I wanted to talk about this story in this section about a player on the New York Yankees named Clint Frazier. He has experienced his ups and downs with the Yankees. As a younger player, now twenty-five years old, he needs to improve his defense if he wants to stay in the big leagues. I know the Yankees are pretty loaded with talent, especially in the outfield. So maybe he can look for a trade, and the Yankees can gain some pitching or something. Anyway, he just got called up from Triple-A at the age of twenty-five. I was just watching the clock after taking a break from working out, and the time was stuck at twelve twenty-five. Eric Sanchez told me there would never be another Albert Einstein, and I can prove him and the entire world wrong. After I saw the clock was at twelve twenty-five, at which time I was about to do cardio, I saw this report that the twenty-five-year-old was called up from Triple-A, and it was because of my Einstein abilities. I hope he makes the most of his call-up and brings that extra spice the Yankees need to get their momentum going strong.

There is another thing I wanted to talk about, and this has to do with the simple math I was talking about earlier and my beautiful mind. I was facing Ray in his fantasy baseball league, and my real creator told me I was down by forty-five points and that he had just benched Anthony Rendon. Anthony Rendon's jersey number is forty-five, and I was down by forty-five points against Ray. So the math was perfect; Satan's (Jack's) number is forty-four, and the people who one-upped me for me to figure this out made me realize that anything with forty-five and forty-six happening is because of me. When Karma catches up with me, it's then that forty-six is more important than forty-five. I ended up losing this week, but because of the equalizer effect I have on the world, everything will even out at the end. I will start winning these matchups in the next year or two when things become more equal in this world. I know I am losing these matchups because of that demon who wanted me dead, but he will most likely disappear from my life.

I wanted to add this part to my book. I developed a significant interest in Damian Lillard when I first started watching him play in the NBA. Nowadays, he is one of the best point guards in the NBA. Anyway, his Portland Trail Blazers team just reached the next round in the playoffs and will play the Lakers, who were the best team in the coronavirus-era NBA. I've been paying close attention to the NBA, as I always do every single year. Furthermore, Damian Lillard's Portland team made it to the next round with a 126–122 victory. I went up to my bedroom and told people to support me, thinking about Damian Lillard's Portland Trail Blazers, and then I looked at my phone and saw they had made another fourth-quarter comeback and won the game 126–122. I was also able to help out other people not just with my magic but with whatever issues they face in the real world. I am happy to help out anybody throughout the day who needs my help.

I talked about Damien Lillard's success in the previous paragraph, and now I want to talk about Chris Paul. He is facing James Harden in the NBA playoffs, and James Harden started the series up 2–0. I was hanging out with my mom on Saturday, when my real creator was out of the house; and Chris Paul leaned on my support, leading them to win the third game of the series, narrowing the gap to 1–2. I watched the fourth quarter and saw how happy Chris Paul was. I didn't even know they were playing, but he one-upped James Harden to win the game. In the next game, he did the exact same thing. I can't remember what I was doing that day, but the Thunder managed to beat the Rockets, evening the series at 2–2. I thought this was very special for Chris Paul, who, I don't think, has never won a title, nor has James Harden. In my opinion, maybe the winner of this series will win it all this year. Hollywood knows there is nothing left to fix in the entire world because of me, and part of this involves breaking all the curses. Both of these guys are waiting for their first title, so it will be special for whoever wins. I view all things created as being equal, and part of this equation is the equalizer. As people die, things become more equal in this world, and it is also kind of like the survival of the fittest. You need to eliminate the unworthy so that those who are more worthy can benefit from their failures. The equalizer is me, Will Coakley, and I was able to help Chris Paul beat James Harden two games in a row. I know James Harden wasn't happy about this, but Chris Paul is very grateful for the help I was giving him.

I thought this was important to mention this right now: I am playing in a fantasy baseball league. My record is 0–4, and I believe two of my losses are because of Avery and that the other two losses are because of Jack. Everything is going to be equal in this world, and this is where my role as the equalizer comes in, making things more equal and ensuring what comes around goes around. I don't want others having say and power in this world because of everything I have been through. It's not fair to me, considering I went through the apocalypse twice before anybody was even talking about it, besides Hollywood. And others want to have say and power in this world. It is not fair, considering that most people haven't been through shit considering everything that I had to go through to get the world into the shape that it is supposed to be in, in the next few years. I also need to start looking at my best interests, and I want to start winning these fantasy matchups; however, it's hard when people who don't know fucking anything about what I am trying to do have power and say in this world.

I wanted to talk about this as well. When I was starting to become myself again and before professional athletes made my life harder for me, many people in the spotlight and across the globe were buying into everything I was doing for people. One of the most important people to me and to the world, and one girl I will never forget, is Carli Lloyd. When I kept playing Lecrae's song that says sin is so bad it's a lie, everyone was buying into it. The people who weren't buying into it weren't receiving the benefits of being on my team. Carli Lloyd was observing me from a distance and watching everything I was doing, and when it was her time to be in the spotlight, she scored four goals for the US women's soccer team in 2015. I was watching the game with my friend Andy Lee, and she was watching our conversations. I said to myself that I wonder if she is buying into my products, and she thanked sin in front of the entire world. I thought that was really cool, and I was just chilling at the bar with my friend Andy and his friend and my acquaintance, Ho Ling.

The other girl I wanted to mention was Ronda Rousey. She was in *Entourage* and *Mile 22* for Hollywood. She started to learn a lot about the world and what my role in all of this was. One day, I was driving with my mom, going home from a restaurant during the afternoon, and I said to myself, "Good, we are on the same page now," and I guess that was meant for Ronda Rousey. Her role in those movies is important, and when the time is right, she will be a big part of my life. They wanted her in Hollywood for those roles for a reason. In her press conference before a match in front of the world, she said that sin was going to help her win that matchup. Unfortunately, her luck wasn't as good as Carli Lloyd's.

There were people in this world who wanted to see me fail at everything I was trying to do, and one of those people was Avery, his empire, and the Mafia. I was at the bar with different friends this time: Eric Sanchez, Cory Carlton, and Alex Shalak. While the matchup was going on, Cory said, "Come on, sin," but he didn't know that Ronda was talking about me. I just kept my mouth shut because I know for a fact that most people in this world don't deal with any demon problems, so they can't blame their problems on the devil when they don't know what demons can really do to someone. I hate these fake fucking empires that are trying to control us in sinister ways. It's our time to take the power back, and I am not talking about other people having power in this world but about these fuckers who run the world taking a step back and letting us win this war with our minds and with the sky. I can't lose. I am in a position where I can't lose, so I am not too worried about it. And I have the supporting cast in all these roles where I always come out to be the winner. Anyway, Ronda Rousey quit MMA, started doing wrestling, and wanted to be more active in Hollywood. She took to heart the people who were hating on her, took a timeout from life, and regrouped with the people closest to her. I am happy that she is important in this world and can be one of my really good friends in the future.

The Arizona Cardinals are giving a significant contract extension to one of their young stars. The Cardinals and safety Budda Baker have agreed to terms on a four-year extension worth $59 million. I was watching one of my TV shows and saw the number fifty-nine show up on the clock, and I also know that Fort Minor is number fifty-nine on my list. And because of whatever he was doing in his life and my Einstein abilities, he was able to get this contract. I know for a fact that in the last two years of this contract, there will be no injury worries in the professional sports world. To be more pessimistic, or realistic, I should say the fourth year is more likely. The deal, which was first reported by ESPN, makes the twenty-four-year-old Baker the highest-paid safety in the NFL.

It surpasses the four-year, $58.4 million extension that Eddie Jackson signed with the Chicago Bears in January. Baker is entering his fourth season with Arizona after the team selected him in the second round out of Washington in the 2017 draft. He earned a Pro Bowl nod for his work on special teams as a rookie and ended up starting seven games at safety that season as well, totaling seventy-four tackles. He started thirteen games at strong safety in 2018, compiling 102 tackles in the process. Baker moved to free safety in 2019 with new head coach Kliff Kingsbury and defensive coordinator Vance Joseph in Arizona. He thrived in that spot while also showing the versatility to line up all over the field. He earned his second Pro Bowl invitation while leading the NFL with 104 solo tackles. His 147 total tackles led all safeties. Overall, in his career, Baker has amassed 323 total tackles with 18 tackles for loss, 3.5 sacks, 14 passes defended, 4 forced fumbles, and 4 fumble recoveries. Baker was entering the final year of his rookie contract but now has a lucrative deal in place that should keep him with the Cardinals for years to come.

I wanted to talk about some of these NBA playoff games and how they relate to me. The one game I wanted to talk about was the game between the Celtics and the Raptors. The final score ended with the Raptors winning 125–122 against the Celtics. I wanted to talk about this score because 125 is always my doing since if God were alive right now, then he wouldn't age past twenty-five, and every time scores end in a number having something to do with twenty-five, then it is my doing. I don't want to see anyone else having power in this world because I have worked so fucking hard and have been through more than anyone else. This includes anyone who was playing me or playing God in this world because it isn't fair, considering that I have been the one saving the world and saving people's lives and have conquered everything so that we can find a solution for everything. The Celtics ended up winning the series, which I am totally cool with because the Raptors just won recently, and the Celtics haven't won in a while. I wouldn't care if LeBron ended up winning just to secure his spot in being the best player who has ever played basketball, but if a new winner happens this year, then I wouldn't be mad at that either. I know these guys are trying hard, and the team that is most deserving will win.

I noticed some of the NFL games on Sunday, September 27, 2020. The first score I wanted to talk about was the game between the 49ers and the Giants. I am not really watching these games too much because I am working out a lot, especially during the first halves of the 1:00 p.m. games, but the Giants got smoked again. This time the score was 36–9. Thirty-six has a lot of meaning to it, and I've talked about the number scheme that I came up with; however, it also matters with age. We *all* need karma to catch up with me sometime during my thirty-sixth birthday year. We are all getting older, and I have had enough—and I think a lot of other people have had enough—of the bullshit in this life. It is unfortunate that the Giants lost this game, but it is also important to remember that even when I am losing, I am still winning because I was able to guide the 49ers to a victory that day. To add to the 49ers, I am following a bunch of them and the team homepage on Instagram, and I liked a lot of their stuff in the pregame. This also led them to victory on this day. When I was liking their shit on Instagram, I didn't realize they were playing the Giants that day. However, good luck to the 49ers and their fan base.

The next score I wanted to talk about was in the game between the Bills and the Ravens. The final score was 35–32, and the number thirty-five is important because big things are going to happen for me and for the world in my thirty-fifth year. A lot of positive changes are going to happen, and people will see it. The Bills beat the Ravens that day with that score of 35–32. The Bills actually came back in the final minutes, and the Ravens were one of the better teams last year. So it is good to see the Bills doing well this year. They deserve to win in the NFL as much as any other team does this year.

The next score I wanted to talk about is in the game between the Browns and Washington. The final score was 34–20, with the Browns winning. Going into this game, the Washington team was 2–0, so it evened out and became equal with this game. The score thirty-four is important too because, at some point, Jack won't get in my way in my life anymore, and I can just worry about my own shit instead of worrying about forty-four and forty-three showing up and Jack getting in the way for all of us to live normal lives again.

The next score I want to talk about is in the game between the Patriots and the Raiders. The Patriots won this game 36–20. Again, the number thirty-six popped up, and it is really important that I step back within the lines so that the world can be saved. There are so many scenes about my life. Anyway, I was able to guide the Patriots and their fan base to a victory that day with the final score of thirty-six. I am rooting for Cam Newton because he is playing for the right reasons. I would say that I am rooting for him to win the Super Bowl, but the Patriots have won so many times with Tom Brady. I might actually be rooting for Tom Brady to win with the Buccaneers, and he might. These are the only scores I want to talk about for this day.

Hollywood said that there is nothing left to fix in the entire world because of me, and this was one step in the right direction. The Padres won their first postseason series in twenty-two years to reach the NLDS.

> From 21-year-old budding superstar Fernando Tatis Jr. to 36-year-old reliever Craig Stammen, the San Diego Padres tossed aside more than two decades of futility and brought joy to a city that's had its sports psyche beaten down for far too long. Stammen and eight fellow

relievers combined on a four-hitter in a brilliant, record-setting that sent the Padres over the St. Louis Cardinals 4–0 Friday night in the deciding Game 3 of their National League Wild Card Series. The Padres won a postseason series for the first time in 22 years and advanced to face the NL West rival Los Angeles Dodgers in the division series at Arlington, Texas, starting Tuesday. Stammen, making his first start in 10 years, said the Padres weren't wrapped up in past postseason failures, including being eliminated from the playoffs by the Cardinals three times since 1996. I was the reason for the Yankees winning since 1996, so that was my doing, as well.

"We're trying to write our own piece of history right now," said Stammen, who mentioned the Padres' return to a brown-and-gold color scheme. "It's icing on the cake to maybe turn the page on some of the San Diego Padres struggles in the playoffs against the Cardinals, turn the page on maybe some of the organizations struggles, the blue Padres, and now we're the brown Padres. Excited to build some memories with the new colors." San Diego is the first team in Major League history, regular season or playoffs, to complete a nine-inning shutout by using at least nine pitchers, according to ESPN Stats and Information research. With starters Mike Clevinger and Dinelson Lamet unavailable due to injuries suffered in their final regular-season starts, rookie manager Jayce Tingler was forced to tap the Padres' already stressed bullpen, and it came through magnificently. San Diego became the first team in baseball history to use eight or more pitchers in three consecutive postseason matchups. "What those guys did this series and tonight, wow," Tingler.

"They've been overworked; they've been overtaxed. Man to man, everybody came up and said, "I'm good, give me the ball. I'm good, give me the ball.' Tonight, for me, was as team-oriented as so many guys contributed again. That's who we are. That's why we're going to continue to keep playing." San Diego's Trevor Rosenthal, who started his career with the Cardinals, struck out the side in the ninth, and the team began celebrating in empty Petco Park. Players gestured toward fans who watched from balconies overlooking the ballpark. Fans crowded downtown and honked car horns and chanted. This was the first postseason series victory for the Padres since the 1998 NL Championship Series. All four division series now feature matchups between division rivals. All seven central teams lost in the first round, with the Cardinals joining the Cincinatti Reds, Chicago Cubs, Milwaukee Brewers, Cleveland Indians, Chicago White Sox, and Minnesota Twins. Tatis, who homered twice and drove in five runs in Thursday night's wild, 11–9 victory, doubled into the left-field corner off Game 3 losing pitcher Jack Flaherty with one out in the fifth and scored on Eric Hosmer's two-out double to right-center. The Padres added on against reliever Alex Reyes in the seventh—on a bases-loaded walk to Hosmer, Manny Machado's fielder choice and an error on third baseman Tommy Edman. Jake Cronenworth went deep in the eighth, becoming the first rookie in Padres history to homer in a playoff game, according to ESPN Stats & Info data.

The Padres rewarded their long-suffering fans by winning one of the most meaningful games of any kind in San Diego in a long time. The city's only major professional championship remains the San Diego Chargers' 1963 AFL title. The Chargers headed to Los Angeles after the 2016 season, leaving the Padres as the only pro team in San Diego, which lost NBA franchises to Houston and Los Angeles. The Padres lost 4–1 to the Detroit Tigers in the 1984 World Series and were swept by the New York Yankees in the 1998 Fall Classic. Stammen, who hadn't started since 2010 with the Washington Nationals, pitched a perfect first inning and made way for Tim Hill with one on and two out in the second. Hill retired Matt Carpenter, got the first two outs of the third and then handed off to Pierce Johnson. Johnson loaded the bases on a single and a walk but struck out rookie cleanup hitter Dylan Carlson.

Padres rookie Adrian Morejon tossed a perfect fourth and struck out two to open the fifth, before Kolten Wong singled and San Diego Edman reached on Tatis' throwing error from shortstop. Austin Adams came on and struck out Paul Goldschmidt, who hit a three-run homer in St. Louis' 7–4 win in Game 1. Adams would up with the win. St. Louis had another scoring chance in the sixth, when Yadier Molina hit a one-out double off rookie Luis Patino and took third on Paul Dejong's grounder. Patino got Dexter Fowler to fly out to the warning track in right-center to end it. San Diego's Emilio Pagan threw a perfect seventh, and Drew Pomeranz walked one in the eighth. The bullpen had been one of the Padres' strengths coming into the

MY THEORY OF EVERYTHING

season, but it lost several members to injuries, including closer Kirby Yates, who led the majors with 41 saves last year. General Manager A.J. Preller replenished the pen just before the trade deadline. Stammen had a seesaw regular season, going 4–2 with a 5.63 ERA in 24 appearances. Flaherty was brilliant, as well, allowing one run and six hits in six innings while striking out eight and walking two.

The next great sports story that happened on this day was the Storm beating the Aces 93–80. The number ninety-three stands for what I did for George Mason in 2006, so I know every time that number pops up, it is because of me.

Sue Bird Set a Standard for Assists in the WNBA Finals

Bird shattered the previous single-game mark for assists in the finals getting 16 in the Seattle Storm's 93–80 win over the Las Vegas Aces on Friday night in the opening game of the best-of-five series. "I think the way that our team plays and the way that our offense is kind of constructed, which actually dates back to even when Jenny Boucek was our coach, it was always about just finding the open player and moving it in a way where it would create opportunities," Bird said. "For me as a point guard, I'm just out there trying to find the open player. But like I said, and I've always said this, assists is a two-person thing, and tonight (Breanna Stewart and Jewell Loyd) playing amazing." The previous record was 11, accomplished eight players before, most recently by Alyssa Thomas last season.

"She really did a good job finding the open person, and we shot the ball really well," Storm coach Gary Kloppenburg said, "Just a tremendous floor game as Sue." Bird also broke the playoff assists record of 14 she held with Courtney Vandersloot of Chicago. The Storm guard had 10 assists in the first half-also a WNBA Finals most-set her own career-best for assists regular season and the playoffs. Most of her assists came to either Breanna Stewart or Jewell Lloyd, who had 37 points and 28 respectively. The record-breaking 12th assist in the third quarter on a pass to Stewart with 7:19 left in the period. Bird is the WNBA career assists leader with 2,888 in the regular season. She moved into third place on the Finals assist list with 68, trailing only Lindsay Whalen (120) and Maya Moore (70). Bird is playing in her fourth WNBA finals, and appeared in her 51st playoff game dating back to 2002. She only played in half of the regular-season games this year as she dealt with a bone bruise in her knee, averaging 5.2 assists. She missed both of Seattle's games against Las Vegas this season.

This piqued my interest because if God were alive right now, he wouldn't age past twenty-five, which aligns with the deal that Robin Lehner just secured with Vegas.

Robin Lehner signs 5-year, $25 million contract with Golden Knights.

It is official: Robin Lehner is staying with the Vegas Golden Knights. The team announced on Saturday that the goalie has signed a five-year, $25 million contract to remain with the team, keeping him off the unrestricted free agent market. The Golden Knights acquired Lehner just before the NHL trade deadline from the Chicago Blackhawks in an effort to provide more depth behind Marc-Andre Fleury. But as Lehner played more games with the Golden Knights throughout the remainder of the regular season and into the Return To Play and playoffs, it became clear that the team considered him their best option. Lehner ended up taking over the starting job and kept it throughout the entire postseason (it was not always a popular decision) as the Golden Knights reached the Western Conference Final. Now that Lehner is officially back with the Golden Knights the focus turns to Fleury and his future. He still has two years remaining on a contract that pays him $7 million per season. Fleury has already said he will not ask for a trade, but it is hard to see how the Golden Knights can realistically keep both. The duo—while being one of the league's best—would account for $12 million in salary cap space in each of the next two seasons, a level that almost no other team in the league has committed to the position (Only Montreal really compares for this season with Carey Price and Jake Allen). Given how close the Golden Knights already are to the cap, they would have to clear salary elsewhere to keep both and still make improvements to the team. The long-term contract provides Lehner with the long-term security he wanted—and has earned—after signing short-term one-year deals (with the Islanders and Blackhawks) the past two offseasons.

I wanted to add to the sports section and talk about my fantasy football a bit. In back-to-back weeks, I found connections that added up to me. The first week I wanted to talk about was when I scored exactly 153 points in two of my leagues, and I lost in the other league. I was 2–0 in one league and lost that matchup but won in my other leagues by scoring 153 points in both leagues. There are important numbers that we encounter in this world, and they are real-world numbers. They are not the numbers that you learn in school or at work but numbers that are applied in the real world. For example, the credit card number that every single individual in this world owns matters, and the license plate number that you have on your car matters. For sports, I like to look up the real-world numbers and names of the players with whom I can identify. Anyway, the second week, I scored 135 points in two of my leagues and won in both of those leagues. I lost in one league and won in two leagues. I thought it was interesting that the numbers of both of those weeks added up perfectly. Also, if you look at it closely, if you flip fifty-three and thirty-five, then the first and last numbers are the same. Everything happens for a reason, and I wanted to discuss these numbers in my fantasy leagues in my book.

I thought this was pretty cool to discuss in my book and important to mention. The Topgolf place that is about twenty-five minutes from my parents' house has the address of 6625. I talk about numbers a lot in my book, but sixty-six stands for me. And if God were alive right now, then he wouldn't age past twenty-five. I guess the magic and everything in my life was right here this entire time, and every address and street sign is important. This Topgolf place has been around for about twenty years, and they named the address 6625. I didn't play well when I went with my friend Ethan Stewart, but I play well when I go with my real creator. Actually, the last time I went with my real creator, I shot a 34 on a par-3 Oak Marr course. I hadn't played golf for a year and I got a score two points better than my previous high. We are always looking for progress in this world, and I actually shot a birdie on one of the par-3 holes. I knew my game was going to get better because once my brain and my mind get fixed and I step back within the lines, then I will be able to do many things better. I know that I was nervous with so many people golfing around me when I went to play Topgolf with Eric. Once my anxiety and panic attacks go away, then I can perform better in front of people. Anyway, I thought it was important to mention in my book that the address of this place is 6625.

Another number I wanted to discuss is that the young Tampa Bay Rays hitter, who is batting .625 in the playoffs, leads the league in 2020, the year of COVID-19. His hitting style and the way he plays kind of remind me of Jackie Robinson. I think they actually came out with this script with mixed messages for this player. I can't remember his name and don't feel like looking it up right now, but at this current time, he is batting with a .625 average. The .625 is self-explanatory because the six stands for me, and the twenty-five is because if God were alive right now, then he wouldn't age past twenty-five. His name is Randy Arozarena. He is a big believer in God, and a lot of these athletes know many of the secrets about the world that I do. I am also sure that he knows why his average was exactly .625 and why he is doing so well.

This was pretty cool to talk about, and it was because of me.

The Miami Dolphins get full capacity approval from governor for 65,000 seat stadium. This could be a huge problem…

The Miami Dolphins have been granted permission from the governor of Florida to allow full capacity at Hard Rock Stadium. You read that correctly. We're talking 65,000 seats. In the middle of a pandemic. The green light comes by way of Gov. **Ron DeSantis**—whose spokesperson **told Andy Slater** the team is now allowed to pack their stadium as part of statewide removal of COVID-19 stadium restrictions. That doesn't mean the Dolphins will rush to allow 65,000 people to watch the team at their next home game…

Slater says the org. still plans on limiting the number of fans to 13,000 at the next home game on Oct. 25. The news comes on the heels of an announcement from the Green Bay Packers—

which just pressed pause on the possibility of opening up Lambeau Field to fans any time soon. "Due to the concerning increase of COVID-19 cases and hospitalizations in the Green Bay area and across Wisconsin, the Green Bay Packers today announced that the organization has put an indefinite hold on hosting fans for games at Lambeau Field this season," the team said in a statement. Plus, with NFL teams like the Tennessee Titans, New England Patriots, K.C. Chiefs and Las Vegas Raiders **dealing with possible COVID outbreaks** among the players…

It just doesn't seem like the best time for a team to pack a stadium with people!

Please be safe, everyone. (boldface in the original)

10 Percent Music

I wanted to talk about this song by will.i.am. I listened to it in high school, and it's called "I Got It From My Mama." He talks about pretty people and suggests we should have a celebration of God's best creation, which could probably get you into a lot of trouble now. Xzibit released his song "X" in 2000. Because of all the progress the world has made since 2000 and all the artists and actors that have been let into Hollywood since then, they all knew it was because of me, but I had no idea until I got old enough to understand these things. I listened to will.i.am's song when I was a junior in high school, when I would go to my training for baseball with my friends, especially this one guy, David Miller. He was one of our best players, and I got pretty close to him, even though he hung out with the "cool" group and I hung out with a bunch of outcasts. I was also close to the other guys I was training with. I wanted to bring this up because I am the reason why all these people became famous at the ages they did when I was just living my life. They let me know they laid the lice in me with Fergie's song, and all these girls all over the globe love me. But everyone is only destined to be with one girl.

When they released all their songs in 2010, it was when I was going through *so* much and had no idea why I kept self-destructing after something good was happening to me. When I was at COMTEK, I was acting like an asshole and could have actually gotten into more trouble than I did, but whoever made those decisions to make me act like that are paying the price. The people who stopped and started letting me live my life again are okay, but I think this is part of the reason all these bad things are happening to Avery and the empire. All their songs from 2010 I listen to all the time because they are important, and after everything was done, then Hollywood laid the lice in me so that they could make sure all of their songs had meaning to them. Then Peyton Manning and company said they were going to put me back in this devilish game again, and he said it to my face on the news. Fergie came clean in her song, and P!nk said that Hollywood will come clean to me when the timing is right. The people that really did bad things to me are either dead or are paying big prices. However, I wanted to talk about how important it was that Xzibit made his song "X" and how all the people in my generation, the younger generations, and the generation above mine all became famous because of me.

Michelle Branch's "You Get Me" starts off by suggesting, "So what if I'm a little out of center?" What she means by this is that I lose my mind and am not like the normal civilian and the average person. I am bit crazy and different from most people in this world, and I am perfectly fine with that. I find many people boring, especially if they are still living the same lifestyles from college. You know, they went to college, started working, had kids, got married, and then expect to retire and die. I don't see life like that. I see it as my dream girl and I being able to spend the rest of eternity happy, and the people and scientists working every single day for a solution for the human race being able find a cure. And all of us can be one happy family. I don't do the nine-to-five anymore because of everything I've been through and have risen above that so that I can run my own business and have set high expectations for myself. I don't compare myself to other people because I am better than most people in this world. As I read in one book, there are outliers in the world, and those outliers are the best people in the world who are just straight-up more talented than the rest of the population. Fortunately for me, I fall under that criteria because I am the best person in the world. Most of those people are in Hollywood, are professional athletes, and are my friends and others that I have met along the way. I am a little out of center because I was born on another level and don't know how to live without being on that other level. It's not manic; it's just because I was born with different DNA, just like what Katy Perry said, and I am not like any other guy in this world. I consider myself different from the average person, and it's not a bad thing. It is actually a really good thing because people love me for who I am, everything I bring to the table, what I can do for people nowadays, and what I will be able to do for people in the future.

In the next part of the song, she says, "I am a little out of tune." She says this because of my monotone voice. My therapist once said that it is a calm, soothing voice, which I very much appreciated. Avery once said, "They don't make them like me anymore," and Kanye West said, "There's a thousand yous, there's only one of me." He was actually talking about the idea that there are a thousand Jacks and only one Will. I have developed a lot of love from so many different people over the past several years, and I appreciate every single one of those people. However, nobody in the world has had it as tough as I have.

Ava pointed out to me that I have a bad singing voice, and I tried to tell her to sing in front of my family, but she was too shy and nervous to do so. They later came out with a script featuring a shy Black girl who sang by herself in front of her mirror and in the shower because she was too shy to sing in front of people. This script was inspired by Ava. Spose and company taught me how to rap and how to sing. I know that I am out of tune, but I can still achieve perfection with my voice because I am determined and am an outlier for a reason. I can do anything when the time is right, and that sets me apart from everyone else. I am not okay with living an average life. I am ready for the biggest accomplishments in life and achieving perfection, not just going to work and not getting the credit I deserve since I am working for someone else when I can get the credit I deserve with what I am doing every single day to save the world and what I can do for my own legacy with my skills and talents.

In the next part of her song, she says, "Some say I am paranormal." She says this because it reflects a part of my personality that is sinister. I don't give a fuck because I spent most of my life not believing in shit. They actually came out with a few scripts titled "Paranormal Activities." These scripts and the enemies of the paranormal person killed off from the planet people who were scared of me and the devil and those who had disrespected me in the past, so it was kind of like a "*Fuck you!*" to those people. I attacked them with death as they attacked me in my mind and life. That might have included people dealing with the devil, and I would put them in their graves, sometimes with other people's guns. When I played Dua Lipa's song, in her song, she says, "I never learned, I never learned." This refers to two people who never learned that we can't deal with the devil anymore; and as a result, two people would die. That could also be included in the *Paranormal* movie. One day, I played that song three times, and there were three separate shootings that night where two people died. Fuck all six of those people; they deserved to die.

Another part of this song is to distinguish me from Avery. I know that in one of Kid Cudi's songs, he mentioned that Avery is trying to be the same as me. I just saw that as stolen paradise because nobody in my life is the same as me. I was mad that people were controlling him to be the same as me because if he is really as scared of demons as he claims, then he is not the same as me. There are other people more similar to me than that Jesus freak is. I can instill the fear of the devil in people so easily if they do me wrong.

In the next part of her song, she says, "Who wants to be ordinary in a crazy, mixed-up world?" Ordinary people are boring, and there are too many ordinary people in this world. I think that most people's conversations are boring, and to be honest, I think many of these people are sick and don't grasp the meaning of life as well as they should because they are not real enough to understand the things that people like me do. I am able to write this third book because of all the things I understand in life. Ordinary people suck. I was always crazy and Hollywood loves me because of my personality. People who are boring fucking suck. Most people go through their entire lives not making any waves or achieving any big accomplishments, just wasting my fucking time. People like Ray, Becka, Rory, Aaron, Andy, and Jack make waves because they are real and add value. There are too many people who don't add value to our lives and are just wasting their breath with their worthless words. Ariana, Jack's wife, and Amy, Rory's wife, understand these things too, and they add value to my life. There are other people, too, who are outliers and crazy and have useless opinions rather than being worthless to me. I can't stand fake people, and I have always been real with people. I know a lot of people didn't like me in the past because of my New York attitude. Granted, I am a lot calmer and self-centered now, but I don't want to talk to ordinary and useless people or those who add no value to my life. I want people who make me a better person. The people from the outside who have subjected me to sinister tests are assholes and deserve the punishments they have received and will get in the future. This is part of the reason the entire part of the song involves my own sinister side and the paranormal part of me that will always be kept alive.

In the next part of her song, she says, "Hey, you were on my side, and they just roll their eyes." She is talking about Avery and that fake-ass empire. They are so fake, and they are falling every single day. There are many of them, so it depends on the day when they are falling and paying the price for what they did to me in the past. Avery will probably end up dead because of the things he did to me in the past. He put me through impossible tests that seemed inescapable. Hollywood relaid the lice in my life so that I could have all these amazing experiences. Avery sent me to the hospital all those times with his empire, hoping that I would die each time. Somehow, I always survived because of myself. I am big and powerful, and he can't do these things anymore because I keep playing "X" every single night to take away his powers and make sure that his say in the world comes from a little bit to none in the next year or two. He has apparently forgotten about the things he did to me but faces karma every day and now finds himself without friends because of the sinister thoughts he put inside my head and claiming that I don't deserve shit. He used to fuck with my mind, and the girl of my dreams knows that they are soft. So she was just waiting for the right time for them to stop and for the right timing for all this to end. The entities that were attacking me were primarily the empires and ISIS. They are so fucking fake and playing these games with me that seemed inescapable, but I always found a way out.

There were other people who attacked me. I once said, "Fuck your belief in God" to Landon inside my house, and that coward posted on Facebook, "Fuck your name." Then he got sent to the hospital and almost died because of it. Avery's mom attacked my mom and now has Alzheimer's. This also relates to Avery's family. Avery and Mrs. Seaman did bad things to me in the past and are paying for it now. Even Steph's cousin is falling every single day because of the things he did to me in the past. Anyway, Bebe Rexha, Dua Lipa, and Diya all implied in songs that nobody is by Avery's side now, and he has lost all of his friends—a sentiment Melanie Martinez echoed in one of her songs. She also said that I am one of a kind and that this one girl knows that I am better than anybody else in the world.

I just wanted to touch on this topic briefly, but she includes in this part the phrase "you get me." I walked into Dr. O'Connor's appointment one day and said, "Dr. O'Connor, you actually get me. I need to find a girl who gets me and not one who wants to argue with me every single day."

Kid Cudi said, "Think twice before you want to be like him. It's like suicide reading my mind."

Before I said that to Dr. O'Connor, I saw on Facebook that he was having trouble trusting people and told his friend, "You get me." A lot of other people started saying that as well, and then Kid Cudi was like, "Think twice before you want to be like him, it's like suicide reading my mind." He regretted attacking me after that. But he is still my people, so I forgive him. However, the empires and the people who aren't mine that were attacking me is pretty unacceptable because I didn't do shit to you, so don't disrespect me. I need to find a girl who I can see eye to eye with, and I have my eyes on one. But like I said, the timing needs to be right, and everything needs to be based on perfect timing. This is all I want to say about this song for the time being.

In Taylor Swift's "Gorgeous," Taylor Swift is talking about her life and also about mine. I was looking for another song to dissect, and this song seems like a good one to talk about. In the first part of the song, she says, "You should take it as a compliment that I got drunk and made fun of the way you talk." She was talking about Joanna and when she was talking to Ray at Becka's wedding. I was really drunk and high, and Joanna was talking to Ray about me. Joanna is an interesting person, and she got really close to Becka around the time when all this conspiracy stuff started happening with me. They were living together, actually, when I was living in Fair Lakes with my friends, and that St. Patrick's Day in 2010 really fucked my world up. I was so fucking scared, and the first person I called was Becka to save me and get me away from the fucking police because I was scared out of my fucking mind and couldn't understand why all these crazy things were happening to me. This includes the light that was illuminating from my sheets on my door and the star wars—when the stars were going crazy in the sky. I don't know who the fuck would do this to someone who was just trying to make a living and start off his career as an accountant. I'm pretty sure that Avery was a part of this and his Mafia crew, and he really wanted to kill me so many times. But thanks to the help of other people in this world, I am always able to get out of these impossible situations with flying colors. This is also how they came out with the scripts for *Mission: Impossible*. Additionally, there are a lot of people in Hollywood who have really good things to say about the CIA. All these situations make my life into a movie, and also, these missions are *Mission: Impossible*. The Tom Cruise character is me, and because of the star wars, this is how they came out with the main character being me with the *Star Wars* movies.

Anyway, over the years, I became really close to Joanna, and she has been a very close family friend and someone I would consider a good friend whom I can count on in difficult situations and someone who would always be there for me as a friend when we both need each other. I feel like we both have had tough times getting into good relationships, so if we are both single after an extended period of time, then maybe we can see where this would go. Vince Vaughn even said in *Wedding Crashers* that he's never been with an Asian before. This Asian girl would be Joanna. She would be a good fit for me, but I think there is someone I have my eye on who might be a better fit. But I will just be patient with my dating scenarios.

In the next part of her song, she says, "You should think about the consequence of your magnetic field being a little too strong." When she says this, she's looking at my solution pit and seeing how I am able to protect myself from the bad things and the evil things in this world, and this is also part of my magnetic field. It helps me stay stabilized, and when she says it's a little too strong, she means that it also causes me problems with social situations, talking, and pretty much being able to be in a stable relationship right now. I don't know what the feelings I am feeling are for sure, so Taylor decided to say it was a magnetic field in this song. This magnetic field and the consequences make me self-destruct, and I use it as a guide to show me what my next best move for myself is and to make the world a better place. My magnetic field is somehow how Hollywood poisoned me, and Calvin Harris said that within my solution pit, the invisible things that I am seeing is a force field. He was pretty much feeding off what Taylor Swift was saying in his song as well.

In the next part of her song, she says, "You're so cool it makes me hate you so much." In this part, she is actually talking about Anna Kendrick. Ever since Anna Kendrick entered Hollywood, around the time I was dating Angie and was the cool guy (not saying that I am not still the cool guy), Anna Kendrick knew that if she was going to make it big, she was going to need to help me out and be on good terms with me for her success to become important in Hollywood. Ever since I took that drive to Pennsylvania, I have taken a real liking to Anna Kendrick because of her *Pitch Perfect* movie. I had no idea who she was until I saw that movie four times in the theaters with Avery, with Eric, and by myself. Then I bought the movie and always watched it. She would be another ideal fit for me, and when the corrupt airplanes in the sky were roaming above my head, I thought that her private plane was going to land in my backyard when craziness was happening in my life with Avery living with me.

When I was sent to the hospital one time because of the price I was paying for being God, there were many skits about airplanes crashing into people's houses, and Anna Kendrick was once again a big part of this skit. Nevertheless, a lot of people actually started dying in plane crashes all over the place, and apparently, everything that I was ever going through was real. There were so many people across the globe who heard funny noises inside their heads because of what I was dealing with in my life, whether they were positive voices or sinister voices. This is how I was able to make my wave in the world, and the "Spaceman" song also made many people hear voices. I didn't know because I was immature and naive, and I thought everything that was going on inside my head was funny. And people who were watching me were laughing. Unfortunately, my real creator took me to the hospital both times against my will. The artist Michael Franti even said, with the Patriot Act, that the CIA took away all my rights. My real creator doesn't understand how important it is that everything goes smoothly from here on out, and he would never understand the things I know about the world. I need to rely on people like Anna Kendrick and others who can help me save the world because nobody else can do the things I can. I actually deleted the will.i.am song and the Grits song that say God needs to help the win because my real creator is helpless. Furthermore, Anna Kendrick felt really lonely waiting for me to come to Hollywood, and she would watch me, probably knowing that I was not coming anytime soon but also figuring out how to get me out of these sinister situations that people put me in. I owe a lot of my future success to her, and there is a reason she made her name big. She is the closest thing to being a queen in this world compared to most other girls.

This part is also about Anna Kendrick. In this song, Taylor Swift says, "I can't say anything to your face, because look at your face. You're gorgeous." This is exactly how Anna Kendrick feels about me. When Jack told me that I am the weird and loser guy in the shows they put out and that I am meant to be with ugly and fat girls (and I have girls like Anna Kendrick interested in me), it made me feel bad about myself. He lost my respect by saying shit like that to me. Anna Kendrick knows that when I show up in Hollywood, I will be showing up with another girl, so she will at some point move on with her life. But ever since I took that drive and went through all my transgressions, she's been laughing and believes that she better move on with her life because there are other girls in my immediate life that I am probably going to be with. Not saying that Anna Kendrick and I would be a good fit, but it's just unrealistic, especially since we are all getting older now. Additionally, people made my life a living hell, and it seems like this is never-ending. We are going to make this life everlasting, but she knows that there are other girls I will end up dating instead of her, as much as she respects the big chief reaper and knows that I will achieve perfection, become rich, and rule the world with my actual soulmate. Anna Kendrick is the next best thing that could possibly happen to me.

In the next part of Taylor Swift's song, she says, "You should take it as a compliment that I am talking to everyone here but you." She was talking about at Maya's thirtieth birthday party, when Avery and the Mafia were playing games with my mind; but I was losing it because I didn't think that Maya deserved to be happier than me, with all these people showing up to her birthday party when I barely have anybody show up to my birthday parties. I was pretty much talking to everyone at the party but Joanna because I got nervous and knew that Joanna and I were getting close, and I didn't know how to act around her. The people who were watching from the outside thought it was funny, but Joanna doesn't want to ruin the friendship that I have with her. And if we were ever to get together, we would need to take it slow. I have a lot of respect for Joanna, but Taylor Swift thought this was a good song to involve one of my family's closest friends with this song and knew exactly how Anna Kendrick felt about me, so she made that pretty well known with this song. I wouldn't have a problem dating Joanna, but if the relationship for some reason went sour, then it would ruin our friendship. I know that both of us don't want that to happen, so maybe it would be better if we just remained friends. I went into the upstairs bathroom and said something, and I guess the cameras showed that Joanna was watching. It caught her by surprise. I think she felt that maybe we could actually build a relationship; however, like I said, I don't think that is going to work. This is all I want to say about this song for the time being.

Flobots' "We Are Winning"—in this song, he talked about the things I talked about with the *Divergent* series about how we are building a new world, and this is part of how they got this script. It was based on what the Flobots wrote in this song. He starts off this song with "Rival gangsters sit down to plan an afternoon's mayhem." When he puts this part in this song, he is talking about the gangs and the crimes they commit. Something needs to be done about this, and a lot of MS-13 gang members have been caught for their crimes thanks to me and the FBI using what is in my solution pit to figure out ways to catch these criminals.

I had run-ins with gangs ever since I was in high school. I threw a party with a bunch of my friends, and there were the popular kids who crashed my party and invited all these random people. They just happened to be a gang that showed up to my party. Some of my friends got into a fight with a lot of their members because my one friend was running his mouth, and I jumped into the fight to back him up. You know what really fucking pisses me off? It's the fact that I was originally diagnosed with bipolar disorder because I have been in fights in the past. Every fight I have ever been in was when I was defending my friends, and that's what I told my doctors. These doctors don't understand right from wrong sometimes; and that fucking asshole of a doctor, Dr. Jacobson, diagnosed me with bipolar disorder since I have been in fights. When I started looking back at my life, I thought that was ridiculous.

Anyway, my friend got into a fight with three of their members, and I jumped in and started throwing punches. Two other guys from my high school then jumped on me and started throwing punches at me, and the next thing I knew, I was getting my face pounded by like six gang members. And they wouldn't stop. I ended up blacking out, and one of my good friends from high school reached for my hand to pick it up. There were a good fifty to seventy-five people in that fight. I looked to my right and saw one of my friends who refused to fight; he was just standing there. My friend Avery was taking a shower and tried to make this fight all about him, and he didn't have my back when I needed him to. It kind of actually reminds me of today when I know there are people I can count on and people that I can't. Avery absolutely falls under the list of people I can't count on. My other friend, Eric, left the party because things were getting out of hand, and he didn't want to get in trouble. People were fighting in my living room and in my kitchen. I started crying really hard and was freaking out because I thought I was going to get into a lot of trouble with my parents and couldn't understand why the fuck this was happening. I actually explained this to my therapist—that with my shadow play, I can end these fuckers if they act up in the world, and the corrupt police can call on me to help them out with my solution pit.

In the next part of his song, he says, "A religious fanatic posts footage of an interfaith service project. A group of teenage boys watches a video of a father playing catch with his son." In these two verses, he is talking about certain things people were doing in this life. When I listen to the part where he says a father is playing catch with his son, I think of my father throwing the ball with me in my front yard. I think this is actually what he is talking about. There was a group of teenagers who were interested because perfection is my direction, and they wanted to be on the frontlines to witness history in the making. When he says a religious fanatic posts footage of an interfaith service project, he is talking about all those Jesus freaks who are on God's mission to save the earth and doing everything they think God wants them to do. This includes the missionaries and people like that who think they have this purpose to serve God in ways that man intended. There were actually people who have died serving these missions, and sometimes I think it's a waste of time. But when Watsky wrote the verse in his song that some people don't ever get a motive to live, he was talking about people like this. I think that a lot of people would absolutely love it if I could actually achieve perfection, and if these young kids want to learn from anyone in the world, I think that I would be a good role model for kids to learn from. I have learned a lot in the past few years about life, about how to be a better person, and about how to conduct myself in different situations in a more grown-up manner. Therefore, I need to be prepared to talk in front of everyone in the world, and this is why people keep on administering all these tests and making sure that I am smart enough and wise enough to pass them with flying colors.

In the next part of his song, he says, "An adult film star posts thumbnail photos of elderly couples fully clothed and smiling. A policeman makes reverse 911 calls instructing residents to take to the streets." The adult film star was my Aunt Sue's friend from Hollywood who showed up at my grandpa's funeral. She was taking photos of the two of them and probably posted them on the secret

Hollywood listserv, and my two grandparents are George's parents in *Seinfeld*. Unfortunately, my grandfather passed away, and my grandma is old now. But this worked for their script, and they based it off my relationship with my grandparents. A lot of people thought that this film star was a bitch. But they are the ones who made me, so I don't disrespect Hollywood. And she was hot as hell. The policeman they are talking about is Lewis Boore. He only ended up getting the policeman gig because of the demons I was dealing with in the past, and his name got brought up as if he was attacking me. But he was actually on my side. The next thing I knew, he was texting me and saying that he was a SWAT officer. I knew he was working with the police because my fraternity brother Stephen Steppe told me, and that is when I found out that the Flobots were talking about Lewis in this song. They also said that Lewis is Thad in a football script, and they also got the idea to write the show called *SWAT* because Lewis joined the SWAT team. Everyone that I hang out with, run into, and touch has an important role in the new world we are building, and those are just some of Lewis's roles.

In the next part of his song, he mentions a patriarch reporting for duty, wearing an orange jumpsuit, and holding a ticket sign. She's ashamed of her birthplace, but retreat is not an option. The person he's talking about is the singer Lorde. I found out she is the person he's talking about because, in one of her songs, she writes that she's ashamed of where she grew up. Lorde is just as important as the other people I have written about, but I haven't talked about her often. I want to download her music onto my iTunes, but I listen to her songs on Miley Cyrus radio on Pandora. She once said that these old men are going to get exactly what they deserve for making our lives a living hell, and she was right about some of them because they were abusing girls, causing domestic violence issues, and controlling us in nonproductive ways. However, she got this expression from her role model, Mr. Big Chief Reaper. Lorde is a good person and cannot go back home because people are scared about what is going on in England. I think it will be safer in the future, but for the time being, she is exactly where she needs to be. They also used this part of his song to write the script for *Orange Is the New Black*. My ex-girlfriend

Ava used to watch this show, and I didn't like it that much. It was pretty much a girls' prison drama. This was loosely based on the troublemakers in this world and was supposed to be based on real-life characters.

I once said that everyone in this world deserves to have credit in the record books, and I meant it. When people try to discredit us, especially me, it really, fucking pisses me off; and I am sick of these assholes controlling us because it is just causing more drama, more anger, and more issues in this world than we ever need. The song that Muse put out, which was featured in one of the *Pitch Perfect* movies, was a perfect song that says they will not control us nor discredit us. My therapist said that nobody is thanking me; however, people all across the globe are thanking me. I know that's not really my therapist talking, but I want the empires to start falling so they will stop ruining our lives. And maybe Avery will die in the process because in *Supernatural*, peace will be attained once that holy motherfucker dies. I am serious because they keep screwing up my life, and I need them to leave me the fuck alone. I will send their "holy one" into the grave.

In the next part of his song, he says, "Women and children, frontline, tune in, stand, and be counted in the belly of the vulture." This line reminds me of the Holocaust and when people are forced to wear masks over their heads during the coronavirus. He says that women and children are counted, and he means that the assholes I was talking about in the previous paragraph are killing the weak and making the strong more powerful. He is talking about the lower class and the Blacks and minorities who live in the streets or in the ghettos. The rich get richer, and the poor get poorer, as is the agenda of an evil man's scheme. I think the people who think like this are so self-involved in their own lives and don't understand that these people need our help and that their lives are equally important to those who go through life with no issues at all. I am actually responsible for killing the flesh, and maybe I should stop because it's not their fault that these greedy and ignorant people are forcing me to self-destruct every day. I think people take what they have for granted, and there are a lot of people who have it way worse than we do. My karma will catch up with me, and I will forget about everything I've been through. But for the time being, nobody in the world has had it worse than I've had it. The worst part about this was that people made me think that I deserved it. I can't stop, and I won't stop. And the fact that the Flobots put this part in their song and that it's on my playlist makes me think that maybe we should start protecting these people as well, especially when the apocalypse is over.

In the next part of the song, he says, "Listen, consider this a distant early warning, the fire's imminent, pollution gathering dust particles through smokestacks." This has a lot of meaning to it. When he says, "Listen, consider this a distant early warning," he is talking about Avery and that he better stay the fuck away from Hollywood because he doesn't belong in the society we are building, and these empires will fall because of everything Dr. O'Connor has taught me about the event when the right man in this world brings to justice everyone who has done me wrong and who has done the world wrong. They also talk about this in *Damnation*, when the God or Jesus character and the priest bring people to justice and say that they are doing the world no good with their actions and bring them to justice.

When he says, "The fires are imminent," he is talking about the new world we are building, which has to do with my solution pit and my cigarette smoking, which I plan to stop. However, the wildfires were my doing, and I didn't even know it. Fort Minor even said in his song, "Who would've thought he'd be the one to set the West in flames?" He is not talking about rap; he is talking about the wildfires that happened in California and also the wildfires that have happened across the globe. Here's the thing, though: Hollywood knows there is nothing left to fix in the world because of me, and my tests started just as early as Ava's did. Except people weren't dying because of my tests, and I don't consider my tests as tests by God; I consider them as tests by people. When he says, "Consider this a distant early warning," he was saying, "Avery, you are not welcome into our world because of the bullshit you have done to Will before Fort Minor even released that song and the bad things you have wished upon him before you even met Will in high school."

The next part that I wrote about is important too. He says, "Pollution, gathering dust, particles through smokestacks," he is talking about the pollution in the world and how it is fucking up Mother Nature and the inside of cities, especially New York City. I actually read about this and wrote it in my book earlier, but Hollywood knew this was going to happen. Or else Flobots wouldn't have written this part in this song. Most people aren't smart enough to pick up on these things, but the pollution in the air is a big problem. And the people that started going green started to do this right.

The next part of his song he says, "New forms are starting to take shape. Once occupied minds are activated, people are waking up. The insurgency is alive and well." This is what caught my eye in the first place about this song. The insurgency are the people who go against the common law and fight for the greater good, even when these bullshit laws make us all follow a certain set of laws. An example of this is when I say that human history has taught us that we go to school, go to college, work, retire, and then die. I am the biggest member of the insurgency, and this is what makes me the biggest divergent because I don't believe this is how our lives should play out. The good people in the 1 percent know this. They are trying to help me build this perfect world, and with the help of Hollywood, I can make all these great things come to life.

I also need the help of the athletes who are buying into my product when I started breaking free and becoming something and someone else, which separated me from everybody else in the world. Everybody else started to wear thin because they weren't understanding all these fantastic things that we can achieve in society. I think Jack's wife, Ariana, is also a divergent because she believes that there should be more to life, and people don't understand that we need to make the best out of what we got on this planet. Rory thinks the exact same way, and Rory is a very good person because he learned from the best not to argue with people and agree with them if you don't understand or if they are wrong, because there is no need to cause controversy in this world when there is already too much evil and drama going on. We don't need these things to affect our lives. It is important that everybody's minds get activated, and every single person, whether they are my first-tier best friend or an outsider, needs to be protected just as strongly as I am being protected. They also have the same right to experience the same heavenly and limitless experiences that I have had. People heard the Word of God through me all across the globe, and this was sort of how I was gaining my wave in the world and how people started to understand that I am fucking awesome and that they need to respect me. The hands of my true believers would love to experience heaven on earth and make this new world we are building into a place of pure faith and science, and all the evil in the world dies because the good people always come out on top.

Outasight's "Tonight is the Night" starts off with "I've been feeling real good. Came a long way from misunderstood, far away from the days when I didn't want to come home because I was afraid of the truth." He says, "I came a long way from the days when I didn't want to come home" because he was talking about when I was dealing with all those conspiracy theories with the CIA and the Russians, and when Katy Perry said in her song that I fell for everything and went from zero to hero because of all the shit that my real creator might have put me through.

I was so fucking scared when I was working at COMTEK. I was working there for three months when the conspiracy hit me on St. Patrick's Day in 2010 with the stars that were going crazy in the sky, and the police came to my house and thought I was crazy. It was kind of like the scene when people thought Russell Crowe was crazy in *A Beautiful Mind*. When Outasight said, "I didn't want to come home because I was afraid of the truth," he meant that my real creator was the "bad man" in *Deliver Us from Evil*, and Selena Gomez said that he is the worst of us. Again, though, Avery is the guy who tried to beat me, but for this song, he is saying that I was scared of the truth as if my real creator is the bad guy in some of these scenes. When I was working at COMTEK, I was so fucking scared about what was going on with me and my body, and nobody was telling me anything about why all these things were happening to me. I really don't know who would do such evil and sinister things to someone, but they couldn't have been good people. I was scared for the entire time I was working at COMTEK, and then the demons actually started attacking me.

My medications, which included Adderall, stopped working, and I couldn't focus at work. I would come home on Fridays because I thought that I was being given productive energy, but instead, the demons inside my head were forcing me to smoke like four cigarettes each hour. I wasn't on that other level that I was on when I was killing it at work. This happened around the time when Susan Sheehan started working as the second person in charge behind Terri Tran at COMTEK. They must have been some really bad people who would do that to someone, but I was scared out of my fucking mind. What happened after that was terrible as well. I ended up finding a new job at a different company because I thought that I could escape what was going on with me at COMTEK. Instead, things started getting worse. I ended up getting charged with indecent exposure because someone or a group of people thought that I deserved to pay that price for being alive right now. I don't know exactly who did that to me, but I want to find out at some point. I have come a long way from how bad things were back then, and I am finally able to live my life again.

The things that were going on with me back then were so bad, that when I came home from work on Fridays—not to my townhouse but to my parents' house—I would lie down, hoping that these demons would go away. For some reason, they would always go away when I woke up on Saturdays. I was pleading for productive energy; instead, the voices inside my head were very evil and sinister, and I just couldn't focus. The Adderall helped me focus; however, I would run out of my prescription every Friday about every two weeks, and that's when the things inside my body started to turn sinister. The medications inside my body weren't working as effectively, and these bad people really wanted my life to end. Luckily, I wasn't charged as a sex offender because of my connections in Hollywood, the 1 percent, and the CIA.

Two months later, in August 2012, I took a trip to Pennsylvania while on another level, and my parents went to my Uncle Bob's funeral. So I was by myself, which was planned by the people who were going to help me get through all this sinister stuff. I broke free from the wrath of society, and it was like *Cribs* was brought to my house and I was giving people a tour of my house. Then I took the trip to Pennsylvania, where I was given many mixed messages about life, and I was happy and then crying. It was like heaven and hell were mixed into one long trip, and Adam and Eve were brought to my attention. There were a lot of crazy things going on, and then my parents ended up picking me up. A police officer called my real creator's cellphone. I thought I was in heaven, but I was just in Pennsylvania. There were many people talking about it, and then it was a turning point for all my lonely nights because they put up a TV screen on one of the billboards within my reach in my car in Pennsylvania.

The Killers wrote in their song that the story looms: you got lost but found your way back home, and that the whole world was going to face an impending doom. After this, Hollywood started releasing all these apocalyptic movies. I still want to live here forever, so I don't listen to apocalyptic songs anymore. They also know that there is nothing left to fix in the world because of me. When people come into my house, fuck around, and mess up the progress I am making, I get really mad and frustrated. I have come a long way from when I was feeling so out of place back then and feel better than I have in my entire life. I am in the best shape of my life, and we need to make sure that this all goes according to the people's plan, and the people who wanted to save me back then. I can achieve my perfection and make sure that the weather is good and that we can all experience those heavenly experiences I experienced. There has to be more to life than what people think life is about. Everything that I experienced can't go to waste, and we need to make this life everlasting so that nothing goes incomplete.

In this song, he also says *who* a lot to signify the elimination of the flesh and people deemed expendable because the world is over-populated anyway. They say *who* a lot in many of their songs because we need to get rid of those who bring nothing to the table and are wasting the resources of those who contribute to this world. With overpopulation, we need more resources for the stronger and wiser people in this world. Like he said, I have come a long way from when I was misunderstood. I thought I was going to die so many times, but I was always able to escape the impossible situations I was in with the help of others and because I am a strong person and a survivor. This is also how I was able to get so many people to buy into my product. There were billions of people across the globe whom I have helped out, and they all know it. People were cheering for me when I left Nationals Park with Jack one day, and Watsky put that in his song because of the good people in this world who were looking out for me and had me branch out to outsiders and those trying to do right in this world. They knew that the world is only alive and surviving right now because of everything I was doing, and it was a miracle that I was even able to go to the game. I left the park, and when the Nationals made a play, they all cheered. Watsky made it specific that they were cheering for me since most of them believe in God and Jesus.

The next part of his song, he says, "As far as I have come, it felt like forever. Days turn to months. Another year passed by but doesn't feel like much. So if I got one chance, I am going to make everyone dance. I am going to have as much fun and figure out the rest when I edge out a plan." When he says, "Days turn to months. Another year passed by but doesn't feel like much," it's because everyone and everything in this world stays the same. I was going through my transgressions and my transitions, but more often than not, people remained the same. I was pretty unpredictable and always thought that there's got to be more to life than what is going on in the real world right now. I am edging out a plan, and I am writing about it in this book. It is all in the scripts that Hollywood writes and about all the progress I have made in people's lives. I don't want anyone or any group of people to take that pride and confidence away from me because I will achieve perfection with people's help and with the motivation and dedication I have within my own world and within other people's worlds. There were even people cheering for me in big groups when they played certain songs that Hollywood put out, such as Katy Perry's song in Italy. I fell for everything and went from zero to hero. Hollywood put the camera on me, and they were all cheering for me because they found hope in the Jesus character who is going to save our lives.

I will have everyone in this world form one big happy family when we are all engaged in friendly competition against one another with acting, singing, and rapping and in every single sporting event. One thing that is important is that karma needs to catch up with me, and it seems like it is taking forever. But it got harder once the professional athletes made my life more difficult, and I ended up missing out on more things. I was feeling down but was a lot wiser and smarter, so it didn't take away from my everyday life; however, the things that were happening to me started turning more sinister again. I am happy that there is always a silver lining at the end of the tunnel; so once this is all over, these assholes stop playing games with me, and I step back into the line, I can have people cheer for me in front of a big audience instead of behind my back.

You know what I figured out? Peyton Manning won his last Super Bowl, and he said, "Believe me, I am going to put you back into that same game again." Before that, everything was done behind my back, and then I started listening to all of Hollywood's songs and Hollywood's scripts and found out that all the positive things that will happen to me in the future have just made me a better and stronger person. Maybe we can't fix the world unless people make my life as hard as it was in the past just to make me a stronger person in the future. I don't have a choice but to save the world, and that is exactly what I am going to do. But I need people's help because this is more than a one-person job. Unlike what most people think, I believe the coronavirus is exactly what we needed to kill a lot of the vulnerable and give these natural resources to the strong. It is kind of like survival of the fittest. We don't need people bringing us down, and the seventy- and eighty-year-old people who were dying because of this was a good thing because they were just wasting their time on this planet; we don't need them around anymore. It is even more important that a lot of the people who were dying were in New York because New York was way too overcrowded, and this was a revolution in New York. We needed these people to die to save the world in the future.

I wanted to write about this part. There is a singer named Starley Hope who entered Hollywood sometime back when I was going through all those apocalyptic things, and she came to my rescue after being welcomed into Hollywood. I hope she can produce more songs, but her song was important. And in her music video, she was lying down while singing. In her song, she says, "If this is our fate, we will find a way to cheat, and we will look to the sky for guidance and say a little prayer. If the answer isn't fair, then that sucks for you." However, at some point, we will definitely cheat fate because we will be forever young. There is one email alert I got called Starlies, and the headline reads, "Find Out Your Life Horoscope for the Day." It also stated the day and date. Her song, when people listen to it, is directly connected to my email when I receive it every day. If the answer isn't fair, then people start dying, but we are maintaining a solid balance of life. And at some point, when people stop having kids, more lives will be protected. In many of the songs I listen to, people die, and they write these songs for me to listen to for a reason—for the flesh to die and for people who don't belong in the new society we are building to pass away.

In one of Hey Violet's songs, she says *don't know* three times, and those are for three people who are never going to understand this life. They are deemed expendable and part of the flesh that can be eliminated. I don't listen to Miley Cyrus's song that says there's no need for two people to go anywhere, because we need the flesh to die to give the strong more power in this world. It is kind of like the Hunger Games and survival of the fittest, giving more natural resources to people who are more important than someone who doesn't belong in this new society anymore. The Starlies email I receive shows everybody's horoscopes, and my sign is the most vital out of all of them. The Killers wrote in one of their songs that my sign is vital. This is also how they got the script called "Scorpion," which was based on the sign of the month I was born. Ava taught me about horoscopes when I was dating her, and then she looked at the signs on my wrist and said that I am going to live a long life. They actually incorporated this part into one of Brad Pitt's movies called *Fury*. They had the girl check the signs on the palm of the hand of the guy, and she said that he was going to live a long life and that he was healthy. This was pretty much what Ava was telling me when she was looking at my wrist. In the movie called *Fury*, they portrayed Adam Seaman as the only member of the crew surviving from World War II, and he was depicted as the guy who didn't belong with all the sinners in the world and the guys in his group. They did this on purpose, and they were going to send him back home from Hollywood since so many of the scripts relate to his life and mine. The positive songs that Hollywood produces about Adam were also part of the reason they were going to send him back home. Hollywood wanted me to be separate from everyone else so that I could understand the lessons they have taught me about life. However, the main reason I am writing about this right now is because I just received an email called Starlies, and I think about Starley Hope every time I get these emails.

Shawn Mendes in "Mercy" starts off the song by saying, "You've got a hold of me. Don't even know your powers." He says this because my powers are very strong, and I don't want to see any numbers besides the numbers that I post on social media and achieve in sports and numbers in general. Jack didn't go through the things that I went through to deserve that credit. Avery didn't go through the things I went through to deserve that credit. My real creator didn't go through the things I went through to deserve that credit. I went through all these apocalyptic things before the average person even knew the apocalypse was happening. If I could thank the corrupt people in the world and Hollywood, I would, but then more and more people started realizing that. And now we are all dealing with apocalyptic things. I was so fucking scared, but now I am strong and powerful, and I don't let the fears I am experiencing affect my daily life. My powers are very fucking strong, reaching all the way up to heaven and down to hell and spreading across the globe as well. I am going to solve every single person's problems in this world just based on the scripts that Hollywood writes and based on the solution pit that I am working with within my reach.

In the next part of his song, he says, "I can't take any more. I'm saying, 'Baby, please have mercy on me. Take it easy on my heart. Even though you don't mean to hurt me, you keep tearing me

77

apart.'" He says this because I can't take any more. I am sick of all this drama, this bullshit, and the shit that I've been through, which only Jesus has experienced at the beginning of time. I am sick of people's personalities and when people don't give me eye contact when they talk to me. I am sick of the people who disrespect me on social media and the drama that Jack brought into my life when I started trusting him. When I wouldn't talk for about ten seconds, Avery would ask, "Why aren't you talking?" I am sick of people saying that I am being quiet. I don't know who started that stupid, fucking trend, but there are so many fucking fake people who don't understand life and bring no value to mine that I don't want to fucking hang out with them anymore. People who talk without a filter don't give a fuck about what you are saying; they only care about themselves. The people who listen more often are the ones you should want to hang out with. I am sick of all this nonsense and words that don't have any specific meaning behind them. The cause of such bullshit and the apocalypse is actually everyone's fault, and it started in 2004. When I heard the voices and when very bad things were happening to me between 2012 and 2013, it wasn't God; it was Jack. He was totally throwing me around my fucking house, and now he is just tearing me the fuck apart. Honestly, I am so sick of the way things have been in this world, and for the world to become sane and stable again, people need to be more like me.

Furthermore, this is what Shawn Mendes meant because Jack keeps on tearing me apart. In Kid Cudi's song, he said, "Like it or not, but you are mean, and look at what I made God teach you." Jack is the devil, and I fucking hate him for playing those games with me back in the day when I was living in all that fear. So many people in Hollywood think that Jack has to pay the ultimate price for all these people dying. He was playing games with me until I took that trip to Pennsylvania and broke free from his wrath, and then he still didn't stop. He was playing games with me when I was dating Ava, and she thought it was Jesus talking to her. But it was fucking Jack. He played games with me at my little sister's thirtieth birthday party, and I looked like an asshole. But now I am much calmer, and people laid it on him pretty badly. However, when I am not around him, he keeps on ripping my soul to shreds; and thankfully, with the help of the people who wrote *Supernatural*'s script, I will get my soul back. Jack knows he can't play games with me anymore, and he is the main person responsible for the apocalypse.

In 2004, the Yankees' tenure ended because of Jack. In 2006, when I started to take control again, then good things started happening in my life. Now that I think about it, 2006 was a fantastic year, and 2004 was miserable. When I was living in all that fear at COMTEK, Jack called me from a DC number, and he was playing games with me at COMTEK that made me unable to work anymore. I was so scared when I was working at COMTEK because of the tests to make me as strong as I am today, but the fact that Jack was the main catalyst behind the bad guys in this world really fucking pisses me off. I would have had no idea if it weren't for the people who told me. Sanchez even said that if I'm getting prank calls, it's probably because of Jack. He said it to my face when we went on a trip to Pennsylvania, and I played it off as if it was his friend Will Morin because I didn't want any drama and didn't believe that Jack really made those moves. When I took that trip to Pennsylvania, I learned that there is a big difference between heaven and hell. Jack is the guy in this world who leads hell, and I am the guy in this world who leads heaven. Jack can lead his sinners into hell, and I will lead my saints into heaven.

In the next part of his song, Shawn Mendes says, "My pride is all I got." I think that Maren Morris says this in her song too. I am a very proud person, and I am very proud of the billions of people I have helped out in this world, the masterpiece I am working on, and the masterpiece of a world that I am bringing to light. I am proud that I am the best person in the world, and no matter what anybody else is going through, I have had it worse. Everyone should look forward to better days in the future. Avery even talked to me about dealing with brain-dead issues, so now I am.

I once told my therapist that I am affected by what other people are going through, which I think is bullshit; but it's hard for me to work and concentrate as well as I once did after Avery was going through his issues because, for some reason, I need to go through the same crap that other people go through. I am a proud person, and everyone is wearing me thin because I hold the future of the world in my hands. I am also talking to my therapist every week, saying that I am a different, more mature, and more level-headed person than I was in the past. She understands the things that I do, and most people only see their points of view. So it is a lot easier to talk to someone who listens rather than to many people in this world who are made of greed. My mom and Rory are pretty easy to talk to as well, but most people only see their own points of view and don't listen to others as well as some people do in this world.

In the next part of his song, he says, "And even though you have good intentions, I need you to set me free." He was talking about my therapist and how I need her to set me free and start living my life again. I am getting help from others; but my therapist keeps on guiding me in the right direction to achieve perfection, obtain all the finest things in life, and be happy and rich one day. I fell into this "prison sentence" in the year 2012, when the Mayans said the world was going to end, so it wasn't a coincidence that I took that trip in 2012. There were Amazons and other people who were praying for the end of times, so they started to fade away as well. Some of them started dying. My therapist is really important, and I love talking to her once a week because she actually gets me and understands the things I am going through. I need to start thinking about myself more often, and because of her, I started to. I can still help others all the time, but at some point, I need to start living my life again too. I can help others by just watching and listening to the words that Hollywood puts out in their music and in their scripts. Like it or not, these words help solve people's problems. My powers are limitless, and these powers help solve people's problems as well. Furthermore, with magic soaking my spine, I am able to help out people all over the globe with babies being born and with sporting events being won or lost, and the athletes fucking love me for helping them out regularly. There are people that I walk by in the streets who smile at me, say hi, and wave because they greatly appreciate the efforts I am putting in to help their worlds, and they can return the favor by helping with the problems in my world.

In the next part of his song, he says, "I'm prepared to sacrifice my life; I would gladly do it twice," and he says it with more emphasis in the second part of his song. When Jesus was alive, he first died at the age of thirty-three, and he was a carpenter until his thirtieth birthday. This actually correlates to life pretty well because one of the turning points in my life was when I was thirty years old, and I had more friends show up to my birthday party. Thanks to my good friend Ethan Stewart, I was able to have this "second coming of Jesus" moment in the spotlight, very effective. When I was reading one of the books, the author said that Jesus did everything he was supposed to until the age of thirty-three. I was a little scared that I wouldn't make it past the age of thirty-four. Nas also wrote in his song in 2001 on his CD called Illmatic that Jesus died at the age of thirty-three. Thanks to people's help, I am still alive and working hard on myself and on other people's lives.

The Red Hot Chili Peppers put in one of their songs that I can't die because I am the "sun dude," and in one of their other songs, which they wrote when they witnessed everything I was going through in college, they said my whole life has been a sacrifice. Shawn Mendes wrote this song, which is really powerful, but obviously, I am not going to sacrifice my life. Additionally, we need to make this one everlasting so that we can all accomplish our dreams and destiny, just like we imagined when we were really young. I also want to write in my book about the Killers' song that says, "When we were young."

The singer Sia has played an important role in my life. In one of her songs, when she writes about how it's hard to lose a chosen one, talking about Avery and that she will help out the guy who saved her life, she was talking about me. When I was a sophomore in college, George Mason went to the Final Four. They carried on this good luck throughout the season and into the postseason because of certain things I was doing that year. Nevertheless, that year, I was planning on doing a dance competition with my fraternity brothers. I was planning and trying really hard to master my dance moves. I would have had stage fright and fucked up the entire thing for my fraternity because of my anxiety. Therefore, I sort of saved Sia's life because she gets stage fright and wears her mask on stage so that she doesn't see the fans, and she pretends like she is the only one in the stadium. She credits all of her accomplishments, fame, and money to the fact that everything I do is special, and I was able to help her achieve our importance in this world with all the moves I was making when I was that much younger. We all know that karma will catch up with me sometime next year or the year after, so we just have to be patient. However, Sia is so aware of the fact that this one mistake I made has made her career. Because of my own personal stage fright, she was able to achieve her own fame. I am very happy that I am able to realize these things now and am able to write in my book about all these events in my life. I don't disrespect or judge people because you never know what a person is going through unless you are walking in their footsteps. However, I wanted to write about Sia's success and how my life depends on her being able to get as far as she's gotten with her musical talents.

In the first part of Michelle Branch's "All You Wanted," she says, "I wanted to be like you. I wanted everything." She says this because I need a girl who can run the world with me, and when I was dating Ava, it was clear that she was a girl who couldn't be hand in hand with me. The main reason she wrote this song was that all you wanted was a girl who cared. When I was dating Ava, I was trying to explain to her all the things I was going through, and I wanted her to understand. But she just couldn't grasp the concept of the things I was going through. Maybe I didn't quite understand all the things I was going through back then to its fullest extent, but she should've made a better effort to try to be a better girlfriend. In another part of this song, she says, "So lonely inside, so busy out there." She is talking about the traffic issues and people who are going through issues in the outside world who need my help. Whether those issues are divorce rates, traffic problems, or whatever demon problems someone is going through, I am always there for assistance and can help out whoever needs my help. Within my immediate reach and what I can see are my family and friends, the sports world, and Hollywood. I put all these people on my list of favorite people; they are before anyone else in the world. I know how to put the good in the good life because it is on my TV all the fucking time. I know these athletes really appreciate my help, and when they don't have to worry about injuries anymore and can just ignore their haters, they can be a lot happier. I was also going through other things when I was dating Ava, such as not getting the support on Facebook from my friends, and she actually started to show that she cared. This is why the Barenaked Ladies said it was "lovers in a dangerous time" and Rihanna said "we found love in a hopeless place."

I completely understand this Michelle Branch song because she knew that Ava was a good fit for that year but not the girl of my dreams. She cared about things that I didn't care about, and she wanted to go out at night when I wanted to stay in. It was things like that that forced us to fight. She picked a fight with me when she misinterpreted Jack saying that we should start working together. Ava twisted his words around and said other things, and then I started yelling at her. We got into a big fight shortly after. Another thing that happened was when we went to Roanoke with the family; she wanted to go out to drink, but I wanted to stay in. I got mad at her for not wanting to stay in with me and be a better girlfriend. She cared about partying way more than I did, and I just wanted to settle down, not go out and waste my money and time. She was definitely a nightmare, and I knew that I could do better. However, to date, she is the best girl I have ever dated. I had issues with my other girlfriends too, and my anger got the best of me in some of my relationships. Now, though, I am a lot calmer. Drinking was actually an issue in every single relationship I have ever been in, and I don't drink at all anymore. Another thing is that I need a girl who can train me to be a better boyfriend, and I think I have found my perfect match for when the time is right. Anyway, Michelle Branch wrote this song because I need a girl who cares about what I'm going through, and Ava just didn't cut out as being the girl of my dreams.

In Selena Gomez's "Love You Like a Love Song," she starts out saying, "Every beautiful thought's been already sung, so I guess right now, here's another one." A while back, I said to myself, "If Hollywood is writing this music for me to listen to, then does that include love songs too?" After I said that, I heard this Selena Gomez song, and she goes, "Every beautiful thought's been already sung, so I guess right now, here's another one." There were other artists in Hollywood who wrote love songs to me too, and that includes Miley Cyrus, Fergie, Bebe Rexha, and other people who aren't coming to my mind right now. I have this relationship with women that makes me desirable to them, and Hollywood made that apparent with their love for me, especially Anna Kendrick. She did a lot of work in this world, much of it for my existence on this planet. Selena Gomez has been through a lot, especially recently, but she continues to survive and be the best person she can be. She made it evident by telling people that I'm the man and that I'm is going to clean up this mess and save our lives the exact way I was born to. It's not just the girls in Hollywood but also other girls across the globe that have shown great interest in me. I have that personality and looks that would make girls go crazy for me. However, every person in this world is meant to be with one person, so none of that matters at the end of the day because there is truly only one girl that I am dreaming and thinking about regularly. Selena Gomez is a truly special person, and I know that a lot of people think that Hollywood and athletes are selfish, only care about themselves, are rich, and have asshole personalities, but I look at it differently. Both groups made it harder for me so I can be the great person I was always destined to be. I see both groups as pushing me every day for perfection and for me to have that personality and be right with my words and example to lead the world with that beautiful girl I dream about every single day. I should also mention that Taylor Swift has written love songs about me too. I am missing other artists, such as Cher Lloyd, who is less known to the general population, but you get my point.

In the next part of her song, she says "with the best of 'em." She is talking about how I am a sinister person. Not all athletes believe in that higher-power bullshit, and I belong in that outlier group of the best people in the world. Even in Kid Cudi's song, when he said, "Some figured I was Satan bound," and athletes would love it if I could actually achieve perfection. It surprised them when they first found out. Anyway, people like Stephen Curry, LeBron James, and Kevin Durant have developed great respect for me for everything I am doing for the world and for them and because of all the adversity, hatred, and the sinister things I was going through in my past. I am even still alive, and I am actually talking big like I can achieve perfection. I know that we are all getting older, but every single day, people are looking for a solution in the world for every single problem that we are going through. Selena Gomez means it when she says I belong in that group of the best people in the world. Indeed, in many of their songs, Hollywood states that I am the best person in the entire world, which says a lot since there are seven billion people in the world, and the outliers are considered the best. Anyway, I know for a fact that nobody in the world has had it tougher than I have and that no one has the heart that I do. Nor does anyone bring more to the table than I do. Given all this information, yes, maybe I am the best person in the world.

In the next part of her song, she says, "You are beautiful, like a dream come alive, incredible, a sinful miracle, lyrical. You saved my life again." I want to explain this part of the song. When she says *sinful*, Hollywood is asking everyone in the world to think twice before you make up your minds between Jack and me. Obviously, those who are smarter in the world chose me, but those who don't understand how fake Jack really is and can't see through his fakeness would have chosen him. She says *miracle* because I am producing miracles every single day for people all across the globe. I have saved many lives and also ended many, but the credit for those lives I have saved goes directly to me. When she says *lyrical*, I have given Hollywood, including Lady Gaga (who also wrote a love song about me), the inspiration to write these lyrics and given them hope past when karma was going to catch up with them; and if they didn't have anything else to write about, I have inspired them to write more and given them more information on what to write about—my life and other people's lives across the globe. Somehow it connects us all together, and I already know that we are all connected through technology, the sky, and the Internet. But we are also all connected through me, everything I do in my daily life, and how I can spread my greatness to others.

When Selena Gomez says, "You saved my life again," I want to give a few examples. She had to get a new kidney, and when she was on the news, she said that her friend saved her life because she donated her kidney to her. The asshole reporters on the Today show were asking her why she said that her friend saved her life, because the assholes of the world wanted her to say that God saved her life. She gave that credit to me and her friend. Selena Gomez's best friend went out of her way to save her life, and Selena Gomez gives the credit to me because Hollywood tracks the moves I make and the lives I have saved. Selena Gomez was obviously one life that I was able to save. Another example is that she was buying a lot of clothes one day, and they told Avery through telekinesis that Selena Gomez is hard to please. Avery thought the voice was mine, but it was people lying or fabricating the truth to him. Anyway, she was embarrassed, and because of my Willpower, I was able to help her out that day. Another example I want to give was when I was using my powers inside my house. I was going to sit down Justin Bieber and Selena Gomez and help their relationship work out when they were dating a few years back, and it actually worked for the time being until their relationship failed. But Selena Gomez watched the highlights, laughed hard, and was very grateful that I was trying to help them out. However, back then, I didn't really know that my powers were actually working and that I was actually helping out people. Recently, I pretty much know what I am doing and how to help out myself and others across the globe.

In the next part of her song, she mentioned that I should listen to all these songs on repeat to get my playlists perfect and to save the world through science and technology with my own technology. Maybe I can even help the Yankees in the postseason in 2020 with my technology. Hollywood wants me to listen to these songs, and they don't really care about what people say, who understands the lyrics, and who doesn't; they just care about my success and what I can do to help out others in the world. I listen to music a lot during the day, interpret their songs, and dissect them, and this is what I am doing with a lot of their songs and getting them on paper, just like what I am doing right now. I actually talked about the Royals manager who said that his technology and phone saved his life one day. I can save lives with this type of weird science. I know it is hard for me to keep my shit together daily because people use their phones all the time, and it is hard for me to keep track of who needs what at any given point in time. But I think that I am getting a better handle on what I can do to save the world. One of those ways is to listen to all these songs and make my playlist perfect for when I make road trips and when I make my final destination trip to Hollywood.

In the next part of her song, she says, "Constantly, boy, you play through my mind like a symphony. There's no way to describe what you do to me. You just do to me what you do, and it feels like I've been rescued. I've been set free. I am hypnotized by your destiny." I am going to dissect this part of her song now. There are a lot of girls who are obsessed with me, including Jack's wife, Ariana, but she made this song specifically about how important and how attractive I am. She wanted to let me know through this song that I am actually the sexiest person on the planet, and when I go to Hollywood, I will be able to live the dreams that I have always wanted to. Of course, I would go with a girl, but all these hot and sexy girls in the world feel the exact same way that Selena Gomez feels about me. When she is talking about my destiny, she is referring to my path to perfection, all the lives I am able to save, and how I am going to clean up this mess with my magic. I have people turn their backs on me all day long, and she wanted to make it specific that everything I do is special and that I am at the very top of the list of the best people in the world. A lot of girls, and even guys, are hypnotized by my destiny. How could a middle-class, nobody accountant grow into the guy who was born to save the world? It doesn't make any sense, but people chose me. I just kind of ran off with it, and a lot of people, including Carli Lloyd and Alex Morgan, really bought into my product and really appreciate all the work I am doing in the world. Those two soccer players found a real liking for me when I was younger and in high school, and they just grew up to win those championships for Team USA. It wasn't a coincidence. Everyone who wanted to be part of my group ended up killing it in this world. Everyone who turned their backs on me ended up with bigger issues and more problems that they brought on themselves by disrespecting me. Selena Gomez wasn't well-known until Maya told me about her, and then I started listening to her music. Now, I have developed a great long-distance friend and someone I can rely on to help me continue with my success in this world. She lets me know very specifically how much she really cares about me, that I deserve to be happy every second of the day, and not to listen to anybody who hates on me because they will face karma in the worst ways.

In the first part of his song "Pretender," AJR says, "I've got lots of problems. Well, good thing nobody knows." This line reminds me of all the issues I am going through regularly. For instance, when I fake on people or when I have to leave parties early, it is because of shadow play and because of all the demons fighting me, telling me to leave parties early ever since I took that trip to Pennsylvania in 2012. Since then, I have been living at my parents' house. A few years back, everybody knew who I was, but now I just want it to be. I also want to focus on my goals and keep my momentum on a high level.

Anyway, another issue I have is with the fear and pain I am going through. When I do yoga sometimes at night, I am living in so much fucking fear that it is hard for me to get through the entire yoga session without wanting to quit. I have quit so many things ever since my hell story began, but I try my best to be the most productive and keep my motivation high, not letting the pains and fear get in the way of my everyday life. I know that Hollywood and professional athletes made my life harder for me after everything was getting better again. I don't think they should have. I have been through so much, and I thought it was because of God. But it was actually because of people. Those are some of the issues that AJR is talking about.

Another issue is the fear I am living in with the light beams, and when I look at the lights, I sometimes see the cross. Another fear is the fear of the sun. There is an expectation that the sun could crash with Earth in ten thousand years unless we do something about it as humans. Fortunately, I can do something about it because I am a powerful person; and at some point, I will look at the light and the sun and see no fear with both of them.

Another issue I am going through is that I am conquering every-thing. Furthermore, when I say everything, I mean everything. I have conquered every single injury known to mankind and every single worst thing imaginable known to mankind. We need to find a solution for all these issues so that we can fix other people's problems that deal with the same shit. Fortunately for me, all my problems always have a way of going away. I went through the apocalypse twice and never talked about it, and the only people who were talking about it were Hollywood, before everyone else was affected by it as well. It actually adds to my story because I am able to save everyone from the apocalypse and become the hero I was destined to become.

In the next part of the song, he says, "I'm insecure. I think like what I'm supposed to." When he says, "I am insecure," he is talking about all my insecurity issues. One of my insecurity issues is that I don't really talk when people disrespect me or when people act fake around me. I don't know how to deal with hate except by wanting to get into a fight with that person, and I don't know how to act fake. I was always a real person and told people exactly how it was, and I started to notice certain people around me act fake and not like themselves around strangers and friends, which would throw me off guard. It was kind of like they were trying to impress the other person, and I don't try to impress people; I always act like myself. I don't give a fuck what people think about me, but some people try too hard. It gets really fucking annoying when people act fake. I know people can change, but stop trying to impress others. When AJR emphasizes *supposed to* the way I said up there, he was trying to get the rapper Spose more fans and more credit than he deserved from the past. I know he wrote the song, "Gee Willikers," which was really disrespectful toward me, but he said that my raps are better than Hoodie Allen's and expressed why the fuck he got all these fans when my raps are better.

In the albums they wrote in 2012, Hoodie Allen didn't disrespect me at all, but Spose did. However, in the 2014 album, Hoodie Allen disrespected me twice. The first time was that he wrote in his song, "And I don't know if I fit in with your society, so chill, take a pill for anxiety and doze off." He is actually on anxiety pills now and wrote his 2016 album as "Intro to Anxiety" because that was karma getting him back for disrespecting me when I was dealing with all my demon problems. The other time he disrespected me, which really fucking bothers me, was that he said in one of his songs, "If you making it bad, well, I'm making it worse." Like I said before, *there is no reason for people to ever interfere in my life and make my life a living hell.* I didn't do shit to people in Hollywood, so I deleted every single song that said I had to live through this hell a second time. It is such bullshit, and I have had so many *Goddamn* issues because of these rich assholes in this world who think they are better than people and made me age this much and go through most of this shit that I never should have ever gone through. I threatened Hoodie Allen, saying, "I am coming for you if you ever dream of making my life hard." If people ever told anyone to write songs to make my life worse, they either died, faced karma with someone in their family dying, or faced their own personal karma because of it. I didn't do shit, and even through 2016, I didn't do anything to anyone until I got stuck deeper. There are a lot of people who died, and if the truth ever got out about why, then a lot of people would get into a lot of fucking trouble for making my life a nightmare. Also, the events that happened leading up to it would put a lot of people's careers in jeopardy.

In the next part of AJR's song, he says, "I'm not really cool. I'm a good pretender 'cause I am just like you… I do not belong here. You all clearly do." I'm going to explain this. He says, "I am just like you" because so many guys and girls in this world have compared their personalities to mine. There is every single part of my personality that can compare to someone in this world, and this is why I am the *only* person in this world who is one of a kind. There are billions of people in this world who are similar to me, but I am a one-of-a-kind person and the only guy in this world who is one of a kind. I am not cool and was never part of the "cool" group in school, but I was always down-to-earth and always kept it real. If I didn't like someone, I would let them know and never faked it to make it.

When he says, "I do not belong here. You all clearly do," he is talking about Avery. Avery is the Jesus character who doesn't belong in this world of sinners. At some point, I want him to join my group of friends, but he kind of is out of place. I have been treated like shit by people, just like him, but he is a loser who has no friends except for me. There are people who care about him, but they just aren't in his life right now. Avery is the lonely stoner who doesn't trust any-body, and there are many people in Hollywood who wish they never turned their back on him when he tried to act in Hollywood because he has been so depressed and lonely ever since. I feel bad for him, and I hope that he could be a big impact on my life in the future. Everyone knows that he is by himself and doesn't trust anyone, but he doesn't belong. However, I have looked at other people in this world, and it doesn't seem like they are cool or belong either. So I want Avery to be more confident and more secure, just like me; make friends; and become a better friend to me. This is all I am going to write about this song for the time being.

Hoodie Allen's "Sirens" had two main reasons for its creation. The first reason is the saying that you can't teach an old dog new tricks, which was part of the reason the apocalypse was happening. The second reason was that the rapper Spose released his song "Gee Willikers," which disrespected me so much and actually made me angry. There was no fucking reason for him to come out with that song. One part of the song I wanted to discuss is where he says, "Got your girlfriend so obsessed with me." He is talking about my rela-tionship with Ariana. I know they are happy together, but Ariana had a bit of a crush on me. And when her relationship with Jack wasn't working, she kept in the back of her mind that maybe it could work with me. I met Ariana for the first time when I was dating Ava in 2014. I thought she was cool and she laughed at all of my jokes, but I didn't think much of it. Ever since then, I have gotten really close to her and really respect her. I wouldn't fuck up that relationship, but Hoodie Allen mentioned this in his song to disrespect Jack for all the times he disrespected me.

The next part of his song I wanted to talk about is where he says, "like we living in the six days." He is talking about God and the Bible with this verse. God created the world in six days, I believe, and there are many revelations that include the number six in the Bible. It is not the devil's code but the code of a God in this world. The number four is the devil's code, which makes sense; and for my names and numbers, the letter D is the fourth letter in the alphabet. So forty-four is actually the devil's code. The number sixty-six is also not the devil's code because it has something to do with the stars in the sky and the universe. One of the authors in the books I read stated that sixty-six is *not* the devil's code and provided several reasons it wasn't, one of those reasons being the moon, the eclipse, and the universe as well. Anyway, Hoodie Allen became specific about it in this song, and the Chainsmokers wrote an entire song that became popular worldwide about my superhuman gifts and about why sixty-six is not the devil's code—because I am not the type of person that it fits.

The next part of his song I wanted to discuss was when he says, "She think I'm James Bond. You just an afterthought." When Hoodie Allen says, "You just an afterthought," he is talking about Jack. I know that many people don't like Jack, and actually, people in Hollywood and elsewhere disrespect him all the time. They are mad that he is still alive, mainly because of the games he played with me in the past and because he is seen as a bad influence on the world. People don't look for people like Jack for guidance; they look to people like me to lead the world and control things the way that God is supposed to. We don't want to hear Jack's voice. Actually, many people dealing with mental illnesses and hearing voices have been taught by me to ignore Jack's, as he is the devil, and you shouldn't pay attention to voices that don't make sense to you. Rely on the person who you can trust to fix and solve your problems, which is me.

The next part of his song I wanted to discuss was when he says, "But the opposite." When he says this, he is talking about the fact that it *is* the opposite: you can teach an old dog new tricks, and that I am actually God. My real creator, his generation, and those above his generation are the reason for the apocalypse and the end of the human race. Hoodie Allen is saying that because of people like my real creator and these old guys who like to control our lives, they are the reason so many bad things are going on in this world. My generation is much better, and we have the gifts and the tools to save the human race. I am not talking about ten-year-olds; I am pretty much talking about people who were born from around 1980 to 1995. We can even stretch that to about 1975 to 1999. Anybody outside that generation is screwing up the world. The hell song explains a lot about the bad things that have been going on in my life, and it was Avery's choice, just like I explained from the script for the show called *The 100*." However, honestly, I know evolution plays a big part in our lives; but every time my real creator walks around me, when I am in control of things, he slows me down. I don't want to hear his opinion on things because he is not like I am. I think more Big Picture, and his opinions on things are wrong a lot of the time. Honestly, my real creator has too much say in this world and too much power; and once his power goes away, then we will all be in a better place and happier because of me, a down-to-earth guy, who cares about people so much, is in control, and will fix all of our problems.

In the next part of his song, it is someone from his gang named Alex Wiley. He says, "I get it for the Lord, I bet you get it for a Lock boy." When he says this, he means that his success and existence in Hollywood are because of me, and he bets that Spose is influenced by my real creator. I've explained a lot in the previous paragraph about how my real creator's generation is actually screwing everything up, and it's people in my generation who are uncovering all the lies told by previous generations. Hopsin mentioned in one of his songs, "Your friends are low lifes. Don't act surprised [that Hoodie Allen took off the way he did while you remained underground]." He should have never released his song called "Gee Willickers." Anyway, I don't think I knew what I was, and we will be here forever because only God can stop Father Time. That is part of my job in the next year or two. I've talked a lot about his song and wrote about a page and a half about it, and that is good enough. Thank you for listening!

The first part of Hopsin's "Ill Mind of Hopsin" that I want to mention is where he says kids are dropping out of school and girls are having miscarriages. Then he says, "I'm embarrassed, and I'm ashamed. I played a part in this devilish game, makin' your common sense perish." When he talks about kids dropping out of school and girls having miscarriages, he's addressing the bigger picture. Kids drop out because they lack motivation and inspiration, and their parents aren't guiding them in the right direction. However, as I have learned, you don't need to go to school to make it far in the real world. Many places ask for a degree, but if you want to work for yourself, then you really don't need one. He says that girls are having miscarriages because miscarriages happen all the time, and it's not necessarily a bad thing because too many people are having kids in this world. It needs to stop. We are worried about overpopulation. And when you have kids, your parents, grandparents, or siblings are bound to lose their lives because of the circle of life. I am serious. Too many people think that having kids is a blessing and a great thing, but I don't. I think too many people are having kids, and I would rather be immortal, believing that only stupid people, to a certain degree, are having kids. Karma will catch up with me at some point, and we don't need any more bodies in this world.

When Hopsin says he is ashamed and played a part in this devilish game, he is talking about how all those bad things were happening to me in the past. I was clueless, scared, and running for my life for about two years straight. I think many people played their parts, like most of the world's population, and I need to learn how to forgive everyone. However, many people are facing karma because it hasn't caught up with me yet. They regret ever participating in this game. People are looking around for someone to blame in this world; and sometimes, you need to look in your own rearview mirror and ask, "What did I do wrong that made my life a living hell?"

I picked up on many clues telling me that many people played their roles when I was scared out of my mind. I don't know if my real creator started this game or not, but I am a bit mad that most people never came clean about what they did to me in the past. I know that Fergie said Hollywood laid the lice in me, and Taylor Swift said in one of her songs, "But not like this." I also know that Peyton Manning and all those athletes gathered together after he won the 2016 Super Bowl and looked at me straight in the face when he was on the news, saying, "Believe me, I am going to put you back in that same game again." Bebe Rexha said they knew exactly what they were doing. I have had so many bad things happen to me since then, and a lot of bad things have happened in this world since then. I know that people were actually dying before they made my life a living hell, and things weren't great for me before the athletes made it worse. When Jesus was alive the first time around, he forgave everyone, including

Judas. I am expecting to do the exact same right now. If people forgot what they did to me in the past, then I won't forget, and I will make you pay for the things you did to me.

In the next part of his song, he says, "You havin' sex with every-motherfuckin'-body you see, with a past so dark that Satan'd jump out of his seat. But still you out in these streets, thinkin' you as hot as can be, without the knowledge to lead." Hopsin is talking about *Gossip Girl* and the girl I was looking forward to meeting when I was dating Ava. She actually came to my street twice to take what she needed from me so that Hollywood could continue their success. The first time I saw her, she was smiling at me and walking on the sidewalk right across from my house. The second time, she was driving her car, and I was on my way to Shakers. They said to take what they need from me but not talk to me because I'm still going through too much. Everyone says that she sleeps around too much, but I don't believe them. I like to see the good in people unless they prove otherwise. Anyway, she is very hot, and she is the one who gossips in Hollywood, talking about people and posting things on what they call their message board so that everyone knows what's going on in Hollywood. I remember when *Gossip Girl* came out, everyone was wondering who Gossip Girl was, and the girl in the real world came to visit my house. I already talked about *Gossip Girl*, but Kate (Avery's wife is supposed to be the Vanessa character in *Gossip Girl*) and Avery is Dan, the only broke character from *Gossip Girl*.

In the next part of Hopsin's song, he says, "You been brainwashed by a fake life that you're used to livin'. When I say the word *fun*, what do you envision? Prolly drinkin' and smokin' out with your crew and chillin' with clueless women you tryin' to bang... Is that all you think life really is? Well, if so, then you're a fucking idiot... Do you even have any goals aside from baggin' these hoes...? Well, let me guess. No... All you do is play beer pong and hang out with the bros... You're a fuckin' adult with no skills at all. You don't read any books or play ball. You don't draw. You literally do nothing at all... Your friends are lowlifes. Don't act surprised." When he writes all this, he is talking about the rapper Spose. Spose should have never came out with that song "Gee Willickers" because it really backfired on him, and now Hoodie Allen has had a lot more success. Spose wrote in one of his songs that he knows his raps are better than that dude and "fuck him and his crew." Hopsin is right. Hopsin is even more right when he says that if you think life is all about screwing women and drinking and smoking with your bros, then you're a fucking idiot. I know people still think like this, but I would rather live healthier than drink and smoke. Smoking weed is not good for you, and I was actually just talking about this with my therapist. Drinking is terrible for you. I might actually never drink again because of what alcohol did to me. I would black out too much and would always get lost on the streets of DC, or I would always get depressed when I drank alcohol. I think that people need to rearrange their priorities in life, or they become nobodies in society. I have risen above the middle class and turned into someone that is bigger than life. I am the biggest rebel to the system, and I will get rich this way. I don't plan on working another nine-to-five job ever again. Spose doesn't read books, play ball, or draw. He mentioned these things in his songs, indicating he doesn't do those things, and this is how Hopsin came out with this verse. There are many people who also don't do these things, and they are wasting space in this life. I am more productive than 99.9 percent of the population with everything I contribute in this life.

In the next part of his song, he says, "Girls, stop actin' like you want a guy with traits like Romeo. Bitch, that's a fuckin' lie. You always talk about how every man's fake and you can't take it and you want somethin' real. Shut up, tramp. Save it. Twice a week, you put on your makeup… and head to the club half-naked with your ass shakin', pullin' a lowlife nigga…and find out he work at the gas station… You want Romeo? Then act patient." This part of the song is about Anna Kendrick. Anna Kendrick was very lonely when I wasn't arriving in Hollywood, and she couldn't find a man. Hopsin talks about two girls in this song: the girl who was Gossip Girl and Anna Kendrick. Anna Kendrick means a lot to me in terms of the development of my transgressions and my perfection. She knew exactly who I was once she became popular in Hollywood and was mixed in with the right group of people. This happened a long time ago, around the time I was dating Angie. They all started at the end and know that I will achieve perfection and that everyone is not focused on the full potential theory, but if they are working out or being productive throughout the day, they are working hard enough to be in the shape they need to be for this to work the right way. I think she deserves more respect in this world, a realization that came to me once I saw *Pitch Perfect*. She suddenly blew up in the world, and everyone was talking about her around the time when I started to gain attention. People need to understand the importance of being on my good side and not disrespecting me. I know nowadays that many people realize this, and for those who are still tuned in to my development, we are seeing a lot of great things in this world. Anna Kendrick is a big reason for that. When I was *really* into her and she was into me from a distance, she knew she had to come clean about who she's dated in the past. Furthermore, she wrote in her book about her past relationships so that we could start on page 1 if we are both still single by the time we meet each other. I don't think we will be, but it just shows how much she really cares about me from Hollywood.

In the next part of his song, he disrespects Kevin Hart by saying, "You hamster-ass nigga, you just stuck in a loop." I understand why he would disrespect Kevin Hart; Kevin Hart is a pretty cocky dude who seeks a lot of attention in this world. For example, during NBA weekends, he would always participate in the celebrity game, seeking attention from the world and acting foolishly in front of everyone. I get it. I seek attention from people; however, I am much calmer now and just want things to be right in this world. Hopsin was very angry with his lyrics in this song; but I love this song, downloaded it, and wanted to talk about it in my book. He also disrespects Drake, saying, "Look at you, a real nigga, thinkin' your life's cool. Girls used to turn me down for guys who were like you…then they regret it because it wasn't the right move." Drake is another person who deserves disrespect because, just like Kevin Hart, he is really cocky and needs to be put in his place. I think that Drake is looking after my best interests and knows that his existence on this planet and the reason for his fame have everything to do with me. The reason he blew up the way he did was because of me, so he will try his hardest to make sure that everything in my life is going right because of all the great things I have done for him. I really respect people in Hollywood, and they know that I am on a different path than most people in this world. If people would just follow in my footsteps, they would become better and stronger because of the wonderful person I have become.

In another part of Hopsin's song, he disrespects Avery and Jack. When he disrespects Jack, he says, "A real nigga don't brag about being real as long as he knows it." When he talks about Avery, he says, "A real nigga stays out of jail…and he keeps focused." Kid Cudi hates Jack and thinks that Jack is the fakest person on the planet and that I am the realest person on the planet. Jack is mean, like it or not, and I am the most forgiving person on the planet. Avery went to jail after his girlfriend accused him of hitting her and putting a gun on her. This happened before the wave of hitting girls and all that kind of stuff with the athletes and people in Hollywood. The two of them, Jack and Avery, I have been unsure about because if it wasn't Avery talking to me too much, then it was Jack. I was looking for my other friends to step up to the plate, but it was always those two who were getting in my way. I think they both have good hearts, but they aren't as strong as people as I am. I believe Jack is very fake, but he is also one of my good friends. I also think Avery is just a loner who is depressed a lot and needs to figure some things out before he comes back into my life full time. This is all I am going to write about Hopsin's song for the time being.

Sum 41's "Some Say" starts off with the lyrics, "Some say we're never meant to grow up. I'm sure they never knew enough… It's too late to live without faith… Don't think things will ever change. You must be dreaming." The next part says, "Think before you make up your mind." I am going to explain what he means by this part. When he says we are never meant to grow up, he is talking about every single person in my generation. The generation spans from twenty-one-year-olds up to about forty-two-year-olds. People need to decide between Jack and me. I am the person people should choose, and before this is all done, people won't even remember who Jack is. I know that he is the little birdie, and I am pissed because I want other people to call me more often. When he says it's too late to live without faith, he is saying that too many people blame things on the devil when they have never experienced any demon problems. And these people who think Jesus is King, well, this statue craze is half the reason the world has been going to hell for the last sixteen years. I am serious. They came out with a lot of scripts in Hollywood where the demon was a person in the real world, and all those scripts were really good. Some of them include scripts for *Lucifer*, *The Blacklist*, and *Empire*. The leading characters in all those shows were the devil, and he was a good guy in all those shows. Jack doesn't know shit about the world. He is also clueless when it comes to understanding the true meaning of life. When Jack says, "Fuck the devil" and "Fuck demons," he doesn't know shit. He has no clue what the fuck he is saying and has never experienced any true difficulties in his life, so I get mad when he says shit like that. (This applies to others too.) When people point to the sky and thank God, I turn my cheek because I am not even sure if there is a God; and if there is, then he is definitely not in heaven. I am not even sure if heaven exists. I think our generation was fed lie after lie about God being great and about Jesus being King. I think all of that is stupid. The Black comedian in Hollywood even said that his only advice is to think twice before you make up your minds because I'm not fucking around and am working with a lot of tools that can end you if you choose the wrong side, or I can really, truly help you if you are on my team.

When Sum 41 says, "Don't think things will ever change. You must be dreaming," he is talking about a range of things. The first thing I want to mention is that I have worked my ass off to save the world, to find the meaning of life, and to actually find the limitless drug, while everyone is living the same lives they've been living since grade school. Every day is different for me, and who I am in the real world is who they display in the movies and TV shows presented to the general population. Another thing is my vision and how I must be dreaming if my vision doesn't happen in the next few years. One of my visions is no more injuries in the world, talking about in professional sports and also in the middle and lower classes, including college kids who are playing in their leagues for fraternities and other Greek leagues. My vision also includes no more traffic, beautiful weather across the globe, and everyone finding their soulmates. My vision is very specific yet also very broad, and I want the world to see it with their own eyes. Another part of my vision includes the "full potential" theory, where the whole world is limitless and achieves my own personal perfection. When he says, "Don't think things will ever change," it is because I am changing every day, and too many things remain the same. Outasight, the singer from Hollywood, even said that things remain the same in the world. I am currently working out three hours a day, reading books, and reading the scripts on my computer that are presented to me so that I can help the world out. My only advice is to think twice before you make up your minds.

In the next part of his song, he says, "You don't seem to realize I can do this on my own, and if I fall, I'll take it all. It is so easy after all. Believe me, 'cause now's the time to try. Don't wait. The chance will pass you by. Time's up to figure it out." What he means by this is that I don't need God's help; I need the help of people. With my solution pit and everything I am working with, helping the human race becomes easier and easier every day. I don't need my real creator's help, and I grew up for most of my life not believing in shit. However, when he says, "If I fall, I'll take it all," I don't think that's the case. I am not going down, and I am not taking the blame for all the bad things that have happened in the world since 2000. I think that people are at fault, especially in recently when things started getting pretty bad for me; it was all because of people. Jack is the monster I am dealing with sometimes, and that Goddamn statue called Adam Seaman still gets in my Goddamn way every fucking day. I just know that I can help people every day, and I don't need some invisible force that certain people in this world rely on. I just think that the Bible and a lot of what we were told is fictitious. I never prayed and never even had God cross my thoughts, and I was always happy. I once thought that Sanchez and I were the only atheists on the planet, but then I started to realize that a lot of people didn't really believe. I am just saying that you need to get your priorities straight and think before you choose between Jack and me. I don't want to see Avery have any more say in this world and especially not Jack. I think the two of them are fucking idiots and don't deserve to be a part of the world we are building. You have to choose between Ray and me or Jack and Avery. It's not really that complicated. Ray and I bring way more to the table than those two Jesus freaks.

In the next part of his song, he says, "Some say we are better off without knowing what life is all about… In some ways, it never fades away. Seems like it's never gonna to change. I must be dreaming." I know a lot about what life is all about, and so do most of the real people in this world. The question is, are you real enough to figure out the things that I have about the world and write three two-hundred-page books about it? I don't think many people would answer yes to that question. When he says, "In some ways, it never fades away," he is 100 percent accurate about that. I have dealt with so many bad things and things that nobody should ever experience, and some of it never completely went away. I have developed a lot of hate, and fortunately, a lot of the instigators and people who were hating on me have died, so I feel a lot more at peace. I just think that there are still too many fake people in the world, and all the answers we seek depend on how free or fake. G-Eazy wrote in one of his songs, "What if the fakes would die and only the real survived, take a look around, I think you might be surprised." You would definitely be surprised by how fake Jack really is, but take another look around and see who else is similar to him. Next, take a look around and see who is as real as I am. Nobody in the world is the same as me, but there are many people who are similar. I am nothing like Jack, and if anybody compares me to that fake Jesus, then they are clearly not seeing things straight. I have worked so hard to get back to normal, and everything I do in this world is special. For someone like Jack or even Avery to demand more say and more respect in this world really bothers me. Both of them didn't go through any of the shit that I was going through, and there is a big trust issue with both of them. I hate when people preach about Jesus; and when I think about those two, who are so fucking fake and are fucking losers, I think they are out of their fucking minds thinking that Jesus is going to save them. Rely on yourself and trust your own instincts instead of pointing to the sky because guess what? *There is no God.* This is all I am going to say about this song for the time being.

Kottonmouth Kings' "Pack Your Bowls" starts with the lyrics, "Now please come and take a journey through life. The experience from what it's like for thirteen weeks… I'm sleeping in my Satan sheets." Okay, I am going to explain this a little. When Johnny Richter says, "Experience from what it's like for thirteen weeks," he is talking about all the pain and suffering that I have been through since 2009. I have been through hell, and I am conquering everything. If people really want to walk in my shoes for one day, they can, but I wouldn't recommend it. I went through the apocalypse twice, and one of those times was when Avery was living here. When the Kottonmouth Kings say, "I am sleeping in my Satan sheets," they're saying that they'd easily chose me over Jack, and whoever Jack was working with faced the consequences of engaging in these devilish games with me. Another part of my journey was when I was in so much fear, and the pains and fear told me to go to the nursery down the street where the kids are and touch the computer. I am lucky I didn't get in trouble, but there was this spaceship over my head. I am not sure who was playing those games with me, but I called my real creator and ran home because there were these weird sensations in my body. My real creator was sleeping in my room for three weeks because I was so scared of all the fear I was living in, and I am grateful that my parents were here throughout the war I was facing with humanity. When Johnny Richter and the Kottonmouth Kings say, "Experience from what it's like for thirteen weeks," he is talking about things like this.

Another experience I should probably talk about occurred when I was smoking a cigarette on my porch, and there was this figure, kind of like a reflection, on my screened-in porch. I looked at it, and it appeared very angry. My therapist even told me that it seemed like someone wanted to hurt me. I looked at the figure, and it punched me on my body. I felt these weird sensations as if it were the hand of God, and I threatened it and stood up on my porch in the backyard of my house. It punched me the second time, and then I came inside because I was so scared. I don't know who did that to me, but I would like to find out one day.

Another thing I should talk about is the journeys and missions I was sent on at nighttime by people and the mixed signals I was given, a lot of which was because of Jack. When he says, "Sleeping in my Satan sheets," it's because time is up to figure out if you want to trust that evil and disgusting person Jack or if you want to trust me, a nice and reliable guy. Anyway, there were many lies, and I was scared out of my fucking mind, thinking that I had to go on these missions, or else I was going to die. I was told so many lies and was walking and running around my neighborhood, especially in the backwoods near my house. Hopsin and Spose both came clean when they said they played their parts in this devilish game, and Peyton Manning said he was going to put me through it a second time. But I was scared out of my fucking mind the first time it was happening to me. Another thing I should say about when he mentions experiencing what it's like for thirteen weeks is that during this devilish game, people kept telling me to hit myself in the face. I kept doing this, and then I sat on the ledge in my backyard. My mom kept trying to get me to come inside, but I was so scared and wanted to kill myself because I didn't know what the fuck was going on with me. I know that Jack played significant parts in the devilish game, and he needs to pay for all these bad things that are going on in this world. I am very serious about that.

In the next part of his song, he says, "A tough choice, but I got to do it my way. I will know who they are for another eight days... Worst part, I thought he was a friend of mine." This is very import-ant. When he says, "Worst part, I thought he was a friend of mine," he is talking about Jack. When the Hollywood rapper said, "Now I am just better off dead, and I know that you want me to be dead," he was talking about Jack wanting me to be dead and pulling out tricks from his sleeves to try to kill me. Tove Lo then came out with a song suggesting, "I am now better off, and I am glad that he's gone." Jack was working with a group back in 2009 and 2010, continuing until 2014 and possibly even after that, to try to eliminate me. I want to know who he was working with and how he got his stupid-ass cheat sheet and fucked those guys up. I aim to bring this to court and let people know that Jack isn't the cool guy everyone thought he was; he is actually a bad person and shouldn't be trusted. When the Kottonmouth Kings say, "A tough choice, but I got to do it my way," they are talking about me taking control of the world. We are all getting older, and things have been shitty for many people. But I know how to fix people's problems with more time. I fix millions of people's issues every single day and can fix every single person's problems with more time. I have to do it my way, or the world would be doomed, and nobody will find the answers they are looking for. I am sick and tired of being treated like shit. I work out hard and work hard at solving issues and being the best person I can possibly be; but I have to do it my way, without guidance from corrupt individuals, including those in Hollywood and others who know which direction to guide me every day. I don't trust Jack, and I am now better off and glad that he is gone. I want to know who he was working with, and I know one of those people was his piece-of-shit cousin.

My good friend Eric Sanchez used to label his phone contact as Jack 2.0 because he was getting prank calls from someone close to Jack, who ended up being his cousin. I am not sure if Sanchez knew who the other person was, but I think he found out it was Jack's cousin whom Jack was working with in the past. Jack was playing games with many people and got a lot of his information from the CIA, but I think there was a certain group of people he was working with. One of those people was Philip Lafayette, who we went to Oakton High School with. Philip died because of alcohol, and he deserved it because he was one of my enemies in the past. I was so happy because I was just listening to the "Pack My Bowls" song and found out that he had just died. I broke free from society more and knew that people didn't feel bad because Philip was always an asshole, just like Jack, who is a complete fucking asshole. I want to know who else Jack was working with and make them pay. Some people figured I was Satan-bound, and when Kid Cudi mentions this, he is talking about Jack. Anyway, for the purpose of this song, I am sleeping in my Satan sheets, and I am the sinner who is living in his world alone, ready to eliminate anybody who gets in my way every day.

The song "Something Just Like This," by the Chainsmokers and Coldplay, starts off with "I've been reading books of old, the legends and the myths…Spider-Man's control and Batman with his fists, and clearly, I don't see myself up on that list." I will explain what he means by this a little. First of all, he talks about my superhuman gifts in this song and why 666 is not the devil's code. This song kind of goes against what I talked about in the last two songs I was explaining, but I will explain this song anyway. When he says, "I've been reading books of old, the legends and the myths," he is talking about the Bible and other books that were read by ancient people. When Coldplay mention Spider-Man with his control and Batman with his fists, this is something they got out of the Marvel movies. I am kind of in control of a lot these days, and this is how they got the character called Spider-Man. He is in control of his own body and uses his web to climb the walls of buildings and things of that nature. In the real world, I can use the web to control things. For instance, when people say something and if they are connected to me on the web, then whatever they say kind of gets put into play and is applied in the real world. I can save lives, and when people put the prayer signal on Twitter or on Facebook, I can throw it into the sky and hope that their prayers are answered. The list he is talking about is the list of the best people in the world. Actually, compared to the entire population and even the people on the list, the group members from the Chainsmokers are actually pretty high up on that list. I stopped making that list a year ago, and it is currently 2020 because I didn't want Jack to have a say in this world anymore and other people on my list. It was bothering me because things weren't going the way they were supposed to for me, and too many people were getting in the way. However, it wasn't those people who were getting in the way that were dying; it was outsiders that were dying. There are a good one hundred or so people on my list who have died, and I didn't know that was going to happen. I made that list because I wanted the competition to be fair, and I didn't even know that I was facing off against Jack. Obviously, people like to break the rules and cheat, so Jack was cheating and using his cheat sheet. I kept taking measures because I don't actually see the tools that I am working with, but I knew that it would hurt his chances. Then he stopped talking about his cheat sheet and now works with nothing. I was sick and tired of losing at everything, and this needs to be fair. Q-Tip actually mentioned in one of his songs that it was a BS competition because Jack wasn't playing fair.

The books of old are good books to read, and I actually do a lot of reading throughout the day, reading about ten to twenty books a month. I have learned a lot about the world that we are currently living in. I don't know much about what happened a billion years ago, but these books come into play every time I read them in the real world and can change the world. I know enough about what happened a billion years ago to understand that it doesn't mean jack shit compared to what's going on around us right fucking now. The books that I read can solve issues for people all the fucking time, and when Atmosphere said, "I hope…you are on page one of your new favorite book," it means that every page in every single book I read can solve up to one hundred problems in the world—every single fucking page. Therefore, if a book has three hundred pages, then thirty thousand people can be happier just because I am taking the time out of my day to help their lazy asses out. That is thirty-thousand people over the course of those two to eight days who are happier just because I am reading a book that is supposed to be fiction, but it is actually real because these people need my help. I am at service to help anyone who needs me. This is just one part of the equation, but it is important. Every book I read has meaning to it, and it always affects my life, but it also can affect those thirty-thousand people by just one book that I am reading. Even if you don't believe in anything, I can still help you out by just simply reading those books.

In the next part of his song, he says, "I'm not lookin' for somebody with some superhuman gifts… He says the testaments they told. The moon and its eclipse. But I'm not the kind of person that it fits." My superhero gifts are supernatural. This means that nobody knows exactly what's happening when I am at work. Everything can appear normal, but it's not for me because I am at work and saving the world. When the Chainsmokers say, "The moon and its eclipse," this was a significant part of why 666 is not the devil's code. It has a lot to do with the universe, especially the moon and its eclipse. When the last eclipse happened a few years ago, I was at home to make sure that it went according to plan. Everyone was super excited, and I ended up working out at around 11:00 p.m. that day, happy to see everyone excited about the eclipse. When he says, "I'm not the kind of person that it fits," he means that when Billy Joel said, "Only the good die young," "I would rather laugh with the sinners," and "We might be laughing too loud," I am not that type of person anymore. I have made some serious changes to my lifestyle, and when people laugh too loud, they appear more fake to me. I don't know why, but a lot of people started to wear thin on me because of how fake they appeared to me from an outside perspective. I don't like listening to the announcers announce the games because they laugh at the dumbest things, and a lot of times, it is not even funny. In my room, I put the TV volume down to zero because I don't want to listen to the announcers talk. I am an honest and sincere person and hate when people act fake around me, so I don't think there is anything wrong with me not wanting to be around people, especially Jack, because I don't want to deal with all the fake bullshit that comes with it.

In one part of Flobots's "Handlebars," he says, "I'm proud to be an American. Me and my friends saw a platypus… I can see your face on the telephone… Just called to say that it's good to be alive in such a small world." I want to explain my meaning behind this a little bit. I think the American pride thing is significant, and we are one nation under God. However, it is good to think outside the box because a lot of Americans are racist against minorities, and they don't treat outsiders very well. Living the American dream is great for people, but it's not that great if you've been living in America your entire life. I know that I am trying to make it in America by getting rich and providing for my family, but this process is taking a long time. Once I can get the ball rolling with my finances, then I will be a lot happier. I think if Avery and I can make a living doing these YouTube videos, then I would be a lot happier. I have been a little down in recently, but I am working hard on my fitness and mental state. I think that I have accomplished a lot in this life and still will accomplish so much more. It is great to live in America, but things have been pretty bad recently. I hope things in this world get better, and I am the person in charge of making that happen. I don't think you need to rely on some invisible force; you can just rely on me. I grew up most of my life not believing, and I don't think that half of America believes. It is a great country to live in, and I wouldn't even think about living anywhere else.

When he says the word *platypus*, it reminds me of my friend Brian Platt. I met Brian Platt when he was pledging for my fraternity, Phi Sig. I was a sophomore and ended up getting really close with a lot of the freshmen that year. One of the guys I was really close to was Brian Platt. Alex Shalak introduced me to the Flobots back when we were still in school and when we were pretty much just getting out of school. The reason the Flobots put this part in their song was when I reconnected with Platt in the future, which I already did, and when he is a big part of the world and my future, which he already is. Brian Platt was one guy who never disrespected me, and he always looked up to me as a person and a role model, even when he was pledging. We would always get drunk and act crazy when we were younger, and he was someone I could always trust. I respected him with all my heart (no homo). I reconnected with him when I was hanging out with my friends Eric Sanchez, Cory Carlton, and Alex Shalak, and I saw Brian Platt for the first time since we were way younger. My relationship with him was pretty much the same, and it was like we didn't skip a beat when we were hanging out. We were still calling each other gay and wrestling on the couch just like we would do when we were in college together. It was great, and I wouldn't have exchanged that night for anything else. I haven't talked to him in a long time and am closer to other people in the world, but I still consider him one of my good friends and know that we will join forces together in the future.

When he says, "I can see your face on the telephone... Just called to say that it's good to be alive in such a small world," he is speaking generally. It is always good to talk to my friends on the phone; and I realize that recently, I haven't really talked to my friends on the phone, mostly communicating through text. However, one person I have been talking to a lot is Aunt Julie. Aunt Julie is someone I have been close to ever since I lived in New York when I was really young. She always took such good care of me, and I am still really close to her. I know that my sisters aren't as close to her as I am, but that doesn't matter. I have been talking to her about once a week on FaceTime and enjoying it a lot. She has taught me some things I didn't know about the world, including that some guy predicted the world would be in chaos in 2020. Rory told me the exact same thing a little while ago, and I believed him but didn't know it was actually going to happen. Rory told me that ISIS was going to cause the chaos in America. He explained in more detail about which Americans were going to be sacrificed and whatever. Rory also told me that Jesus was going to come down from the sky in 2019 and only bring certain people to the promised land. Jesus never came down from the sky, but Spose and Jurassic 5 both put out songs saying, "You don't have to ask him. You are already in." They are talking about me and imply that Jesus wasn't going to actually come down from the sky and that a God figure was already living. My therapist told me that it is a big world, and I have been thinking that way ever since she said that to me. Everyone used to say it's a small world, but you have to get out of your own small world to see the bigger picture so that you can enjoy more of life and branch out of your circle to meet more people. It is great to be alive in today's world, and I wouldn't want to live in any other generation because my generation is going to be the one that solves all the world's problems and uncover all the lies that were fed by generation after generation after generation. I am happy to be alive right now; this is the only life I have ever known, and I believe I will be the one to save us, just as Hollywood shows in the scripts they release. With billions of people in this world, I don't think it is a small world.

In the next part of the song, he says, "I know how to run the business, and I can make you wanna buy a product...me and my friends understand the future. I see the shrinks that control the system." I want to explain this part a little bit. When he says, "I know how to run the business," I think he means that I now know how to run the businesses with all these ideas that were presented to me. I can sell and market my products, and I can do the back-office work and the accounting work. I understand the future pretty well, and I think Sanchez believes he knows all these things about the world. But he doesn't know most of the things I know about the world. I know that it is important that the technology we are using to fix the world needs to be enhanced and perfected. I know that Sanchez said certain things, but it is important that I play my role, bring back gravity, and answer all the possible prayers that I can possibly answer every single day. I know that shrinks control a lot of the system and medicate people because they think that those medications are needed for that particular person, but the system is fucked. These doctors don't know shit, and I am sick and tired of taking my fucking medications. I was misdiagnosed with bipolar disorder when I was twenty-two. The doctors at the mental hospitals think that someone is bipolar for the stupidest fucking reasons, and they have no clue what they are talking about. I actually think that people who aren't bipolar act crazier and more bipolar than people who take medications. They also actually said that people who are diagnosed with mental illnesses are smarter than the rest of the population. Anyway, I want to talk about P!nk's song before the two hundred pages runs out on my third book.

In P!nk's song "What About Us," she says, "We are billions of beautiful hearts, and you sold us down the river too far." I always tell myself, and I think people are aware, that the devil keeps tearing my soul apart. This devil is Jack, who keeps selling me down the river too far. I've helped out each person in this world at least once. Some people, I have helped out several times, others a few times, and yet others several times. When P!nk says that people are still searching for answers, I know that I can provide those answers when the time is right. As of right now, there's no cure for cancer or any illness known to mankind. However, I am conquering everything and can help people with the answers they are looking for. I know people are searching for answers to why Mother Nature has been so bad, and I can control Mother Nature. I can answer people's prayers and help them out every single day. I will keep on killing the flesh because I am so Goddamn sick and tired of the things that are going on in my life. I don't give a fuck about any of these Goddamn people dying. Anyway, I can help athletes every single time they step onto the playing field. I can help people win their fantasy matchups. I can help girls get pregnant and help them find their soulmates or their significant others. I need about two to three more years to completely save the world, but every second in my life is a highlight. And I know for a fact that I am doing the right thing every single day.

P!nk said in her song that Hollywood came when I called. I was suffering from sleep deprivation, and also, the world was fucking ending around me. I know that most people go about their everyday lives as if this is the way we are supposed to live. I don't see it that way. I think that heaven and Earth need to combine into one force and that we all need to be on the master pill and on the heaven pills that I have been on in the past and sometimes currently. When Hollywood came to save me, I was screwed. I thought I was going to die with my eyes open. I know that it is possible, and I was so fucking scared. I don't think anyone should have made my life any harder than it already was. I went through the apocalypse twice before anyone was even talking about it, which I mentioned in this book, the third book I am writing. In another part of P!nk's song, she asks, "Will you be ready to talk in front of a big audience?" I think people need to train me to speak better in front of others and maybe quiz me a bit more. When I say that people need to quiz me, I don't mean sinister tests, which I have been given in the past. I mean productive tests that make me a better person. I am ready for all this shit to be over in my life and for everyone to become one big family. However, there are still many improvements we need to make as a society and things that people need to do themselves to make the world a better place.

I enjoy helping others out and carrying this weight on my chest, but I am serious when I say that others need to carry their share of this weight as well. I know that the Gorillaz said I am useless, so I am going to delete that song because I am quite the opposite of useless. What I am doing for the world is a lot better than any money you could possibly make and better than any progress you think you are making in your own lives. I can change the world with the steps I take and the magic I can produce. I don't think many people in this world contribute as much as I do, and I know for a fact that nobody in this world has had a tougher life than I have. I mean, I don't know where my story begins; so when Fun says, "Ten years of this. I'm not sure if anybody understands," that song makes no fucking sense to me. I am not asking God what I stand for; I am asking people to help me the fuck out. I don't need God's damn help, and I can do this on my own. I need people to help me the fuck out to save the world. When people put that Goddamn prayer emoji on the Internet, it fucking pisses me off. Who the fuck are you praying to? *There is no God.* I don't give a fuck if I am hell-bound or whatever. I don't think any god would allow humans to do the things they have done to me. I just think that people need to get their priorities straight and take accountability for their actions. Don't wait for God to judge you; seek people's approval. I am not going to read that stupid-ass, fake Bible because that is what is expected of society. I am going to apply what I know to the world and make good things happen for others.

10 Percent Entertainment

I wanted to talk about this article because Maren Morris wrote that one song, "Meet Me in the Middle," which made me see life a lot more clearly.

Maren Morris and Ryan Hurd
Welcome First Child

Oh baby, why don't you just meet your parents in the middle? Country singer Maren Morris and her husband Ryan Hurd have welcomed their first child, a son. [I know that we need to stop having kids, but I am still going to write about this.] The couple announced the birth Monday on her verified Instagram account. "Hayes Andrew Hurd. 3/23/20. Love of our lives," she wrote in the captain of a series of photos showing her, Hurd and the baby on the day their son was born. The award-winning country star scored a major crossover pop hit in 2018 with producer Zedd titled "The Middle." Hurd, a singer-songwriter who was written hits for country artists like Blake Shelton and Luke Bryan, shared some of the same images on his official Instagram account. The couple married in 2018.

I have been into working out a lot recently, so I wanted to write about this article. This article talks about Vin Diesel's intense

Bloodshot workout. Part of the reason they got this script was my life and my bloodshot eyes when I wake up in the middle of the night. I hope this changes at some point, but he is fucking up bad guys in his movie.

To play the comic book superhero Ray Garrison, aka Bloodshot, Vin Diesel had to look the part. Luckily, He's Vin Diesel. "Vin obviously brings a huge physicality to the roles he plays, and it was definitely not something we were going to shy away from," Bloodshot director David S. F. Wilson says about the film's lead in ET's exclusive clip. Producer Dinesh Shamdasani adds that Diesel is a producer on the action film for a reason. "The first day he was on set, you could just see all the attention get to him, and he understood it and then he used all that power to help the production and help guide us," Shamdasani says. "It's why he's a producer on the film, because he legitimately did the job. And he just elevates everything because he demands a higher level." Showing his guns in the gym, Diesel picks up giant weights, dishing, "Every morning, I come in here and I've got to get a good quick workout, and then I go to each crew member and I tell them how much I appreciate their work efforts and how much I appreciate their expertise." His co-star, Lamorne Morris, quips, "He's given me life advice and advice on how to approach the business of it all. It's great of him—someone so old, so bald—to partake that wisdom on someone so young and handsome and beautiful." Bloodshot went straight from theaters to digital purchase on March 24.

I wanted to talk about this story because I listen to M.I.A.'s song to give people luck with their betting in sports and casinos.

Singer M.I.A. Reveals She Doesn't
Believe in Vaccinations for Kids

M.I.A. says she doesn't believe in vaccinations for kids. The 44-year-old "Bad Girls" singer took to social media to explain her position on Wednesday. "If I have to choose the vaccine or chip I'm gonna choose death," she wrote. A follower asked her why she took this stance, and M.I.A. (real name Mathangi Maya Arulpragasam) wrote, "Most of science is in bed with business. Business is in bed with banks, banks are in bed with tech, techs in bed with us, we're in bed with corona. Corona is in bed with science. So on..." She also opened up about the time she was forced to vaccinate her child for school. "Yeah in America they made me vaccinate my child before the school admission. It was the hardest thing. To not have choice over this as a mother," she explained. "I never wanna feel that again. He was so sick for 3 weeks then Docs had to pump him with antibiotics to reduce the fever from 3 vaxins." M.I.A. further elaborated and said she felt like she was taking a choice away from her child. "As an adult you have choice! By then you've built your immune system. You have a choice as an 'adult' wishing you all good health."

"Don't panic you are ok. You are not gonna die. You can make it without stressing the medical systems. Just breathe. You are going to be ok. You can make it through without jumping in the frying pan. You are fine. All the vaccines you've already had is enough to see you through," she added. M.I.A. has one son in 2009 with environmentalist and investor Benjamin Bronfman. They met in 2008, later became engaged, but separated in 2012.

Here is someone who hasn't been talked about as much in recent memory because of other people taking the spotlight from her.

Jennifer Lawrence's Mom is more Proud of
Actress' Charity Work than Oscar

One proud Mama! Karen Lawrence, the mother to actress Jennifer Lawrence, admitted that she is more impressed by her daughter's charitable endeavors compared to her Academy Award win. "Honestly, yes, because, I mean, not to take anything away—that's an amazing award. But I think at the end of our life, we're gonna wish that we left some legacy and it doesn't have to be a big legacy," the Camp Hi-Ho founder told US Weekly exclusively on Tuesday, March 24, while promoting her collaboration with Operation Parent. "I try to think in terms of 'How do I want to be remembered? What can I do to make my mark?'" Karen continued, "We all have an ability to make a difference and make a mark, even a small mark because it passes down. I don't really believe anything feels a whole lot better than being able to give back and beginning able to help someone else. I think when you're depressed and feeling really bad, go out and do something for someone else. You're gonna feel a lot better about your situation. It's just the way it works." Jennifer is a four-time Academy Award nominee. She walked away with a win in 2013 for her role opposite Bradley Cooper in Silver Linings Playbook.

Since cementing herself onto the A-list, the 29-year old Hunger Games actress has used her platform on numerous occasions to give back. In February 2016, Jennifer donated $2 million to the Kosair Children's Hospital in her hometown of Louisville, Kentucky. At the time, the star confirmed that her donation would help launch the Jennifer Lawrence Foundation Cardiac Intensive Care Unit within the medical facility. "As part of my effort to help these children and caregivers, I challenge the entire community to get behind this cause and help my gift by raising an additional $2M to support all of these brave and inspiring children," the X-Men: Apocalypse actress said in a video message. Jennifer launched the Jennifer Lawrence Foundation in 2015, which supports organizations such as the Boys & Girls Clubs of America. Separately, she has advocated for Planned Parenthood and Thirst Project, among other charities.

I wanted to talk about this article because I am really interested in what they will come out with in the next *Space Jam* script. I still listen to these songs from the first *Space Jam*, which came out when we were mad young, and they come up on cue because people such as Don Cheadle want me to think about it. The headline reads, "Paul Scheer Claims Don Cheadle Will Play the Bad Guy in Space Jam 2."

A number of the main characters in Space Jam 2 are already set. LeBron James will, of course, play the film's protagonist, while a handful of NBA and WNBA players will presumably get their talent stolen from them by a bunch of aliens hell-bent on taking down the Looney

Tunes in a game of basketball. Other roles are still up in the air, including the role of the film's main antagonist, whomever that may end up being. In the original Space Jam, that character was named Swackhammer and was voice by Danny DeVito. This time around, an unlikely source may have revealed who will be the biggest thorn in the sides of LeBron, Bugs, and co.

Paul Scheer—who you know from the League, the podcast How did This Get Made? And a whole host of other things—appeared on Clip City. The Athletic's Los Angeles Clippers podcast hosted by Jovan Buha. Scheer was asked about the acting chops of former Clipper Blake Griffin, and around the 39:50 mark, he discusses doing a Space Jam live read with Griffin a few years back. He alludes to the film's upcoming sequel, at which point he drops that Don Cheadle is in line to play the bad guy. "Actually Don Cheadle, who I do Black Monday with, he's the bad guy in Space Jam, and he said Lebron's really great," Scheer said at the 40:15 mark. Cheadle's involvement in the film isn't new-it's been reported in the past that he'sh hopped onto the project, and he's actually spoken about being in the film. He was asked about this a few months back at the Televisons Critics Association Conference in January, but Kept his close close to the chest, saying "No, I'm not playing myself. I actually can't tell you what I'm playing." Now, thanks to Scheer, Cheadle's role looks like it's becoming a little more clear.

This is one of my girls in Hollywood, so I wanted to talk about her new album. I think I've heard some of her songs on it.

Dua Lipa Releases New Album "Future Nostalgia"

Dua Lipa dropped a new album that might just blow your mind. "Future Nostalgia," the English pop star's second studio album, was released on Friday. "Thank you to all my friends old and new, to love, happiness and keeping an open heart. Welcome to Future Nostalgia," she tweeted Friday. The album features 11 tracks, including "Don't Start Now," which was released in November. The singer took to Instagram in December to announce the title for the album with a cheeky post showing a tattoo on her arm with the album's name. She's been working on it since last spring. The songs, which are a mix of disco and '80s pop, delve into Lipa's experiences with heartbreak, new love, and her long-lasting friendships. "It's a fine line, so I wanted to bring something that was reminiscent of my childhood and at the same time make it really current," she told Apple Music. "I remember listening to songs by Moloko and Jamiroquai, which would make you want to dance no matter what time of day it was. I wanted to recreate that feeling." The Future Nostalgia 2020 European Arena Tour was set to kick off April 26 in Madrid. But due to the global coronavirus pandemic, it had been moved to 2021.

This is also a cool story because my real creator and I were just talking about how Rihanna hasn't come out with anything recently.

Rihanna Finally Gave Us a New Song, Sort Of

It's not a new album the world has been begging for, but it's a start. Early Friday, Canadian singer PartyNextDoor dropped his new album, "PartyMobile," which features Rihanna on the song, "Believe It." Rihanna announced the new single on her verified Twitter account. Folks have been more than excited for new music from the singer and makeup mogul since she dropped her last album, "Anti," in 2016. "Best make me believe it/Best make me believe it/Believe you won't deceive me," she and PartyNextDoor sing on the chorus. PartyNextDoor has written songs for Rihanna, including her hit, "Work," so it makes sense that she would guest on a track with him. She's been hinting for what feels like forever that a new album is coming. Even her former frequent collaborator, Drake, is growing antsy. Drake and Rihanna on Wednesday both hopped into DJ Spade's Instagram Live, and the rapper had a message for her. "Rihanna, drop R12 (the album) right now," Drake now.

I wanted to write about this story about Alec Benjamin, who most people don't really know about; but if he is in the news, that means he is making progress in his life. Some of his songs that I have listened to in the past speak to me.

Alec Benjamin Debuts Coronavirus Song "6 Ft. Apart" During Billboard Live-at-Home Concert

The singer-songwriter unveiled a very timely new song titled "6 Ft. Apart" on Thursday morning (April 2), and an hour later, he sang it for the first time during his Billboard Live-at-Home concert. The singer-songwriter began his short-but-sweet Facebook Live session with the new tune, which he just penned Wednesday while quarantined at home. It's actually very pertinent, because the song is about the current state of affairs in the world," Benjamin said. "It's about COVID-19 and this whole social distancing thing. I'm not saying anything, I'm just like, this is how I feel." Because the song was so new, Benjamin struggled with the lyrics at first—though it could've been the fact that he'd pulled an all-nighter to finish the track. "I haven't really done that since college." He said, "and I haven't been in college since I was a freshman, so it's been some time." But he pushed through and delivered the poignant lyrics, depicting how man many be feeling at the moment: "I miss you most at six feet apart/When you're right outside my window but you can't ride inside my car." Benjamin also played snippets of his songs "The Book of You & I" and "Steve during the Live-at-Home, which raised money for Meals on Wheels America.

I wanted to talk about this story as well: "Fountains of Wayne Co-Founder Adam Schlesinger Dies at 52." I was listening to his song "Stacy's Mom" a lot, but he was eliminated from society because I am through with the pairs. Also, Eric Schlesinger and Adam Seaman are more important in the world than he is, so he was expendable.

Adam Schlesinger, the prolific singer-song-writer and co-founder of the rock band Fountains of Wayne, died Wednesday at age 52 after complications related to the novel coronavirus, his lawyer Jaime Herman said. On Tuesday, his family confirmed that he had been hospitalized with COVID-19 and was on a ventilator. His attorney told Billboard he had been in the hospital for a week. Schlesinger, who was born in New York City on Oct. 31, 1967, and raised in New Jersey, racked up more accolades for his music over the years, including Oscar and Golden Globe nominations for writing the title track to the 1996 comedy "That Thing You Do!" The song was chosen out of 300 submissions when the movie's writer and director, Tom Hanks, put out a call for a Beatles-esque" track that could carry the film.

Fountains of Wayne's biggest hit, the tongue-in-cheek "Stacy's Mom," earned a Grammy nomination in 2003 for duo/group pop vocal and helped land the band in the best new artist category. He started the band in the mid-'90s with his college friend Chris Collingwood, and they became critical favorites for writing, as one newspaper put it at the time, "Insanely catchy pop songs, creating hum-all-day ditties for the '90s with a classic '60s feel." Schlesinger would go on to win a Grammy for best comedy album in 2009 for his work on Stephen Colbert's "A Colbert Christmas: The Greatest Gift of All!" It was one of the many projects for which he wrote songs for TV personalities, as he worked with a host of stars. Over the past several years, he became a fan-favorite writer on the CW's musical dramedy "Crazy Ex-Girlfriend," and he won the Emmy Award last year for original music and

MY THEORY OF EVERYTHING

lyrics for the song "Antidepressants Are So Not a Big Deal." A Tony Award nominee for the 2007 musical "Cry-Baby," he was also well known for his work in the Broadway world, and previously won two Emmys for co-writing the opening and closing numbers on television broadcasts of the Tonys ("It's Not Just for Gays Anymore" in 2012 and "If I Had Time" in 2013). When the news of his death broke Tuesday evening, tributes flooded in on social media.

Selena Gomez Is Quizzed on Her "Friends" Knowledge and She's Pretty Rusty

Selena Gomez is a self-proclaimed huge Friends fan, but could not believe how many questions she missed when Interview magazine quizzed her about the beloved NBC sit-com. "All right, look, I'm not gonna lie. I've been watching some Will & Grace lately," Gomez quips after she finds out her final score. In all fairness, Friends has not been accessible on any streaming sites since the beginning of the year and will not return until May 2020 when it will be available on HBO Max. Not to mention, some of the questions are pretty tough! Gomez can't recall the Hollywood star's dressing room shower that Joey Tribbiani gets caught in (Charlton Heston) and remembers Joey walking Phoebe Buffay down the aisle to marry Mike Hannigan when it was Chandler Bing. "We gotta edit some of this because I'm letting a lot of people down," Gomez jokes. She does, however, remember the name of Joey's stuffed Penguin (Huggsy), and the neighbor who leaves everything he has to Monica Geller and Rachel Green when he dies (Mr. Heckles).

When all was said and done, Gomez got 18 out of 29 questions right. In real life, the 27-year-old singer is friends with Rachel herself, Jennifer Aniston. In January, when Aniston guest-hosted The Ellen DeGeneres Show, the pals talked about how they first met—and it sort of sounds like something that would happen on Friends. "Well, nobody knew who I was, and you were in the bathroom wearing a black dress," Gomez explained giddly to Aniston when they were both on Ellen. "I think we were at, like, Vanity Fair, something, event and I was there with my mom. And I walked into the bathroom and I saw you… and my heart, like stopped…you were everything that I wanted." The feelings were mutual, with the 51-year-old actress telling Gomez, "You've always been so sweet. You really are a genuine 'Friends' fan. It's amazing. We've known each other for years. You've been to my house. We've had pizza. Girl after my own heart, do we love a pizza or what? We love a pizza."

I wanted to talk about this article because Jessie J is one of my girls, and Channing Tatum is a cool dude.

Channing Tatum Is Spotted with Jessie J, Sparks Reconciliation Rumors

Channing Tatum and Jessie J just can't quit each other! A source told ET at the start of April that the 40-year-old actor and 32-year-old singer had broken up after rekindling their romance three months prior. However, it now appears that they are on again and quarantining together. On Wednesday night, Jessie was spotted riding on the back of a motorcycle with Channing in

Los Angeles, California. The Magic Mike star was also seen outside of the British pop star's home that same day. While it may appear that these two are back together, a source tells ET that Channing and Jessie are just friends right now, nothing more. The sightings come just a few days after Jessie wished Channing a happy 40th birthday on social media. "Happy 40th birthday to this special man right here," the "Domino" singer wrote, alongside a photo of Channing standing waist-deep in crystal clear ocean water. "You are truly one of a kind. I am so grateful you were born, and even more grateful that we met." Another post was a short clip of the actor in swim trunks and a tank top—shot with a retro, film-grain filter—as he jumped from a platform into the ocean at an unidentified tropical resort. "Keep living your best life," Jessie wrote over the video. Earlier this month, a source told ET that Jessie and Channing's breakup was amicable, noting that the couple tried to make it work, but in the end, they realized they were better off as friends and it was time to move on. Here's more on the on-again, off-again pair, who were first romantically linked in October 2018.

This article also intrigued me. The headline reads that JoJo intentionally refrained from sex for a year.

JoJo made a big decision in her personal life that greatly influence her upcoming album, Good to Know. The 29-year-old singer tells ET's Katie Krause that while making new music this past year, she abstained from sex. JoJo says she refrained from becoming physical with someone because she'd "been in relationships from the age of 14."

"I never really had to think about being abstinent because I was just in a relationship," she explains. "I've always had a boy in my life and I've always had a safety net, whether it was real or not. I've always, kind of never truly been on my own. So it was an exercise that I wanted to put myself through, and I'm so glad it did." JoJo says she learned a lot since taking sex out of the equation when it comes to dating. "When you have a sexual connection with somebody, it can really confuse things. So taking that out of my life for a good year just brought some clarity and it helped me," she shares. "I loved saying no. Not like it was really hard but if I went on a date, there was no coming inside. There was no after-dinner drinks, and I just liked that." The pop star adds, "It was a powerful thing for me and I think that it informed the album. It informed the woman that I am today. I'm a lot more choosy. I don't want to be in a relationship just to be in a relationship. I like the relationship I have with myself today." Though JoJo wasn't having sex during the making of the album, some of the songs are pretty sexual. "I just love talking sex. I love sex. I love talking about it. Even when I'm not having it, I love talking about it," she admits. "I really wanted to channel all my creativity and my sensuality and keep it for myself. But that doesn't mean that my imagination doesn't run wild and that I don't have a healthy appetite for imagination." In addition to bringing her fans new music amid the coronavirus pandemic, JoJo also came out with a quarantine edition of her hit song, "Leave (Get Out)." "I was just entertaining myself because I was bored in the house and I was doing Instagram Live and someone in my comments was like, "Stay in, right now," she says of the inspiration behind the rendition. "After I got off my Live, I just played around and wrote some new lyrics and had my lyrics had my mom filmed it and that was it." Expect to see more of JoJo this year! Her new song, "The Man," and its music video are out now, while her album, Good to Know, comes out on Friday, May 1.

I wanted to write about this article in my book because Kendrick Lamar released a song in the *Black Panther* movie, which was supposed to give me more publicity, and this song was written so well.

The Weeknd Refutes Claim He Copied Yeasayer for Kendrick Lamar "Black Panther" Collab "Pray for Me"

Back in February, Brooklyn rock band Yeasayer announced its intent to sue the Weeknd and Kendrick Lamar over their song "Pray for Me." In the lawsuit, the now-split band claimed the two artists illegally sampled their 2007 track "Sunrise" for the Black Panther: The Album closer. It was alleged the song used the same "distinctive choral performance," and now the Weeknd has responded to the allegation. In court documents obtained by Complex, and as reported by the Blast, the Weeknd has requested the lawsuit be dismissed. "Each and every allegation contained in the complaint not specifically admitted herein is denied," read the documents. Attorneys for the Weeknd wrote, "The sound recording of "Pray for Me" does not capture any actual sounds from the sound record, "Sunrise.""

Additionally, he is asking for his attorney fees to be paid for by Yeasayer. When Yeasayer filed the lawsuit, it was claimed that the band recognized their own voices in the track. The alleged sample in question has been described as "comprised of male voices singing in their highest registers, with animated, pulsing vibrato." The band split near the end of 2019, but fans first pointed out the moment on "Pray for Me" was similar to "Sunrise" when the song debuted back in 2018. The Black Panther entry was produced by Frank Dukes and Doc McKinney, but no samples were listed in the credits.

I wanted to talk about this article. I don't really know who this singer is, but we are still worried about overpopulation. This singer died of natural causes.

Country singer and songwriter Cady Groves, known for hits like "This Little Girl" and "Oil and Water," died on Saturday at age 30. Her brother Cody Groves took to Twitter to confirm the sad news with a sweet photo of the two of them acting silly together. In addition to confirming the news, he revealed she died of natural causes and referenced their two brothers, Casey and Kelly, who died in 2007 and 2014, respectively.

"@cadygroves has left this world. Details are limited right now but family is trying to get them and will keep people updated. Rest in peace little sis. Hope you're reunited with @kellydgroves and Casey," Cody wrote Sunday.

In a 2015 interview with Arena, Cady revealed that her brothers both died at age 28, noting that Casey was believed to have been murdered. After his initial tweet revealed to the world that the country singer died, he responded to a comment asking if it was a hoax, writing, "I wish it was a sick hoax." He also fended off rumors that it had anything to do with the coronavirus pandemic. Eventually, Cody posted a lengthier note offering more details about Cady's passing.

"I hate that I even have to do this, but apparently the world and internet is a cluster of twisted misinformation. In my original post I had stated we had no information to try and prevent that, but to expel rumors I will provide an update" he wrote. "The medical examiner has completed autopsy and there was no indication of foul play or self harm. Simply put, Cady Groves died of natural causes." He continued: "She had some medical problems last fall and our best guess at this point until further testing is complete is that they had resurfaced. Please respect her name and family before sharing information that did not come directly from here." Cody concluded his post by noting that Cady was in the process of releasing a new album that she was really looking forward to sharing with the world. "Cady was really looking forward to the next few months and release of her new album," Cody's post concluded. "Our latest in-depth conversation (Since most were witty banter) was her sending me songs to critique and give feedback on." Hours after posting the lengthy statement, Cody seemed to lament choosing a lighthearted photo to himself and his sister in which he's making a silly face to announce her death. He shared a different one along with a tweet noting the change as well as further eulogizing his late sister. "Boy... if I had known my post would have been plastered all over the Internet and tabloids, I would have chosen a more flattering picture!" he wrote. "But thank you to everyone who has shared kind words/stories about @cadygroves. She truly loved her fans and friends she made along the way."

I wanted to write about this article because Eminem has meant a lot to me, and I had just written about an intruder going into Ariana Grande's property. The article headline reads, "Eminem Confronts Intruder in His Living Room."

Eminem confronted a home intruder in his living room after the suspect slipped past his sleeping security guards, according to a report Thursday. The 26-year-old Mathew David Hughes smashed a kitchen window with a paving stone and climbed into in the rapper's home in a gated community in the Detrioit area around 4:00 a.m. earlier this month, TMZ reports. The smashed window triggered Slim Shady's alarm system, waking up the rapper who found the intruder in his living room, the report says. But the intruder didn't try to steal anything. Apparently, Hughes just wanted some face time with the rapper, whose real name is Marshall Mathers, TMZ reports. The alarm also woke up the security guards, who rushed into the house and detained Hughes until cops showed up, according to TMZ. A representative for Slim Shady told XXL, though, said Eminem was the one who detained Hughes till cops showed up. Hughes faces a pair of felonies, home invasion and malicious destruction of a building, was held on $50,000 bond on April 6.

I wanted to write about this article because when I was going through those evil tests when I was twenty-four and twenty-five years old, one of the tests was for kidney and liver failure.

On Wednesday, rapper and singer Young Thug revealed that he had previously been hospitalized for kidney and liver failure. During the virtual music livestream Offset and Friends, hosted by Offset and featuring Young Thug, Rich the Kid, and Saint John, Young Thug went into detail about the harrowing experience, saying that he narrowly escaped death. "So, I kinda just stayed in the bed, and I was like, 'Yo, call the ambulance. I can't move my body.' Then later... when the ambulance came, I couldn't' get out of the bed," said Thug, who has been arrested for drug possession and undergone substance-abuse counseling in the past. "They had to get me out of the bed, basically. I felt like my whole body was numb, and I couldn't move. I went to the hospital, and I had found out that I had liver and kidney failure. And I kinda had sorta passed away, like, I kinda died. I was in the hospital for, like, 17 days. I left the hospital. My mom didn't trust it. So I left the hospital, went to another hospital. They was like, 'Man, you got liver and kidney failure. You supposed to be dead. Basically, you've been dead.' I've been killed before." Thug then launched into "Killed Before" a track off of Super Slimey, his collaborative mixtape with Future, in which he sings the refrain "everyone know I've been killed before." He ended his performance with a message to the livestream audience: "Drugs aren't good. Don't do drugs."

I wanted to talk about this, and this girl is another person who means a lot to me. Her name is Selena Gomez, and she was diagnosed with bipolar disorder. Here is an article where she talks about her issues.

At just 24 years old, Selena Gomez has spent a lot of time in the spotlight. She's one of the world's biggest pop stars and the most popular person on Instagram, with 113 million followers. But as she reveals in the April issue of *Vogue*, fame hasn't been so easy on her health. In the interview, Gomez opens up about checking into a psychiatric facility last summer for feelings of depression and anxiety that emerged while she was on tour, which she calls a "lonely" experience. "My self-esteem was shot," she says. "I was depressed, anxious. I started to have panic attacks right before getting on stage, or right after leaving the stage." The singer says she spent 90 days in the treatment center in Tennessee, where she took part in individual therapy, group therapy, and equine therapy, which uses horses to help treat mental health conditions.

"Animals can be very therapeutic since they show an unconditional positive regard," says Linda Esposito, a therapist and licensed clinical social worker. "Group therapy can also be a helpful tool to recognize you're not alone and hear about others' experiences, in addition to one-on-one therapy. While a 3-month stay in a residential program isn't doable for most people, it's important to seek help from a therapist if you're dealing with burnout, depression, or anxiety," she says. "Ask a trusted friend or family member for a recommendation, or do research online to find a therapist who's right for you."

This is not the first time Gomez has been to rehab. In January 2014, she spent time at a treatment center after being diagnosed with lupus, an autoimmune disease that can cause skin rash, achy or swollen joints, fatigue, hair loss, and other symptoms. She has since gotten treatment for lupus and is now in remission from the disease. Now, Gomez still sees a psychologist 5 days per week. She credits dialectical behavior therapy for completely changing her life. This type of therapy is often used to treat complex or long-term mental health conditions and typically involves individual sessions, group therapy, and phone coaching. It focuses on mindfulness and acceptance, while working with your therapist to change negative behaviors.

Another way Gomez is taking control of her mental health: staying off social media. Instagram had become "so consuming to me," she tells *Vogue*. "It's what I woke up to and went to sleep to. I was an addict, and it felt like I was seeing things I didn't want to see." As a result, she's now lying low on Instagram, even deleting the app and letting her assistant post for her. "Seeing the perfect pictures posted to social media can be especially detrimental to people prone to anxiety, depression, and low self-esteem," Esposito says. "Feeling similarly attached to your smartphone? It's not a bad idea to take a break and go cold turkey, the way Gomez did," Esposito says.

10 Percent Endless Connections or Signs

I talked a lot about signs and connections in my second book, but I wanted to touch on that subject again right now. There are two important people in this world that preach the Word of God and Jesus on the Internet, in their podcasts, and across the globe. Those two people are Joel Osteen and Joyce Meyer. I mentioned that they named one of the main characters Joyce in *Stranger Things*, and they talk about Joel Osteen a lot in Hollywood. The two of them are connected because both their first names start with the letter *J*, and their last names are very close, ending in *M* and *O*. Joyce Meyer is really important because she buys into my products and everything I am doing positively in this world. They didn't come out with her character's name in *Stranger Things*, Joyce, by accident. They wanted her to be more important not only in the world but in my world. They wanted her to understand that the things Hollywood talks about are important and that everything that I do is monumental. They actually named the little boy Will in *Stranger Things*.

When it comes to Joel Osteen, he has been preaching the Word of Christ for as long as he was old enough to preach. I didn't know anything about him until I woke up one morning at two, and my TV was on the cable channel. He was preaching in front of his followers. He sounded interesting and like he knew what he was talking about. Then Joel Osteen was mentioned when they came out with the script for *Damnation*. I already mentioned in my last book that this is how they said it was important that Donald Trump approved that one thing that would benefit the farmers, even if it wasn't good for other people in the world. That was written in the script for *Damnation*. The main point for *Damnation* was that there was a preacher and a Jesus character who were struggling to make things right in this world, and they were working together to feed the poor and make the rich suffer because they weren't looking after the world's best interest. They would go around killing their haters and feeding the hungry and those who believed in their products.

Kanye West went to meet up with Joel Osteen not too long ago, and I think they were talking about me a little bit and how I saved Kanye West's life after he kept on calling himself Jesus. If Jesus were alive right now, he would eliminate from the world the people who were playing him because that is just a rule if Jesus was resurrected. A lot of people have died because they were playing me, and this is *not allowed*. I might be God, but this is why I explained to my therapist that it was really important that Kevin Hart told me to just trust the process and that he wasn't going to make the same mistakes that others have made in this world. Kevin Hart actually got into a really bad car accident, and I wonder if that had something to do with him giving me that solid advice. If it was because of Avery, then Hollywood is right in giving me that advice that Avery needs to go at some point for the world to find peace. They actually mentioned in the script for *Supernatural* that peace can only be attained once the chosen one has died. Anyway, will.i.am said that he doesn't want to sound like a preacher, but we need to be one family united together.

I think this coronavirus can help us unite into one family, but it is important that karma catches up with me, or everything that we have planned for my future will go to waste. Also, I have said this before, but people are working on a solution for the human race every single day; and since I am conquering everything, scientists and other people are looking at my life and seeing how we can fix my problems rather than focusing on the efforts of others in the world. Joel Osteen is very important, and so is Joyce Meyer, in helping unite the world into one big family.

10 Percent Intruding into the "Stars" of the World

The next script I wanted to talk about is for the movie *Ghosts of Girlfriends Past*. It's another Matthew McConaughey movie. They write about this in a song that I was just listening to as well. I can't remember what song it was, but still. When I finally get everything in my life under control and get with the girl of my dreams, I will put every single girl in the past. Not saying that I won't still talk to them, but I'll put them in the past. One of the reasons I was born was to make this entire world form one big family. I had visions a long time ago about how my exes were messing with my head, and then I was able to put them all in the past. I started crying with one part with Jackie Cook, the girl I dated when I was about twenty years old. My real creator kept asking me what was wrong, and I said, "Ex-girlfriends." It was one of the skits that people ran by me. I know that a lot of people in this world wish bad things on their exes and go through the rest of their lives never talking to them ever again. This isn't how I think because of the tests that I have been through. I believe that I will be friends with every single one of them in the future, but I will just focus on one girl instead of *all* of the other girls in this world who have been interested in me throughout pretty much my entire life. They ran this by me again after the skits were all done, and I was ready to commit to my dream girl and do everything possible to keep this relationship going for the rest of eternity. I never actually saw this movie, but it all makes sense in terms of my life and why they made it a Hollywood success. Lauren Reynolds was one girl that they put inside my head when the "Spaceman" song came out in 2008 by the Killers, and they ripped me out of my bed in 2013. I think she has moved on with her life, and I put her on the back burner because there are bigger priorities in both our lives.

I was talking to my therapist about the coronavirus, and she actually worded it perfectly with what script this was meant for. It has everything to do with *The Maze Runner*, and those who are infected were the ones who were trying to kill the regular human beings in this world. I know that people want to talk about other scripts, but if you are *real* enough to understand this script, then you would know that this is exactly what they are talking about when they released *The Maze Runner*. My mom once told me that the girl the main character is meant to be with did some terrible things to him in the past, and I listened when my mom said this. She was talking about the movie, but it still relates to me in real life.

Anyway, the *Space Jam* part is accurate with the athletes and how aliens took over their bodies, and people couldn't understand what the fuck was wrong with them. They eventually all got their talents back and were able to play. They even said it in *Supernatural* when the main character (me) said there are no more sports. This is just temporary, but I know that Hollywood fills me in on their secrets. Other people tell me things too.

Dr. O'Connor was 100 percent correct when she said it relates to *The Maze Runner*. This is the perfect script they are talking about.

The next script I wanted to talk about is actually pretty funny, and the script was written when I was dating Angie when I was twenty-one. The movie is called *Failure to Launch*. The movie, another Matthew McConaughey film, is about a guy who lives at home and cannot land a girl. He brings girls home just to break up with them because he is scared of commitment and uses his parents as an excuse to not land a permanent girlfriend. I used this excuse when girls used to talk to me on the Internet through dating sites because I knew there were too many variables in my life to actually be with any of these girls long-term, but I was also mad because every single fucking day, stupid-ass shit always gets in my Goddamn way. I used to bring girls home all the time, and my parents have met every single one of my girlfriends, whether they were short-term or long-term. I haven't dated a girl in a long time because of one girl who keeps keeping me from landing a girlfriend, and I am completely fine with this because I can be patient. I've been with awesome girls in the past, but that is the past. This is why we are talking about *Ghosts of Girlfriends Past* and *Failure to Launch*. I need this one girl to set me free and get my shit back in order. I am continually helping people out all over the globe and getting my shit in order every single day, so I am not worried about it. I need the people who are helping me out every single day to keep helping out, and we will figure this world out together and take that last trip to Hollywood to talk in front of everyone.

I talked a lot about the *Supernatural* show in my last book, but I wanted to talk more about it here. In each episode of the show, the two brothers are solving demon problems for people and saving lives. This is kind of what I am doing every single day with people who have dealt with demolition or demon problems, or even if they are drug addicts or alcoholics.

I have done this throughout my entire life, but I have just started to figure that out now. For instance, I said in my last book that Josh Hamilton was cured in June 2006, and that is the number sixty-six, which pretty much stands for me. So people know that I have had the magic inside me this entire time and that the world will be saved because of me. Nevertheless, I have helped many people with their actual demon problems in the past several years, and I have encountered these people in restaurants, stores, and sporting events. Some of these people have made the sign of the cross when I passed them. Many people have recognized my face, and a lot of people have acknowledged my name. Many people have given me a head nod and a wave, and they've shown appreciation that I am alive right now. For instance, a very good example of this is the demon problems that a high school friend, Zach Bush, was dealing with in high school. Kid Cudi clarified this for me, but apparently, I saved his life back then. I had to do it again the second time since people put me back into this game again. He knows it, and he knows who saved his life the second time around. So he put the pieces together himself. Another part of the *Supernatural* show I wanted to mention was that someone who didn't really know who the brothers were for a significant part of the seasons was writing a book about their lives and thought it was fiction. He was having these visions and wrote their story of their everyday lives, and the brothers started getting mad about it. They used him for their benefit to get help to save the world and to fight off the bad things in this world and use all of his help for positivity.

I wanted to add to the *Supernatural* script with some observations I made. The one part I wanted to add to, and I talked about it before, has to do with the character Lilith, who, in real life, is my little cousin Lily. In the show, Lilith is an evil character who is working with Lucifer and trying to destroy all the good things in the world. In the real world, Lily helps me solve problems and destroy my enemies and the people who are overpopulating the world. Anyway, I was on the porch with my mom, smoking our afternoon cigarettes, and we were talking about Lily and something she was going to do in the church, like a communion or some shit like that, when we heard a little girl scream outside our house.

My mom was like, "What the fuck was that?"

Then I told her, "Lily is a bad character in the show *Supernatural*, and the scream we heard is something Lily was doing with her technology that put someone in his or her grave."

The next part I wanted to discuss was that they added a character to the show *Supernatural*, and the character was based on someone I met in a restaurant when I was having breakfast with my family. I was eating at Silver Diner, and I was talking to myself, which I do frequently. I said, "I don't fuck with gay shit. That means I can't fuck with you now." I looked ahead of me, and the guy waved to me like he was really happy that Jesus was alive right now This is what Xzibit meant when he said that in his song. Jesus was Jewish and gay, so the notion that Jesus is not supposed to like Jewish people and gays still doesn't make any sense to me. But whatever. He was a believer, and I guess I had just helped him out recently. He was a believer of Christ and wanted to talk to me, but I like to distance myself from outsiders because people in my family wouldn't understand how well I can connect with outsiders. Anyway, in the show, he helps me defeat the evil and bring the world to justice.

In my life, Hollywood and the writers of the books I read pretty much know how my days are going to go every single day, which is okay for me, and I am not mad about it, but sometimes when they take credit for the things that I do, I get frustrated. For instance, Anna Kendrick wrote her book called *Scrappy Little Nobody*, and she got that title because she entered Hollywood around the same time I was dating Angie. That is when she started making her waves in Hollywood. She was observing Angie and me date and watching how happy and miserable we were together. Anna Kendrick helps me out every single day, and once she was more adapted to the Hollywood life, they started teaching her more and more. She then started understanding more about the world and what her role in this society was. It was for my benefit and hers. We are working as a big family, but we are trying to tell people to let those who know what they are doing do their jobs. Everybody else should just live their fucking lives.

Another instance I got mad was when Kevin Hart wrote his book, and it was called *You Can't Make This Stuff Up*. He got this from when I was watching the Michael Bay movie *Transformers*, and people put this thought inside my head. This is how Kevin Hart got the title for his book. I am dealing with some serious shit in real life, and they take things that happen in my life and get rich and famous because of it. I need to start gaining more publicity not just within my world but on TV. I am okay with this because they started at the end and know I will get my name all over the record books, and the fact that I am writing books is really important. It was really important that professional athletes put me back into this game because we needed more clarity on the bigger and smaller issues in this world. When Zach Bosh nearly went through the same thing he went through in high school, he was scared; but this time around, he knew exactly who saved his life. Everything I have been going through in my entire life has been real, and there's been a lot of good and some bad.

I wanted to talk more about the *Supernatural* script. There is one part that I wanted to discuss. The two brothers sell their souls to demons and buy their ticket into hell because of people close to them who they care about. In real life, I sold my soul because I thought I had to, to make the world a better place and to provide more natural resources for people currently living to better their lives instead of people wasting my time on planet Earth. I know that a lot of people like when the stocks are doing well, so I play the song "X" so that every time I play that song, people are looking for progress in the world. This simply means progress for the human race, and it doesn't matter how it gets done. I just need the people who are noticing these positive changes to help me out every single day. The two brothers ended up killing the demons in the show, so I wonder how that affects my life.

I wanted to add even more about the *Supernatural* script. They talk about something called the Reaper, who takes people to the afterlife after people's times are up on the planet. If the Illuminati didn't give me proper credit on who lives and who dies, then I just walked away when I was at COMTEK. This is also how they came up with the script for *Mr. Right*. Madonna said in her song that the boy with the cold hard cash is always Mr. Right. Anna Kendrick stars in this movie, and it is about an assassin who kills people after him because he betrayed their trust. Anyway, the Reaper is not necessarily a bad person, but this person is given an order by God to take people into the afterlife after they die off planet Earth. I am the Grim Reaper, and this also has many responsibilities, one of these responsibilities is to help guide these people in the "better place" after they pass away. However, like I said, we are going to be here forever, so most people don't have to worry about the afterlife. The two boys made deals with the Reaper because they didn't want to die, and they made deals with demons and sold their souls, which bought their tickets into hell because they wanted to help out people in need.

I've talked a lot about the *Supernatural* script, but I have more to add to it now. There was this one guy, twenty-nine, talking on the news about how he was given his last rites and then ended up staying alive because of a miracle. I was just watching this one scene in *Supernatural*, and the guy ended up staying alive in the script. There was one guy that I read on Yahoo News who died at the age of thirty from the coronavirus, and this guy was twenty-nine and survived the coronavirus. People say that bad things happen in threes, but all those people were wrong; bad things happen in twos. In this case, it happened with one because I was able to save this guy's life, especially when I was listening to the Third Eye Blind song where he said that bad things were going to start happening in ones, and Hoodie Allen said in his "Silver Linings" song that we were going to try to add some motherfucking zeros. Also, good things will start happening in sixes. Everyone won't win all the time, but this will be a trend that we will start to head in for the future.

I also wanted to talk about this other story. There was one guy who had a near-death experience, and he talked on the news that God saved his life that day. Recently after that, I was talking to my friend Ethan Stewart, and I was explaining to him some of the things I was going through. I said to him I didn't think God saved me after telling Aaron how much I believe in God.

Eric was like, "Haha, you said that God didn't save you after you were talking about God with Aaron."

I realized that I saved that guy's life because I can't believe now that I am reborn, and I am saving people's lives all the time. If you are deemed not to be saved, then you will die; but the people's lives that I have saved, they most likely will know about it or already know about it.

Tim Allen also talked about the Reaper in his show *Last Man Standing*, and he also said, "Don't lose the friends that you have, and keep in mind the people that are closest to you." The two boys look after the people that are closest to them first and then try to help out as many people as possible to keep them safe from the demons. This is kind of how I operate. However, I need to keep in mind that it is important that I help out the people closest to me and then branch out to other people. I do know this one fact: nobody in the world has had it tougher than I have. I've even dealt with the coronavirus but refuse to get tested for it. It always heals up and then comes back sometimes; but hopefully, people who are helping me out from the outside can pick up on these trends and make sure that we find a solution for the coronavirus, as we are trying to find a solution for the human race. The Reaper was a term I wasn't familiar with until I heard it in the *Supernatural* show and then when Tim Allen repeated it in *The Last Man Standing*. I know that the people who are aging in Hollywood are doing everything in their power to expedite this process and make sure that I step back into the line, the process of healing is all healed, or karma catches up with me so that they don't have to face the Reaper and deal with the afterlife. Unfortunately, this became a little bit out of my control once people made my life a living hell, and I was defenseless against these attacks just like I was when I was at a younger age. I was given the hardest tests in human history so that I can be the best person in the world in the future. My future holds many promises and will be great. I have had many opportunities to get with so many different girls, but I know that every person is only destined to be with one person. So the girls who have been interested in me can move on. I am seeing much better clarity on my life as I have matured and see clearer than I have in my entire life. It is important that I talked about the Reaper, and if you are free enough to understand this, then props to you. Many people don't understand the things that I have written in my book because they are not as free as I am and as other real people are in this life.

I wanted to add more about the *Supernatural* script because I can relate to a lot of these episodes, and they all speak to me. In the last episode I was watching, they were talking about a movie star named Vince, and he was dating a redhead girl. There is one girl I am interested in, and the Vince movie star they got from the scripts written for *Entourage*. The Vince character in the *Supernatural* show ended up being a bad guy because he was possessed by Lucifer, the devil. In the show *Lucifer*, he is a funny character who helps the police solve crimes; but in the show *Supernatural*, he is actually Jack and is the bad guy.

There is also another part I want to talk about in the *Supernatural* script. There was one episode where a girl was scared of a storm, and the other police officers were wondering why she was so scared of a storm when she should be focusing on taking down the bad guys. The storm actually ended up killing her, and it was formed by the evil girl who was trying to destroy the world. The evil girl was Mary, but the other girl was on the good side of things. At the end of this particular episode, she ended up as a good girl and went to heaven with God with happiness. In the real world, I expect something like this to happen; and regarding the storm, they were talking about dust storms and other storms that were forming at about 3,500 miles per hour in America or somewhere in the world. This is how they got this part in the script, about the storm. They made the God character a creative, complex person who was easy to relate to the people in the world. They came up with this part based on all the believers in the world who want answers, and I can supply them with those answers when the time is right. This book will help me dissect the information in the real world for those who are interested in what is going on with the world.

The two brothers are very similar to the two brothers from *Prison Break*. Both of the brothers in these shows are Avery and me. I am the main guy, and Avery is always my sidekick. I don't think Jack has a very good personality. Also, Jack is kind of boring, so he doesn't entertain people as much as Avery does and certainly not as much as I do. So Jack is always the bad guy in these shows.

A lot of the *Supernatural* script is based on the apocalypse. The two brothers are in survival mode, and they help people with their demon problems and also with everything that involves the apocalypse. I went through the apocalypse twice in the real world, and the first time was when Avery was living here. I was scared out of my fucking mind and later found out that it wasn't because of God; it was actually because of the devil, Jeff Veltri.

I was reciting Bible verses and pretty much connecting each verse to the universe and to people's lives. Later on, I was able to connect Bible verses to the professional and collegiate ranks and make their games more productive and efficient. I was going through so much and got sent to the hospital for my mental illness twice because I was paying a price for being God and the devil. I would rather pay a price for being God because this is the only way I will fully win in this world. There are a lot of songs that Hollywood put out saying that I am God.

Anyway, when I was going through the apocalypse the first time, I think people were watching me and observing; but I heard this funny noise that said, "Will, we have to do this the Bible way."

When this voice came in, it wasn't talking about the good parts of the Bible; it was talking about the worst parts of the Bible. In addition, they mean that the world is going to end and that humankind goes extinct. I am the only person in the world who can fix these problems, and the brother on the show *Supernatural* is Avery. He is supposed to be the Jesus character, and I am supposed to be all the God characters in *Supernatural*.

When I was going through the apocalypse the first time, I was dancing on my porch and rocking out to some of the songs that were stuck in my head, and Anna Kendrick was there for my support to make sure I would get through this smoothly. She was the main person I was thinking about who could really help me out. There were other people who were helping me out, especially Atmosphere, the rapper in Hollywood. He wrote the most meaningful song about the apocalypse and even mentioned my name in the song. People started to talk about it, and they even talked about it on ESPN.

Another person who came to my rescue was Emmy Rossum. She is really important and plays a very important role in my future and my current well-being. I said earlier in the book that she was the main girl character in the script for *The Day after Tomorrow*. This script has to do with global warming and the apocalypse, and it has a lot to do with my life. Atmosphere is wishing me a better day every single night so that I can wake up and have a good day through the entire day. This was her first role, and it had everything to do with me. The other film she was in that I can relate to is *Shameless*, and this has everything to do with these dirty girls who want to meet the man of their dreams by doing funny business inside their homes when I am just chilling inside my home.

I was reciting so many things from the Bible when I was going through the apocalypse, and it was just a fucking nightmare. I was able to recover from this and move on with my life. Then I dated my soul sister, Ava, for about a year. The next time I went through the apocalypse was equally scary. I didn't sleep for a week or longer than that because I was pretending like I was immortal and like nothing could bring me down. However, it really backfired, and I actually went through these issues because Peyton Manning said to me,

"Believe me, I am going to put you through that exact same game a second time."

After I stopped sleeping and everything in my life was going to hell, the world, in my eyes, was over. There was no sign of life, and the human race was extinct. P!nk said, "Hollywood came when I called, and you fooled us," "We are billions of beautiful hearts," and "You [Jack] sold us down the river too far." Anyway, I saw people on the streets about four, five, or six days later and knew that everything would be okay. I asked my real creator if we could take a drive around the neighborhood so that I could make sure that there were still people alive. I was scared out of my fucking mind. People were continuing on with their lives but making sure I was okay, that we can solve these issues as a team, that I can get all the help I need to fix the world and myself, and that things will go a lot more smoothly in the future.

I talked about this other script before, but it is actually really important. The script is for *Collateral Beauty*. It pretty much talks about how humans are connected to things, especially things that are important in life. This comes from Einstein, but I have used these things in our lifetime to help other people out. One of those things is love. I am able to put relationships together, with or without people knowing. There is this one girl in Hollywood who is helping me out with this. It was written in the script for *Shameless*. Most girls in this world, at one point or another, have done bad things in their bedrooms, using me to find their soulmates, and I have fixed their relationships together. The one crazy freak in Hollywood stands for love, and she is helping me put relationships together. The other thing is time. We are all connected to time. I have helped out so many people by just looking at the clock and figuring out the signs that connect. For example, every time the number twenty-five appears on the clock, it helps out people who believe in God. I am just a human being, after all, and have made mistakes. Another example is when they were playing *Jeopardy!* and the clock just turned on the thirty-ninth minute. It was directly connected to the score on the *Jeopardy!* game, and the woman ended up winning the game. I hope she appreciates the help. They were making examples of me, and once I step back into the line, I won't get in trouble anymore. However, in the movie, Will Smith's friends set him up for failure so that he could look like he was mentally unstable when he was fine, and they were messing with his head.

Maren Morris is helping me keep my shit together, and the people who have watched me from outside have made me feel like this has been a blessing for all those people who have figured out who I was. When "Remember the Name" was playing at every stadium, it was great. I didn't really notice other people talking about me, but some of them, I did notice. Most of it was positive. I went to one game with Ava, and they were playing the "Remember the Name" song. I stood up from my seat and was like, "Holy fuck, they are playing my song." I turned around me and started clapping when the Giants scored. The word spread; and the next time I went to the game with Joanna, my real creator, and my sister, one guy was like, "God damn it, I'm drunk. I heard that Will guy was at the game."

His friend was like, "I heard he's a Giants fan."

He didn't mean this in a sinister way; he was just saying so that they could figure out who I was. I don't like controversy, and when people argue about sports, I don't speak because it is sinister. Another thing I don't like is that people go to church on Sunday mornings and then yell at the players. My therapist once told me that it's a good way to live like Jesus and not hate. I am trying to follow this motto and practice what I preach. I just don't understand because they go to church and see everything as equal, but then they talk shit online and yell at the players on the opposing teams. It's very immature, and I wish ill fate on a lot of these people sometimes. It's just straight-up annoying sometimes.

The last part of the *Collateral Beauty*" script was death. We need to cheat death, and this is what Will Smith said in *Hitch*. We need to make this life everlasting because nobody really knows what the afterlife is made of. We know what this life has to offer, and in Watsky and Bebe Rexha's songs, they say we turn to dust when we die. I would rather be a human for the rest of eternity than a spirit, a ghost, or fucking dust. They pretended they were invisible to make Will Smith in *Collateral Beauty* look crazy. This is some of the unnecessary bullshit that I have dealt with. I never chose this path, and my real creator is too stupid to help me out. I have to figure this shit out on my own with the help of the people in this world who know what they are doing. I don't need God's damn help. He gets credit for the things that I do, and I fucking hate that. If I am God, then God bless you, but my real creator will never understand the things that I do. So I deleted the will.i.am and Grits song that says God needs to help the win. If God were going to help the win, he would've helped by now. I gotta do this on my own, and if people can't get what they want, it's all because of me. I am sick and tired of people looking to the Goddamn sky. Nobody up there is helping us out. It's all because of me. These stupid-ass athletes wanted to put me back in this devilish game again, and now Kobe Bryant is dead. And they can't play sports now. They know that karma needs to catch up to me, but the evil people are getting exactly what they deserve right now. Everything in my life seemed so fucking simple a long time ago. These bad people who wanted to make my life a living hell back in the day are facing karma every single day. Those bad people are the Mafia. I refuse to be scared of them. Additionally, when people think of the Mafia, they think that they are scared of them, but they don't fucking scare me. Anyway, this is all I am going to talk about for the script for *Collateral Beauty* for the time being.

The next script I wanted to talk about was the one for *Deep Blue Sea*, which was written in 1999 and included people like LL Cool J and Samuel L. Jackson. The Killers came out with their song "Spaceman" in 2008, and people think they might cross over and are stuck between the devil and the deep blue sea. The people who were hating on me because of some of the moves I was making back in 2013 started dying. It wasn't an option for a lot of people, and I figured out that I wasn't the devil. But the people who really did fail this test started dying, and it was their own fault. That was just one part of the process in which several people died, and I think that particular test is over now because everyone who was going to fail that test did fail. They all died because of it. The movie *Deep Blue Sea* was really good, and it involved deadly sharks who were killing the humans. LL Cool J was also in one of those *Space Jam* songs that they released back in the day, and I listen to that song sometimes. The people who are dying these days are dying because of the actual apocalypse that is going on. We are still worried about overpopulation, so I say that we just let the flesh die because they are weak people. We need more natural resources for strong people.

My therapist actually told me that there are positives we can take away from the coronavirus in terms of people not using their cars as much, giving Mother Nature a break from all the automobile usage and people's activities in this world. I know that many people think it is sad about the people in New York who are dying. However, we are especially worried about overpopulation in New York, and we need people of all ages to die. But I was only going to take this as far as people were willing to take this with me. We still need to try to find a cure for the coronavirus so that people can start living their lives again. I thought I should write about *Deep Blue Sea* because the Killers became really famous for their "Spaceman" song. There are still people intentionally making my life worse, and they will pay if they haven't already. I don't know who, but I will find the answers soon enough. After they came out with the "Spaceman" song, Andy Grammer came out with the song "Keep Your Head Up" in 2009. In the "Spaceman" song, he says that the spaceman says, "Everybody look down." Andy Grammer's "Keep Your Head Up," which was played in the first *Pitch Perfect* movie, came out afterward. Back then, I didn't know the things I now know about the world, but it is all a process. And it's no secret that we are all getting old. People in this world who made my life harder need to fix everything they have done to me and make things right again in this world. The apocalypse actually started in 2004, about the time when I graduated high school and about the time when the Red Sox started winning their World Series. It is kind of weird because 9/11 happened in 2001, and that was when the Patriots started winning their Super Bowls. I wonder if there is a reason why the apocalypse and 9/11 happened. Is it because of events that were happening in Boston? Anyway, I do not think I am the devil anymore, and I think that people need to believe for our lives to get better. However, if you can't get what you want, it will be strictly because of me since nobody in the world is as powerful as I am. And anybody that stole this paradise from me will face repercussions. This is all I want to write about *Deep Blue Sea* for the time being.

I think I have talked about this script before, but I wanted to discuss it again, as I mentioned in the above section. The movie is called *Pain & Gain*. This movie featured Mark Wahlberg, Dwayne Johnson, and Anthony Mackie. They got the movie title based on a Fort Minor song, and in the song, he says, "One man's pain is another man's pleasure. One say infinity, the next say forever." Right now, everybody has to get their shit together. In the movie, one pretty funny scene that I was talking about is similar to when Aaron and I were presenting our products to Andrew Ke; we looked like a bunch of amateurs, just like how they showed the characters in *Pain & Gain*. Another main focus of the movie was three guys who really believed in lifting weights, getting bigger, and making a lot of money. I want to just pretty much focus on Jack and me for this part. We talk about lifting all the time and how we can make each other better with our workouts. The other guy I would talk to about lifting was Avery, but he has been pretty much MIA for a while now. I am a lot bigger now because of people like Tim Tebow, Mark Wahlberg, and Dwayne Wade motivating me to get bigger, keep focused, and not let outside distractions deter me from doing exactly what I need to be doing to make myself the best version and the best person that I need to be—and to further the world's goals to make this world the best possible world since the second coming of Christ.

Things were never perfect in the world, and Jesus made that pretty clear when he was alive a billion years ago. They even put it in a song that we need to make the world the best version of the world that God and Jesus said it was when they were alive at the beginning of time. We need to make this world the best version of the world that we could possibly make it until the end of time. I always like the part of the movie when the Mark Wahlberg character was like, "I am blah blah blah, and I believe in fitness." For those who are still watching me, and when I am by myself and getting big and making my positive moves, I say, "I am Will Coakley, and I believe in fitness." I think it is so funny, and perfection is my direction. Mark

Wahlberg was even a part of this when he was a part of the script for *Invincible*. I talked about this script when they named the characters Vince and Johnny. I am supposed to be Vince, and Jack is supposed to be Johnny. Jack is also Johnny Drama, I am Vince in *Entourage*, and Mark Wahlberg was a part of that as well. So they easily connected the dots for these two movies.

The next part I wanted to talk about was the coronavirus and how everyone has to wear those stupid-looking masks, including the people working at grocery stores and those who are getting sick. When the three idiots in this movie were trying to kill the people who were setting them up for failure, they wore masks in the hospital. This image ran through my mind, and I figured out that they predicted this part of the virus when my real creator got a bit sick and started wearing that mask. The two guys got the death penalty for the things they were doing, but I think Jack and I will be fine because the things both of us are doing are too good to be true. Also, we cannot get caught for doing things so innocent without actually breaking any laws.

I talked a lot about the show *Shameless* in my last book, but I wanted to discuss it again here. In some of the episodes, Frank looks to the sky and curses at God for being such an asshole, looking down at us and not doing *shit*. He smiles down upon us, makes us live in pain and fear, and doesn't fucking do anything about it. I look at the sky sometimes, but it's not to pray; it's mostly to curse him the fuck out for being such a piece of shit and ruining my life. So many people did so many bad things behind my back and talked so much shit behind my back, and God didn't do anything about it. He just sits in heaven and looks down at us with his blank fucking, Goddamn face. People will never understand the things I have been through because I have been through everything humanly possible, which has been very positive and very negative. People are used to going to school and then college, working, retiring, and then dying. I don't see life as being like that. I feel like we need to find a solution for being limitless, and with all my heavenly experiences. Anyway, the scene they came up with in the script for *Shameless* when Frank and company kept cursing out God, they had a very good reason to do that.

Every single character in *Shameless* plays an important role in society. For instance, the main character, Lip, who I think they came up with because of my personality, was created based on Sum 41's song "Fat Lip." I have set up so many relationships through my magic, and it's been inside me since I was young enough to start jerking off. I have established so many relationships with girls being shameless and doing their thing within their own privacy, not really talking about it until recently. Missy Elliott put in one of her songs, "Ain't no shame, ladies. Do your thing. Just make sure you ahead of the game." All the hot guy characters in this show were combined into one human being, plus the other guys who are sidekicks, to all the benefits I am giving to society. I think the Frank character is really supposed to be my real creator, and he is funny. But the Lip character is the most real character out of all of them. This whole *Shameless* thing goes back to when I was in high school and college, even though I didn't know about it.

Nowadays, and I've mentioned this before, but I need to get my mojo back before I enter another relationship since the actual apocalypse happened with the scripts for *I Am Legend, Deliver Us from Evil,* and *X-Men: Apocalypse*, which was probably the scariest thing I have ever been through—probably the scariest thing besides Avery putting me in this crazy position to answer everybody's dumbass prayers and making these invisible pains enter my body. My real creator has no clue what any of this actual higher-power stuff means, so I deleted the songs that say "God help the win" because there is no God helping any wins in this world, unless that God is me. This is all I want to say about this script for the time being. Another character who is crucial is the Black girl, V. They came up with her name because of Veltri and me being stuck in the deep details of the devil. The devil is in the details, and it's written in Veltri's last name. His first name is Jeff. Sometimes when I look at the street lights, the lights are illuminating at my eyes in the shape of a *V*, and this is how they came up with the girl's name. They also wanted to add a Black girl so she can somewhat resemble my soul sister, Ava, and for when Ava comes back into my life.

The series *Divergent* came out around the time I was dating Ava, and it has become really important in my life because all of these bad motherfuckers in this world who control us can't control some of us because we are the divergents in this world. I am the biggest divergent in this world, and that is why they called me Four in this script. Bea Miller, one girl whom I listen to quite often, wrote a song about this script; and her first songs were released in 2015, about a year after Ava and I broke up. This script is really important; and we are building up a new world, which they showed in the third movie, with no clouds in the sky and beauty all over the place, with different colors and stuff in the sky. The Jeff Daniels character in the final movie was supposed to be Mr. Drewer, and they are supposed to finish what some of them wanted to finish—the corrupt people in this world who put me through all these tests so that I can be the best person in this world. It is important because he was the bad guy in the final movie in this series because they laid pretty hard tests on the two best people in the world that they ended up passing, but they weren't able to pass that test unless they defeated this Jeff Daniels character. I made promises to Pat, Joe, and Matt that I would bring their father back to life after karma caught up with me, and I know some of the tests he put me through that were pretty difficult. In the book, the main character dies, and I didn't like that too much. So in the movie, they changed that around and had the main character living through all this bullshit. They changed that up so that I could be happy with the ending, and we could see more silver linings in this lifetime.

I thought about writing about the *Divergent* series because they named the new Raiders stadium in Vegas Allegiant Stadium, and the second book, I think, was called *Allegiant*. Hollywood started at the end and when everything was ready to move forward, so they knew this move was going to happen. And all the people responsible will get their credit. The stadium is also at an address with four 3s in it, and 3 stand for Anna Kendrick. Her motivation and my powers have led the Raiders to transform into a better team, and I was actually just thinking about Jon Gruden the other day, the head coach of the Raiders. The spirits also flock to me every day when they need my help in the afterlife, and the Stadium is on Al Davis Road. He was the owner of the Raiders, and I think he passed away. But I would have to do research on that to make sure. This move happened right on cue and for a reason, and I wish the Raiders the best luck in the upcoming season.

I wanted to talk about this script, and I think it is equally as important as the other scripts I have written about. The script is for the show *Lost*. The first part of this script I wanted to write about was that the two characters, Omar and Hurley, were mentioned with the first and last names in this script. The two friends from my past are Stephen Hurley and Omar Syed. They came out with this script knowing that I was going to reunite with them in the future. I knew Omar from playing soccer in high school. I played with him in my travel league, and we became really close to the point where I would rather hang out with him instead of the people at my high school. We had the cool group on my soccer team and the rest of the people. I was a part of the cool group, and there is one guy, Reggie Bennett (who I am still friends with), I talk to all the time. They made the Omar character Middle Eastern just like my friend on the soccer team was. The other guy, Stephen Hurley, was a friend from high school who hung out with the cool kids when I hung out with a bunch of outsiders and pretty much formed my own group in high school. I became close to Hurley when we were playing baseball in high school. He was a part of my group playing baseball, and we became close because we both rode the bench in our junior years with the guys who were better than us because they were better politically than we were. There were only five juniors that made the varsity team because our team was stacked, and Hurley, Slesinger, and I were a part of that group. I still talk to Slesinger now and actually play in a coed softball league with him, and he is one of my close friends. Hurley was an interesting character, and I would love to be friends with him in the future. I am a different person and more mature, and all of our separate groups were meant to fall apart and come together again in the future, so I will be friends with Omar and Hurley in the future. We are going to be here forever, and those two guys are a big part of my future plans, so they mentioned them on purpose in the show "Lost." The other part I wanted to talk about was that the grown man with those crazy abilities and that monster ability was my real creator in the show. I am the cool guy who solves the problems because he is smart and knows how to fight pretty well. The old guy was a good guy but he had crazy abilities that were pretty evil in the show, and that character is supposed to be my real creator.

The next script I wanted to talk about is the one for *Office Space*. The part that I have images of was when one worker kept on getting demoted. He was a funny character in the show, and they ended up putting his cubicle downstairs, away from everyone, because everything in the show and all the moves they were making were political. When I went to visit my cousin Ray one time, his cubicle was in a similar place to the guy's cubicle in *Office Space*. It came to my head right away, and I started laughing, but it wasn't funny because Ray was dealing with this harassment in real life. A group of people laid the worst in the best in this world just to make us stronger people in the future, and you bet your ass that Ray is in the top one hundred best people in the world and that I will get rich with him. Another example is when I was working at COMTEK; and again, because it was political, Janice and I were given cubicles far from the accounting department when everyone else was given a room so they could have their privacy. There was one Asian girl who ended up working near us. In *Office Space*, the owners of the company really liked the main guy because he blamed all his issues on his bosses not pushing him hard enough. This kind of reminds me of how I don't really try that hard and still get really good credit for my work ethic. He was saying that he didn't have a work ethic because his bosses weren't pushing him hard enough.

To go along with the above script and what I said about Ray, I wanted to talk about the script for *Horrible Bosses*. This script was based on three guys who were trying to make a living, and they were pretty stupid and funny, working together. They didn't really know how to operate a business and were actually being played by rich people who thought they could use them because of their ignorance. Ava said that in the show, I reminded her of the Charlie character. I thought it was funny because she didn't mean it in a sinister way. When I was working with Ray and we were trying to recruit people to do our graphic designing and things of that nature, we were looking at hot girls, and that is how the Jason Sudeikis character was looking to recruit people to work for him—by hiring girls who were hot, even if their skill level wasn't good enough. That part was designed for Ray and me to look at girls' looks instead of their skill level. The other guy would probably be Rory because the keys to my success lie with Rory and Ray, and they are both connected because they both know business and are smart. I wouldn't want to work with anyone else in the world besides these two guys.

The one thing that made me very angry was when Jack started comparing me to Charlie in *It's Always Sunny in Philadelphia*. He was doing it in a sinister way, unlike Ava. Jack got disrespected pretty hard for the way he was talking to me, and he wouldn't stop until I told him to shut the fuck up. Then he realized that he needed to stop. He brought up this topic again, and I told Rory that I didn't want to talk to Jack anymore because he was acting like a bully. Next, Rory told Jack how I felt about Jack because Rory didn't want me to lose Jack as a friend.

Jack called me on the phone the next day and said, "Are we okay? Like, I was just joking," blah, blah, blah.

I said, "Yeah, we're cool."

I just can't deal with anyone's bullshit after all the crazy fucking bullshit I've been through in my life. Jack got under my skin more than anyone else ever has, and Hailee Steinfeld said that in one of her songs. Anyway, these two scripts are about guys who are the best of the best and are just trying to make it big to help the world, and since we are on our pursuit of happiness, I thought I should write about it.

I have talked about the script that was written called *Taken* with Liam Neeson and Maggie Grace, but I am actually dealing with some of this shit in real life. They came out with the new script for *Robin Hood* because the girl I was talking to on the Internet was named Robin, and all the people who were dying were dying because of the missions she was sending me on. Anyway, I talked to this other girl I met on the Internet, and she also lost both of her parents, just like that Robin girl did. I figured out that both these girls are damaged, and it has something to do with a gang ring or some shit like that where they abuse the girls and use them to gain profits from innocent people. They use hot girls to catch the attention of innocent guys on the Internet. With my powers and my shadow play, I can end this at some point with more time. I need the next year or two with focused energy and effort to end this type of bullshit that goes on in the world. I am the right guy for the job, and they would not have come out with the script for *Taken* had they not seen me as the right fit for the guy to help these poor girls out. They don't know any better, and I can get them out of the ruts they are in if they are really God-fearing girls. They are brought up in a bad environment and led down the wrong path, but the guys who run them, I can end. And if they mess with me, I will be strong enough to fuck them up. I would need the powers of the courts in the United States to end them the right way without getting into trouble. In the script, Liam Neeson uses guns and violence, but I can do this with shadow play and help these poor, innocent girls out. I also talked about how they came out with the script for *Taken* because there is one girl left in our generation who hasn't been taken yet, and I will be the one to take her. I don't know if I can wait that long, but for the right girl, I can be as patient as I need to be.

I wanted to talk about the script for *Old School* a bit. There is one scene that keeps playing through my mind. People used to compare one of our fraternity brothers named Brian Platt to Vince Vaughn, and there was one scene in *Old School* where Will Ferrell takes a joke too far.

Vince Vaughn goes, "Don't overcelebrate it."

When I was hanging out with a bunch of my fraternity brothers and other friends to watch a boxing match, Brian Platt was one of the guys I was hanging out with, and it was when so many people kept saying, "God damn it" and "Jesus Christ" a lot. Everyone was losing their minds. Brian Platt was always really funny to me, and I always got along with him very well. He was saying "Jesus Christ" on repeat, and I kept laughing while everyone was being so serious. This was when Cory Calton or I was supposed to say, "That's great, but don't overcelebrate it." They came out with this line based on of how funny Brian Platt and I were acting that day.

Then he says, "Do you think that Jesus was the most boring guy ever?" and the entire room went silent.

I was like, *What the fuck is going on?* but apparently, that was because of the concentrated power of Will.

The next time I ran into him, people were calmer, and it was at my friend Alex Shalak's birthday party.

He mentioned, "Coakley was acting especially crazy that day," attributing this to his having listened to the Gorillaz song that suggested I might be Jesus Christ. He knew something was up when the entire room went silent, their serious conversations abruptly stopping. Those empires also had Brian Platt watch my highlights in the past when I was acting crazy.

Brian Platt then went, "Yeah, but Coakley was acting especially crazy that day," referring to a different memory from college.

Another aspect of *Old School* was that these college girls, who have fallen in love with an older guy who is not available to them, was based on the *Old School* script. I am meant to be the Godfather, with the other two guys being Aaron and Jack. I will achieve perfection with all of them cheering for me, and in the meantime, I can help them out whenever they need my help—whether they need that extra boost in finding their boyfriends or if they require assistance with tests.

I can also mention *Wedding Crashers* because all the girls Vince Vaughn was involved with in *Wedding Crashers* were crazy hot, mature, and eager to find boyfriends. Many of them I have hooked up with their soulmates based on the activities in my bedroom. One of those girls is Tim Tebow's fiancée. These girls also include all my sisters in Hollywood and practically every girl across the globe since I was in seventh grade.

This script is really important and kind of put me on the map in terms of my football skills, how Fort Minor came out with the song "Remember the Name," and how Snoop Dogg released his infamous song "What's the Name?" Rihanna and Drake also released a song along those lines. The movie I am talking about is called *Remember the Titans.* They developed this script based on the rivalry with the interracial team from back in the day and how they faced discrimination from all the White teams in the conference, ultimately defeating them because of their chemistry, even if they weren't more talented on paper. However, Hollywood was also thinking about my direction and how it would impact the big leagues. Will Smith revealed that they write these scripts based on my life, and this script was a perfect example of how I became so famous in the world. They came out with *Remember the Titans* as in "Remember the Name Will Coakley." The two team captains in this movie are the most important players, and one of those guys ends up in a wheelchair and dies. The other guy, however, kills it, while the injured one struggles. I think the character I am supposed to be is the Ryan Gosling character, Alan Bosley. He was a skinnier dude who played cornerback or wide receiver in the movie. These would be the two positions I would play against the pros. He was one of the main guys in the movie who got along well with the Black players. His personality is similar to mine; and although he wasn't one of the main characters, out of all the characters in this movie, the Ryan Gosling character would be the best fit for me. Anyway, I was on my couch, reading one of my books, when this movie came to mind, and I thought I would write about it.

I thought I had talked about this script before, but I will mention it again. I might have discussed it in my previous book, but this script is the one for *It's Always Sunny in Philadelphia*. In one episode they made, they talked about how the gang was going to solve global warming. The main character, Dennis, turns the AC on in the bar and has girls dancing to his music in the bar in an attempt to solve global warming. There are a few points I want to bring up about this script. First of all, before storms come, I can see Mother Nature inside my house and outside. Hollywood is working every single day with me to try to solve global warming, and one of the ways is to control Mother Nature. When she acts up, it is usually because of the things my mom is doing, since Rosa is Mother Nature. They brought this part up in this script because we can solve Mother Nature inside my house and outside, on my porch, every single morning. Every single morning, I will chain-smoke my cigarettes in an effort to illuminate the sky and try to fix Mother Nature and the sky. Watsky even mentioned in his song that soon, in this room, it will be just me, my soulmate, my mom, and me with all the elements.

The other part of this equation I wanted to bring up was these single girls dancing to the beat of the music. There is a group of girls that they are talking about specifically in this script who think I am sexy, and for this one script, they were trying to meet the loves of their lives. They put the exact number of girls in this episode, which equates to the number of girls in the real world who thought it was a good idea to rock out to my music and do their thing to find their soulmates. Will.i.am included in one of his songs a message for ladies to not lose their tracks, going into specifics about these specific girls.

We can solve global warming within the next two years, no longer than that, with the help of people who know what they are doing in this world. People aren't as naive and stupid as they used to be, as long as you are real enough.

Like I am saying, the girls who know what they are trying to do with me aren't dumb and understand that they are using me for the right reasons—to find the loves of their own lives. People who are real enough to understand these things about the world are the type of people I rely on every single day to help me save the world. This includes a lot of people, actually. Like I said, many people understand things, as the entire Nationals stadium was cheering for me when I left the stadium with Jack because they saw some of the highlights of my past and all the bad things I was going through. They won't specifically name it, but they knew a lot of it was because of Jack. They were happy that I made it to the stadium. The songs and Hollywood knew that I would appreciate them putting me in the spotlight so that the entire stadium would cheer for me. The crowd was also becoming more aware of the CIA and the evil tests they put me through. It was a miracle that I was still alive because of all the sinister things I was going through; and Jack was the main conspirator behind my back in the past and sometimes in the present, which is part of the reason they were cheering for me. Once I am able to achieve perfection, everyone who is able to get past the apocalypse will love it, and they will be cheering for me all the time. Thanks to the clever lady, she will be by my side the entire time, and we will have people over all the time.

Another point that I wanted to mention right now was that I said I want to make Jeff Bezos money, but I don't want to be selfish with it. I want to make that type of money so I can share it with every single person in this world who makes it past the apocalypse healthy and spread the wealth to the lower, middle, and upper classes equally. Everything will become more equalized in this world in the next few years. With every single death in this world, someone or a group of people always benefit. The *Equalizer* script with Denzel Washington was made because everything becomes more equalized in this world with every single death that happens. People cheer for these individuals because they are striving to make things right in the world and will save our lives, thanks to what was written in the stars and because of what he is working on within his solution pit. People are very grateful for those working hard behind the scenes to make sure things are right in this world and prevent bad things from happening when they are not supposed to, because we can always count on me, and people are more than aware of that.

I wanted to talk about the script for *The Grudge*. The first movie was released in 2004, and they just came out with a new one in 2020. They also released other ones in different years. The movie is actually a scary movie. The person that I hold a grudge against is Satan, or Jeff Veltri. He is the little birdie who whispered his famous words to God that I was conquering a world of fear. Thankfully, the fear is all gone, and he will live for a while. The words out of Jack's mouth were "God's like, 'Everybody, shush. Bryce Harper is up, hahaha.'" First of all, the way he said it was very sinister, and the way he said it seemed really fake too. I thought about it for a little while, and Hollywood kind of guides me in what my next best move is. They made me figure out that Jack was actually the little birdie. The movies are scary, but they are scripts that were written for all eyes to see and for me to interpret. Hoodie Allen then came out with his song saying, "You the one they love, so if you disappear, they'll hold a grudge… [Jack] could have had it all, but then [he] lost it." When the world existed the first time around, Jesus ended up forgiving everyone, including Judas.

This time around, I don't know if I can forgive Jack, especially since Hollywood puts out so many songs suggesting I shouldn't forgive him, and he is the one who wanted to see me dead. He kept on playing games with me and did that indecent exposure to me. They included a part in *Supernatural* where Lucifer (Jack), who is the bad guy, is homeless, doesn't have anything left, and lost all his power and all his friends, and his crew goes down to nothing. Jack is still fucking playing games with me, and in two of their songs, they said goodbye to Jack's hopes and dreams since he took everything away from me and is still fucking up my life, so venom will be his only source of income at some point.

One of the reasons why I write so much negativity about Jack is because we were at a fantasy football draft one year, and we were watching TV before we did our draft. They showed a commercial with Charlie Day in it, and Jack started doing his sinister laugh. (He is also supposed to be the bad guy in *Happy Gilmore*.) He then turned to me and said, "Look, Will, it's your twin." He then said that he was the reason I quit dip, but he was watching me and knew that my teeth actually got worse after I quit dip. And I will still pass that test with flying colors despite going up against the most evil creature known to mankind. They put a lot of their songs about being a believer and that Jack is Satan, and I am the God figure who is supposed to save the world despite every curveball that Satan throws in my direction. Jack was such an asshole. He then started talking about how I deserved to be with all these ugly and disgusting girls in the world when I have had all the hottest girls in the world interested in me. He lost it all, and he will lose more when he loses everything. Venmo is his only source of income.

Anyway, this is what they are talking about when they came out with the script for *The Grudge*. Who knows how long Jack has been playing these games with me? But I don't think I can forgive him for the things he has done to me in the present and past. There was another song written by Tove Lo that said I am better off now and happy he is gone. I got stuck pretty deep, but then Jack continued to fucking play games with me. And then Tove Lo said that I am better off now and happy that he's gone. The other guy in Hollywood said that I am better off dead and he knows that he wants me dead. I didn't know what other guy he was talking about, and then I figured out he was talking about Jack. After he came out with this song, Tove Lo came out with the song that says I am better off now and glad that Jack is gone.

I wanted to talk about this other script for *The Maze Runner*. I have talked about it before, and I read all the books and discussed it a lot with Dr. O'Connor. Dylan O'Brien was the main character in the scripts that were written. The main female character, my mom said, did some bad things so that they could be together at the end of the day. Furthermore, when this is all said and done, she did some bad, clever things because she knew they were meant to be together, and it was bad things that she did so that everything would work out for everyone and that we could be soulmates for the rest of eternity. Dylan O'Brien didn't get the credit he deserves, and they were talking about actors and actresses who didn't get the credit they deserve. This is kind of what's been going on in my life and how these assholes want to discredit all the progress I have made in this world, and they are really fucking my shit up every single Goddamn day. Dylan O'Brien is an underrated actor, and they were talking about him in this one article I was reading. They also talked about Drew Barrymore, and there is a girl who I know that Bryce Vine wrote about in one of his songs who is going to be the next Drew Barrymore when this is all done, and all the tests are done, and when we are on our way for full potential and perfection to be accomplished.

The *Maze Runner* series was built on a guy who was chosen to go through all these hellish tests by people who don't show their faces to the public, and he needs to pass these tests to be the best person in the world. My tests started when I was crazy young, despite what some people said. Anyway, in one of Fort Minor's songs, he said, "The devil's got a fresh new place to play...like a maze you can never escape." I am sort of in that maze now, and I need to pass these tests every single day. I don't mind, though, because I sort of know what I am doing; and with the help of people, I can get through these mazes to reach the main goal, which is to form the world into one big family at the end of the day. I can solve problems every single day with what I do in my life and escape from this maze every single day to help out my family, friends, and strangers. I can help athletes peak and reach their full potential. I can bring birth into life.

Everybody in this Goddamn world loves kids. I don't know why. I would rather be immortal than have a kid. I am not saying that people who have kids can't be immortal, but a lot of their parents died because they had kids. And I don't think that will be an issue with my family. People wonder why grandparents and parents have died after they have had kids. It all has to do with evolution. Here is what you need to do: fucking stop having kids. It is that simple. Your legacy doesn't mean jack shit when you are dead. It doesn't fucking matter anymore, and you're not alive to see your legacy live on. Fuck your legacy. Stop having kids, and let's be here forever and make this life everlasting.

Anyway, Dylan O'Brien also came out with a movie where ISIS totally fucked up his marriage and killed his wife, and he took it personally and trained hard to get back at them. Dylan O'Brien is definitely an underrated actor because this movie was fantastic, and this is how I feel about some of the sinister tests that ISIS has put me through. I don't trust them, and we need this war overseas to end. We don't trust the government to make this happen, so *we, the people*, will stop this war overseas and make sure the right people come home safe. The cemeteries where previous people have been in wars are filling up pretty quickly because of old people dying who were in wars in the past and because people who fought in Afghanistan and Iraq are still dying. About twenty veterans commit suicide every day because they can't deal with the pain and suffering of a broken limb or whatever the fuck they are dealing with. All these problems can be fixed, and when I am go through the scripts for *The Maze Runner*, then I can solve these devilish tests that people put on me. One of those tests was the devil just a nose make. The girl who wrote that song is named Henderson, and she was talking about the noises Jack was making inside my body. Now he is making those fucking annoying sounds in my speakers when I am listening to my music. It is really driving me crazy, and he is a bad person who can't be trusted. I don't trust half the shit he says to me, and he is obviously someone I won't be able to trust in the future.

The next script I wanted to talk about was for the *Planet of the Apes* movie when James Franco was the main character. He developed this one drug where the apes could be tamed, and they were like science experiments. They could do all these crazy things when the drugs worked effectively. The drug made an ape talk just like a person, but he ended up forming a revolution against the people who started these tests against him because he couldn't stand what was going on with him and started killing people all over the place because it was like a fucked-up bad experience and experiment. Nevertheless, he also gave this drug to his real creator, who was experiencing dementia or something like that; and then, with this miracle drug, the real creator was able to play the piano clearly and perform tasks as if he was in the prime of his life again—maybe like a seventy-year-old was able to do things that a forty-year-old, or even a thirty-year-old, could do.

I thought about my real creator one day, as he is developing a lot of memory loss, and there are things that he used to do in the past that he can't do anymore. I thought about this one day, and the next day, they said they have made progress with Alzheimer's research and research for dementia. My friend Garrett's real creator just died from dementia, and I feel bad for him. He is someone who has always supported me and been nice to me, and he really doesn't involve himself in hate, kind of like me. I don't think he likes Jack that much, just like me and millions of other people across the globe. Anyway, this miracle drug is supposed to solve some of our problems. Obviously, not all of them, but it can help us with many problems. A lot of our other problems can be solved with faith and science at the same time.

In the *Planet of the Apes* movie, the ape is also a sign of a Jesus character; and in one of the movies, they put him on a cross. Actually, a lot of people were cheering for me in this movie because people were watching me when I was driving and Kid Cudi's song popped up, "You Were Playing Him, Now You Know."

I don't trust all people's intentions, but I know that there are still billions of good-hearted people out there who are trying to reach out to me and need my help. Many of them know exactly who I am, so I don't need people discrediting me or controlling us in sinister ways to make our lives worse than they already were. Perfection and progress are what we are aiming for, and anyone who gets in the way of that will start dying. When people talk shit about me behind my back, then bad shit starts to happen to them. When you play games with me and wonder why you got laid off your job and lost all your friends, then wonder why this is happening to you, you have to think about the consequences of the only person in the world you shouldn't have done certain things to. I am talking about Avery. When he looked into my eyes and told me to die, it was so fucking bad that day. Thankfully, the CIA got it to stop, and I was able to keep on living my life. It was apparent that Avery was the only guy in the world who tried to beat me. Karma will catch up with me, and I will live forever with the girl of my dreams. If people still want it, then they can have it, but don't come into my house and ruin my life because you feel bad that yours sucks. This is all I want to say about this script right now.

The next script I wanted to talk about was the script featuring Sandra Bullock, the script for *Gravity*. When she was nominated for this award, she was in front of the camera and said, "I started to understand the meaning of life a lot better after being a part of this movie." The whole point of this movie was that the male main character was going to bring back gravity into the world with all his positive movements, and it was actually a movie that involved outer space. However, just like what Tinie Tempah said in his song and what Sanchez was talking about, I am the man for this job; I can bring back gravity, let the flesh die, and feed those in need and those more important than the flesh that is dying every single day. People think the Lord works in mysterious ways because of everything I am doing in my life every day. I stopped liking Sandra Bullock because in *The Blind Side*, they disrespected the player who wore number 66 on the opposing team, making him look like the bad guy because 666 is supposed to signify the bad guy. People who wrote this script and the ones that were primarily responsible for making me the bad guy faced their karma, and maybe they still are. I like Sandra

Bullock and always did, but when I started to learn more about life and understood that people hated on me behind my back when I was going through so much bullshit, that was so fucking ridiculous. I was depressed and suicidal for a while, and I fell into this rut by accident. And people still hated on me. Just like what Miley Cyrus said, don't listen to all the people who hate, because all they are going to do is make your mistakes for you. This is exactly what people have been doing when I am talking about people making my mistakes for me.

I never deserved to be hated on at all since I am the only one in the world who is solving people's problems for them. Anyways the *Gravity* movie is based on two astronauts who survive after an accident leaves them stranded in space. I know how to solve the gravity issues in the world once we are all connected to the sky through technology, my powers, science, and religion. For instance, when Lizzo released her song saying that Hollywood doesn't love me anymore, it just turned me completely off from ever listening to any of her music. It went from one of the hottest Black girls in the world (Fergie) to some fat, insignificant Black girl named Lizzo. I'm not going to listen to a word she says about them not loving me anymore, and Fergie is a way better person than some fat pig who thinks she is better than people in this world. She actually got evicted from where she was living in Hollywood, and she fucking deserved that punishment. Fuck that fat pig.

I am the man for the job to save this world, and a lot of this involves bringing back gravity and making sure the skies, especially in urban areas, are clear all year round and that we can be safely on the ground when the sky is perfectly normal. People think that God is answering their prayers, but they are actually talking about me. And anyone who was dealing with any sinister things in their lives, I am able to help them all out every single day. All the best people in the world have dealt with hate at some proportion, and they just keep the train moving forward.

Unfortunately, a lot of the haters in this world are not the atheists of the world but God-fearing people. I don't understand. For instance, people go to church on Sunday mornings and then end up yelling at the players, coaches, and other fans when they were just told at church to be peaceful. There is something seriously wrong with that. You know, I grew up most of my life not believing in shit. I guess I sort of believe now because I have more weight on my shoulders trying to save the world every single day. I will save the world, and when Sanchez said, "I will tell you exactly why we are here right now," he was talking about gravity and overpopulation. That is less than 1 percent of the reason we are here right now. I mean, this is important, but it is just one part of all the reasons we are here right now. He also said, and Rory mentioned this too, that humans aren't supposed to be alive right now and that this was all done by mistake. I don't believe that at all, and I know that I was born for a reason, which is how they came out with *Bourne* movies with Matt Damon.

Everyone always thinks they are Mr. Right, but nobody is more precious with what they say except for me. I am the one with the future in their hands and the one who went through the worst tests known to mankind. I don't want to see anyone else have so much say and any power in this world besides me. I have been through everything and the apocalypse twice before anyone was even talking about it.

To add to this section, when Avery came into my house and said he had superhero gifts, I said, "I don't care, dude," which sounds really good because I don't really like to cause controversy. However, I was mad on the inside because I worked too damn hard to let anybody else have power in this world besides me, and nobody went through the hardest tests known to mankind like I did. I went through the sum of all fears to get to where I am going to be in the future. This means the sum of every single fear that you can possibly imagine. They even talked about this in *Divergent*, how you need to eliminate your fears and that those who are fearless can be the leaders of the world in the future. I am still going through some bullshit that I wish I wasn't going through, but honestly, I don't want to hear about your minuscule problems when I have dealt with a lot worse things than you will ever deal with in your lifetime. We will be forever young, but honestly, I don't care about your dumbass problems when I have dealt with so much worse.

I know I've talked about this script a lot, and it meant a lot to me, especially when I was in the hospital and misdiagnosed with having bipolar disorder. The script is for *Silver Linings Playbook*. It was really the first script I could relate to when it came to Hollywood, and my therapist wonders why I don't talk about it more because it means so much to me—about happy endings and how this family, an anomaly, can be so funny and so dysfunctional and always find a way to make things work out in a weird way. One part I wanted to mention was that Jennifer Lawrence won an award for her role when I was actually in the hospital, when I was paying a price for being God. O.A.R. and Katy Perry both mentioned in their songs that I knew it was right here this entire time, and it was pretty ironic that she won this award while I was spending time in the hospital for being God. The next part I wanted to mention about *Silver Linings Playbook* was that I was in the hospital, and it was one of the first books I ever read when I started reading books, which was when I was around twenty-six years old.

In the script, Bradley Cooper is interested in other things besides sports, but his real creator, Robert De Niro, keeps talking to him about his sports betting and about how he needs to be under control, always take his meds, and not act out. When the Bradley Cooper character got into a fight at the Eagles game, his real creator got very mad at him and said it was bad juju for him to get into this fight and that this was the reason they lost the game. My friend Keith Mann said he didn't really like the Robert De Niro character in this movie. The Bradley Cooper character is obviously me, and I can never seem to do anything right and always get in trouble with my real creator with all his Hitler rules under his roof. It is also pretty funny because I like to read my books while the games are going on, while my real creator is trying to talk to me about sports; I would rather read my books and somewhat watch the games. I always like to think the sports teams I want to win are winning when I am happy that day. However, I always know the winning teams are *always* because of me.

The next scripts I wanted to talk about are actually those for the *Avengers* movies. The first character I wanted to talk about is Iron Man. The Iron Man character is supposed to be me. He had a bad accident where he had to get a new heart, and his heart is powered by technology where he makes a machine. He also kills the bad guys with his technology. In the real world, we are supposed to separate my heart from my chest so that we can live here forever, and this was supposed to be a part of the process. He is also the funniest character out of all of them. I am a really funny person, so they made this character; and with the heart that I have now, considering Iron Man's heart, we are supposed to be in sync. Also, he's a ladies' man and a billionaire. I will keep my eye on only one woman in the future, but there are so many hot supermodels and other girls all over the place that have been interested in me. In terms of the billionaire stuff, I want to make that type of money and spread the wealth to everyone in the world. I told many people that I want to make Jeff Bezos money and spread the money to every single person in the world.

The next character I want to talk about is Captain America. This character is supposed to be Avery. The Captain America character was frozen in time and was actually born during the time around the World Wars. I think Avery was born in 1901, and he was alive during all those wars. Who knows his family tree, what the fuck was going on with his life, why he entered my life, and what these empires thought about the tests they would throw my way to make this world complete? Avery is a strong person and doesn't have any superpowers except for the fact that he is strong and a White boy who can fight. Captain America and Iron Man butt heads a lot because they don't see eye to eye on many things. In the past, Avery and I used to butt heads when we would hang out a lot because every time I spent too much time with anyone, we started getting into arguments. It's things that I am doing and the things the other person is doing as well. I hope people from the outside can pick up on these trends, and we can find peace within ourselves and help solve the world crisis with marriages and with fights within our own circles.

The next character I wanted to talk about is the Hulk. The Hulk is supposed to be Jack. Jack is a big dude who can fight and can scare people with his muscles and strength. The Hulk character is also a genius who can solve math problems for people and is very good with science. Jack can defeat the bad guys with his muscles, while I can use my technology to defeat the bad guys, and Avery can fight the bad guys off with his fighting skills. The Hulk character is also a character who tries to find peace in the world, so this is a good role for Jack, who wants peace in the world just as much as I do.

The next character I want to talk about is Thor. Thor is supposed to be Aaron. He is also a strong-built character, and Aaron is very strong. He can help God control the weather. Aaron is also supposed to be Moses, and he can help me with people's demon problems and with controlling the weather. The Thor and Hulk characters are very strong, while Captain America and Iron Man are more strategic. The Hulk and Thor fight each other in one of the Marvel movies, and it would be a good fight to watch if Jack and Aaron fought each other.

The next character I wanted to talk about was the role that Jeremy Renner played. That character is supposed to be Sanchez. The Jeremy Renner character works closely with the people who started these tests. This may actually be true in the real world—that Sanchez knew all these tests were being run on me and that Sanchez was trying to help control me so that I would stay under control. I don't see this character as being anybody else except for Sanchez. The Jeremy Renner character is good with bows and arrows, and he can use this weapon as a means to fight off bigger enemies with his craft. Sanchez was always able to fight people because he was quicker than his enemies, and he would always put up a good fight against people bigger than him. And if going against anyone around our size, he would always win. Jeremy Renner is an important character because he works behind the scenes to fight off the evil in this world and can help with the whole mind-control thing, which is something they mentioned in one of the *Avengers* movies. He is also good at helping Iron Man make new friends; and Sanchez is a very friendly dude who can help Iron Man branch out to more people, create more peace in the world, and help spread the word on all the good things that I'm doing in the world because I work behind the scenes a lot with the creators of the world.

I've talked about this script before, and it is actually really important. The movie I wanted to talk about is *Wanted*. There are so many signs and mixed signals in this movie. First off, the main song in this movie is Danny Elfman's song called "The Little Things." It is so good, and my friend Avery and I used to rock to this song after we watched this movie in the theaters when we were younger. In this song, he includes a lot of very important points; and the two that I want to mention right here are that

- everything that's been bad in my life has nothing to do with God,
- I am actually God,
- there is nothing left to fix in the entire world because of me, and
- I am working with a box full of tricks.

When the main character was taught how to kill people, they marked Xs next to the people he was supposed to kill. The people who trained him are the Illuminati. He is hopeless and has a shitty life until he is brought upon this crazy life that was waiting for him, and he becomes rich and learns how to kill people. Nevertheless, Xzibit's song "X" plays when things go wrong in my life, and I mark an X next to the targets of the people who are next in line to leave the world. Danny Elfman said to let the headlines wait; and this is what he is talking about because if the Illuminati didn't give me proper credit when I was at COMTEK, then I just walked away, just like what Madonna said in her song "Material Girl." Furthermore, the characters in this movie are important too. His best friend was such a shitty person and a shitty friend, and the main character gets mad at him and kinda beats the shit out of him. This is very similar to my best friend in the real world, Adam Seaman. At the end of the movie, he goes from shitty best friends to cheating girlfriends to Janice and billing reports. This is me taking over. I am pretty much taking over, and I have to save the world the way that I am supposed to and the way that I was destined to. Ava never cheated on me, but this is the girl he is talking about in this part of the movie when he said cheating girlfriends. Actually, Hollywood released a song saying that I never cheated, and I deleted everybody from my Facebook account because they were making me uncomfortable. Janice is really important, and she was actually my best friend when I was working at COMTEK, when I actually did have a normal life.

In the movie, Janice is his boss and a fat piece of shit who had a shitty childhood. She thinks she can boss him around with her orders. I had shitty bosses at the government contractors I was working with. I have now risen above all that and have become this entirely different person who is saving the world. This is what I was talking about. I was this average, middle-class accountant who was just hanging out with his friends when all this hell happened to me. And now I am doing everything that I am doing for so many different people and have led a different life than my parents and my friends could have ever imagined I would be living. I like the person that I have become, and it is so cool that I have become as popular as I have become in the world. I love the feeling when I break the chains that Jesus put on this world. This goes along with my hospital visit that I had when I was younger, and I ended up getting so fucking scared back then. Nowadays, everything I am going through is real. Hollywood knows there is nothing left to fix in the world, and it is all because of me. I started playing that Vertical Horizon song that says, "'Cause you're a God, and I am not… No, never again… And I just thought I'd let you go." I started playing that song again because they made my life worse again, so I started killing some of them again. This is also how they came up with one of their new scripts one for the movie called *Retribution*. I was sick and tired of people controlling us and moving us in the wrong direction, so I started eliminating some of these old men from the world.

The next script I wanted to talk about was *Summer Catch*. The best part of this script is that the guy, who never had a shot at making the big leagues, has a chance to prove himself in front of all the scouts during one summer. His girlfriend, Jessica Biel, is from a rich family, and he falls in love with her. Her real creator doesn't approve of him because he thinks he is dirty and a low-class piece of shit. Anyway, I might have to prove myself with my baseball skills when I am set up on my path to perfection. I will ace all my tests because if I am not the best person on the planet, then why did I go through all these sinister tests? The main reason, however, for me writing about this script is Giancarlo Stanton. There was a teammate of Freddie Prinze Jr.'s in this script who was this cocky dude who wore a bandanna and always disrespected Freddie Prinze Jr. because he thought Freddie was a loser and didn't belong on the same level as he did. When I am watching the Yankee games (and it sucks now, but Stanton is hurt), he reminds me of the character played by this character in this movie. Stanton is probably an asshole to some people in the real world, but we are going to be here forever. So over time, I want to be friends with him. His personality is perfect, and I think Hollywood actually made this character based on the future and how Stanton was going to have an impact on the world.

Right now, I am watching *Lucifer*. I don't care about the negative things people say about this script. I was perfectly happy being the devil in this world, and a lot of people were loving it and buying into this product. They came out with this script when I was listening to Lecrae's song that said sin is so bad it's a lie, among other sinister things in this world. In the script, the devil is the main character, and he falls in love with a police officer who is destined to be with him. He also helps the police solve crimes and puts the actual bad guys behind bars. At one point, Jack said that it doesn't sound realistic that the devil would do good in this world. I don't think Jack knows shit about the world, and I feel like he is the dumbest and fakest person I have ever met in my entire life. You have to look at the big picture. In the script for *Supernatural*, the two brothers, Will and Avery, were helping the world by curing it of all its demon problems and saving the world that way. In the script for *Lucifer*, they bring Avery into it as a part of the solution, but Lucifer is the guy who kills and puts the bad guys behind bars. Jack is too Goddamn stupid to understand these things. In one of the episodes, they brought it back to 1946, where Lucifer is in love with the mother of one of his closest friends. The girl who is his closest friend kind of reminds me of my sister. In this episode, they actually mention my name and Avery's name. They also called the mom Lilith, who was the devil's mistress in 1946. In *Supernatural*, Lilith is the little girl who causes the two brothers so many issues with her demon powers and is a nuisance to the brothers. I like to think of this Lilith character as my cousin's daughter Lily, and she helps me kill my haters and the haters of people in Hollywood who portray me in their movies, eliminating these fuckers from society. She does this by just fucking around with her technology. Lucifer's brother in the show is actually Jack. He goes into Lucifer's life, fucks everything up, and intentionally does things that can make him seem like an enemy of the people and an enemy of other people in this world. Lucifer makes a very hard effort to make sure that people still respect him and tries to get his life back in order. This pretty much reminds me of the real-life Jack, with everything that he has done to me and how he really fucked up my life, which I am trying to get back in order.

I wanted to add more about the *Lucifer* script. The first part I wanted to mention is that Sum 41 came out with a song a long time ago that says it seems like everything we were told seems like it's not true. This is part of how they came out with the script for *Lucifer*. In this song, he also says that some say we are better without knowing what life is all about. Fortunately enough, I was free enough to understand all these things about life, and this is part of the reason I am able to write three books so far about my life. Anyway, in the script, the Lucifer character never lies, and he is the devil. The devil is supposed to be the worst person to ever exist on this planet, according to the Bible, which was, by the way, written by a person. Anyway, it is really hard for me to lie, and this is part of how they came out with this part of the script because the lies that were told to me back then were bad lies. I also didn't know that anything going on with me was real. People on my side of things in Hollywood are only suggesting that people think twice before they make up their minds if they want to be on my team or on Jack's team.

Jack has been known in the past for the lies he has told me and for all the fun and games he has played with me. Like I said in the previous paragraph, his brother, the archangel, who was also a bad character in *Supernatural*, comes into Lucifer's life and totally screws it up. He goes out of his way on purpose and fucks everything up. He is the master liar and is supposed to be the angel, but he is actually way more fucked up than the devil is in both these scripts. Michael actually speaks English, while Lucifer speaks every language in the dictionary and speaks as if he is from a foreign country. They face off in this script; and then God, who is Black, intervenes with their fighting and says that he doesn't like to see any of his children fighting. They made God the Black guy from the Allstate commercials. This is how the last episode ended, with God saying, "Everybody, stop. I don't like to see any of my children fighting." I thought it was cool because I did a little bit of research and knew that they were going to make a God character in the last season.

Furthermore, the Maze character, who is also a demon in this show, is Maya, my sister in real life. She is just as crazy as he is and wants to fight him for reasons he has no idea about. She is mad at him because she thinks that she deserves to have a soul when Lucifer said that's not possible because she's a demon, just like he is. The Maze character also reminds me of Fergie a little bit, and Fergie tries hard to think about me when she wants to envision a guy that she would like to date after breaking up with Josh Duhamel. She just ends up meeting losers that aren't her type and tries really hard with one guy, but he just doesn't give her the satisfaction that she wants. Anyway, they definitely came up with this Maze character because of my younger sister. I know that we might have had our differences in the past, but nowadays, she has been one person I can really relate to. She always laughs at my jokes, and we usually see eye to eye on things. Also, my mom is currently living with her and seems to be happy with the way Maya is respecting my mom's wishes and giving her mom all the support she needs when they are living together.

The next part of the show I wanted to mention involves the Dan character. He is someone Lucifer always picks on and is kind of big and goofy, and he doesn't appear as someone who people should actually respect. This character, I figured out, reminds me of this guy, Andrew Truell, who was in my fraternity and died of liver cancer—or however you say it. Part of this reason was that he was an enemy of the demon. The biggest demon in this world is me; and if you are the enemy of the demon, just like what Eminem said in his song, then you are pretty much done. In the script, Dan saw Lucifer's demon face and then got really scared, sided with the angel Michael, took his advice, brought his police gun to Lucifer's apartment, and tried to shoot and kill him. He definitely shot him, but Lucifer survived because the devil is free from death. In the real world, I guess, with all this bitterness since college, Truell turned into one of my enemies, and he was the second Phi Sig to die. It should only be two Phi Sigs, since bad things happen in twos or ones. I don't think any other Phi Sig in my fraternity should die. I am not going to speak about all the Phi Sigs in the world, but at least in my fraternity, this should be it in terms of people dying in my fraternity.

The last part I wanted to mention about *Lucifer* is that in the last episode, they mention time stopping. However, it wasn't stopped because of the good character Lucifer; it was stopped because of the bad character Michael. In one of the Imagine Dragons' songs, he says that everyone is praying for the end of times—meaning, the devil, Jack, does harm on the world. In a productive manner, I will be able to stop time when it comes to Father Time, and we will be here forever because I am the only one with the power and powerful enough on this planet to do this. Actually, a long time ago, I had a dream that Dwayne Johnson gave me this power to stop time. The song "Hell Song" by Sum 41 says, "Everybody's got their problems. Everybody says the same thing to you. It's just a matter how you solve them, but what else are we supposed to do?" I am older now and wiser, so I think I have a handle on how to solve more people's issues and this problem. It was crazy how they displayed it in the show because everybody just stopped, and then Lucifer and Michael started fighting each other. The other characters picked sides until God was like, "Everybody, stop. I don't like to see my children fighting." Anyway, I know that I will be able to make time stop.

Another part of the script I wanted to discuss was that Lucifer lost his mojo. I talk about how I need to get my mojo back in the bedroom because I was going through all the apocalyptic events and am conquering everything, and now I am trying to get back to normal. So I need to be able to get my thing downstairs to work properly again. I am trying hard, but anyway, they talk about this in the script—that his soulmate stole his mojo after they had sex, is actually able to use it to her own advantage because his powers are gone now, and uses it instead. In the show, however, when I talk about mojo, he talks about getting people's truths and desires out of people, and this is one of his powers. He lost this ability after he has sex with his soulmate for the first time, and now he is mad at her until he finally gets his mojo back. They brought this part up because once I finally get my mojo back, then I can have a normal sex life and finally, hope-fully, hook up with the girl of my dreams.

There was another script I wanted to talk about, and this script is for *Blue Bloods*, featuring Donny Wahlberg. The first part I wanted to mention about this script was that they got the script based on of my friend Mike Sanacola, who became a cop in New York, and he was my childhood best friend in New York. The conversations the family has at dinner remind me of the conversations that my family has when we are all happy together. The Donny Wahlberg character kind of reminds me of myself. Bridget Moynahan reminds me of Maya. When the two of them argue with each other at dinner (and it is kind of a comedy at this point in the script), it reminds my mom of when I talk to Maya, and we are both acting funny. The Tom Selleck character is very familiar to my real creator. When my real creator does that dumb thing with his glasses, acting like he is the head of the CIA or FBI, it reminds me of the Tom Selleck character in *Blue Bloods*. The script is also important because it involves important police people who catch the bad guys in the world. This script is loosely based on of a true story and off of my life, but each episode has meaning behind it. And if the FBI and police ever need my help, then I am here to help them out. This is all I want to write about this script for the time being.

This script has a lot of meaning to it, and I talked about it in my previous book. The script is called *Happy Gilmore*. In the script, Happy Gilmore wanted to play professional hockey but wasn't good enough, so he ends up playing professional golf, makes a killing, saves his family with the money, and gets the girl of his dreams in the show. The first part I wanted to mention was that the girl of his dreams in the show is named Virginia. There is one Train song that I listen to that reminds me of this girl in Virginia that I am interested in, and this is how they named the main girl character in this show Virginia. She is the perfect match for Adam Sandler in this script, and I have a good feeling that I can make things work with this Virginia girl in the future. The next part of the script I wanted to talk about was that he takes two steps before he hits the golf balls and hits them four hundred yards without any issues, and everyone wonders how he is able to do this. Then his mentor shows him how to actually play the game of golf instead of just going based on his instincts.

When I was in high school and at the driving range with my high school friends, including Adam Seaman, Taylor Ryan, Ethan Stewart, Amanda Zank, and Josh Borders, I started to hit the ball like Adam Sandler was hitting the ball in this movie. I was hitting the ball a good 250 yards without any issues, and they were all like, "Holy fuck, that is amazing." Nowadays, I am trying to get the help of people around me; but when the time is right, I want to be shown how I can make my golf game the best possible so that maybe one day, I can compete with these guys. I know some of the pros are helping me out every time I go onto the golf course. Actually, I went golfing with my real creator when the coronavirus was dying down, and I played my best round of nine holes because we are all looking for progress in this world. Even though I didn't play golf for a year, my game still got better. I shot a 34 when a par score would have been a 27. This was the best I have ever played in my entire life. I even shot a birdie on one hole, which is a 2. My real creator didn't believe me, but at my full potential, I expect to shoot a lot more birdies instead of pars and bogeys. Pars aren't bad, but I expect to shoot a lot better, and I am raising my level of expectations so that in the future, I can compete with the best in the world. The other parts of the script that come to my head, I already wrote about, like the importance of the ninth hole at Oak Marr and about the homeless population in Portland, Oregon.

The show I am currently watching is *Ozark*. There are a few things I can say about this script and how it relates to my life. The first part is shadow play. God did everything he wanted to do, so I can use my box of tricks to end all the corruption in the world. The family that Jason Bateman is with is running away from their town because they got in deep with the mob bosses, and they needed a place to get away from everything. I can use shadow play to take down the mob and make them pay for all the bad deeds they did in the world. The next part of the script I can talk about is where they are working at a casino. There is a lot of heavy competition with the casinos, and people who count money always get caught. I also wanted to say that the casinos always win because they structure their system in a way that the house always wins, and the players usually go home with less money than they came with. Well, the wife of the guy fixes this problem with her competition by using some type of device and technology to make sure the house loses all its money, their casino can buy the other casino, and the couple can make a lot of money. However, the Jason Bateman character doesn't agree with what his wife is doing but kind of keeps his anger to himself. I am just saying here that there is stiff competition in the world, and I don't think everybody is following the rules like they should. This place that is kind of segregated from the world is a good getaway for this family to go to, and I am currently on season 3 and will continue to watch until the series finale happens. I hope for the sake of all the people that contributed to this script that the series goes a long time. It will probably not last as long as *Supernatural*, *Grey's Anatomy*, and *Criminal Minds*, but I wish them the best of luck. And they know they can throw their backs on me whenever they want.

Another part of this script I wanted to mention was that the couple is going to therapy to try to work out their issues. It kind of reminds me of my therapist and how she listens and tries to solve the problems of people who are going through some serious bullshit; and she is, according to people, the best therapist on the planet. I feel sorry for people who have to go to couples' therapy, but relationships are really hard. Hopefully, in the future, couples can start to see eye to eye with each other.

I wanted to add to the script I was just talking about, which is *Ozark*. Wendy, the wife in *Ozark*, discriminates against her brother's illness because he is bipolar. When people act like this in the real world, it really annoys me. This world is bipolar, and people not diagnosed and prescribed meds act more bipolar than people who are on meds. The brother actually finds out all these secrets about the family and causes a scene when they are trying to open up a casino, saying that Wendy and her husband are working for the mob and that she has ordered kills on people. They just play it off like he is crazy and that nobody should listen to a word he says. He gets sent to the hospital and feels like hell because the hospital is a fucking nightmare for anyone to ever get sent to against their own will. After he gets out of the hospital, he approaches their business partner. Wendy warns against approaching the business partner and threatening her kids because she will order kills against that person. The first place he goes to after he gets released from the hospital is that person's house. Wendy, however, is the reason her brother ends up getting shot and killed (the bipolar guy)—because she told her partner exactly where their location is. Jason Bateman usually plays things pretty well, but Wendy is out of control. I also don't think I like the person she is portraying in this script. She keeps telling everyone that her brother is bipolar and crazy and that he is talking out of his ass, and that really annoys me because there has been research done that says bipolar people are actually smarter than the rest of the population. Anyway, one of my goals is to get the entire world off mental illness medications so that our memories aren't so foggy. Actually, there has also been more research done that people who take meds have better memories than people who aren't on meds.

The next part of the script I wanted to talk about involves Frank Mills. They named this one character in the show Frank Jr., who is a mob guy, and he was the Tommy character in *Power*. He beats up Ruth and stomps on her, and she is afraid for her life because of this guy stomping on her. They came up with the name Frank Jr. because of this one guy who lives around me named Frank Mills. This Frank Mills guy is part of a gang. He came to one of my house parties when I was in high school and started a fight with my friend, and I went in to defend my friend and started throwing punches. The next thing I knew, after I blacked out, I had six pairs of feet stomping on me. I blacked out the second time and then saw one of my friends reaching up and grabbing me to bring me back to life. Again, as I talked about with the gangs and Mafia, shadow play can end all this type of madness in the world, and I can bring all these types of people to justice. I need more time and more resources, but with everyone in

Hollywood who wants to make things right in this world, then I can fuck up the worlds of people like Frank Mills.

In the script, they named the family name the Byrdes. I think they came up with that name as in "the little birdie." When you are talking about families, I think the family who should be titled the Byrdes are the Seamans. Back in the day, when I was around twenty-four or twenty-five years old, Avery was playing a lot of games with me, and in this day and age, it is pretty clear to me that he tried to beat me and kill me back then. Luckily, everyone saw all of his attacks coming, and they were always able to get me out of the ruts that I was always in. Avery is Jesus, right? So everything comes good with Christ. In this day and age, I don't fucking think so. It is clear that the Mafia and Adam, with his Jesus title, tried to beat me, and peace will only be attained once my wayward son (Adam) is dead.

Honestly, I hate the fact that Hollywood ever liked him as my partner in crime because it is so obvious to me that he tried to beat me back then; and then when I started taking over and he came back into my life, he forgot about all of it and couldn't understand why he kept on self-destructing and why all these bad things kept on happening to him, his family, and his other family (the Mafia). I am going to lock up every person who ever put a finger on me, and with the new songs that Hollywood has produced, none of them are respecting him. Anyone who disrespects me pays the price. We have people who will make them feel humiliated and like shit because of the way they treated and disrespected me.

I wanted to write about this script. The script is for *The Sinner*. I will give my audience a little play-by-play on how they got the title and the writing for this script. In the year 2012 or 2013, I was ripped out of my bed because I was making all these sinister moves, and I was sent to the hospital. This is how the Killers came out with their song "Spaceman." It was Saturday night, at about eleven, and I thought everyone was coming to my house to say hello or something like that. Instead, something really bad crawled up inside my system. It was God, the devil, or something else. Then I had to go on my bed, and I was like, "Holy fuck." I called Ray, and he didn't answer. knew I was fucked, and I thought I was going to die. I woke up the next morning with all these bad and evil things entering my mind, and my real creator called the police on me. It was a mess of a day, and it was on a Sunday, the day of the gods. I got Tasered by the police and broke metal handcuffs in half that day, and it was just bad. The bad things kept entering my mind, and I asked the police officer to kill me.

He was like, "I'm not going to kill you."

I was acting up, and he ended up Tasing me. The next thing I knew, I woke up, and a girl and other people were rushing me to someplace else in the hospital and were worried that I was going to die. I ended up living, and they took me to a mental hospital. Bebe Rexha actually wrote in her song that people brought me back to life that day, and that it was like Jesus was resurrected or something. I was definitely on the wrong train, but I am not going down for all these bad things that happen in this world. Actually, because of my actions that day, Black people are so paranoid about the police; and if those events never happened to me that day, then the Black Lives Matter movement probably wouldn't have started.

Anyway, to go along with the script for *The Sinner*, I was walking with Aaron and Steph one day to go to a party, and we were talking.

I was like, "I am a sinner."

Steph was like, "Aaron's entire family are sinners."

Many times after that, I would laugh at the exact same time as other people at parties or in the real world, like my family. I sort of set that trend in the world as well—the laughter among people so that they can see eye to eye. Furthermore, this is why Mac Miller included "still setting trends" in his song, enabling new artists and movie auditions to happen in Hollywood—so more people can reach their dreams. He put "still setting trends" in that song because I am still setting trends in this world.

When I was in Florida with Ray, my cousin—the same guy I called on that Saturday night when people ripped me out of my bed—there was this Christian girl going around spreading the Word of Christ. My parents and sisters were there, as well as Ray's family, and Ray went, "If you're a sinner, then you're just going to drop dead." Right there, I felt weird again and out of place because of my history of self-destructing after professional athletes put me back into this devilish game the second time. We all went to eat lunch, and I asked Ray a question. He acted as if I wasn't there, just talking to my real creator. At that point, I decided I had had enough, so I went up to the hotel room until Ray and Lauren went back home. Then I could just hang out with my family. I hate the way people act in social situations sometimes, and Ray was pissing me off that day. Anyway, this is how they came out with the script for *The Sinner*, where the guy arrests the bad guys in the world who are actually doing bad things but is nicknamed the Sinner.

The next script I want to write about was a Mark Wahlberg movie that was released in 1995 called *Fear*. Hollywood came out with this script, and Mark Wahlberg has been a big part of people branching out for me, how I got my name out there, and on my pursuit of happiness and perfection based on what was written in this script and the songs that followed. I have been living in some serious fear ever since I knew that tests were being done on me like I was some kind of fucking science experiment. I didn't know all these scripts had meaning to them, especially those written in the '90s. Anyway, the main character in this movie is a psychopath, and I think that my soulmate believes that in the past, I had some of these same characteristics. I am a lot calmer and have my shit together now that I have matured. I have been going through a world of fear for a long time now, but my tests started when I was young, despite what Ava thought when I was dating her and despite what the Fun song said—that after ten years of this, I'm not sure that anyone understands. That song is fucking terrible and should have never been released in the first place. If nobody else knows where to begin with their stories, then why is mine just ten years?

Fear is something we can all work with, and fixing me up is part of the recipe for saving the world. I am the key part of this new world we are building, and fear has made me pretty psychotic. Anyone who has been going through the same shit would go crazy too. I know that this one girl in my life was the clever girl, and she feels bad about the tests she had me go through so that we can be together in the future.

But sometimes, it really fucking sucks—the fear that I have been going through. It is a combination of demons, spirits, and pretty much the worst possible conditions known to mankind. They came out with this script, and people knew that Mark Wahlberg would really blow up in the 2000s with his other scripts. This is all I want to write about this script for the time being.

The next script I want to talk about is the one for *The Adjustment Bureau*. The first thing I want to say is that Matt Damon is at war with the Illuminati. They keep changing the course of history so that things in his life are so screwed up that he can't save the world in a timely manner. The biggest part is that in the movie, Matt Damon has his eyes set on one girl. They ask him to look for other girls because it would fuck up the world's plan if he gets with this girl. They keep on changing his course and her course so that he never sees her ever again. He is so fucking determined to make sure that he gets to be with this girl that he has his eyes set on, so he doesn't care what they say. They end up being together and living together happily ever after. There was this one Black guy in the movie, Anthony Mackie, who goes behind the Illuminati's back and tries to help out Matt Damon. I ran into this guy in DC in the real world, and he said, "Keep your head up" when I was crossing the street at a traffic stop. This guy in the real world continues to help me out, along with all the other help that I am getting from people. He tells Matt Damon that they are humans who just live longer than the average human. That saying is exactly what Rory told me when he explained to me about the Illuminati before I even knew who they were. Actually, they were testing me at COMTEK when I thought it was my actual fraternity who was testing me. In the movie *Wanted*, the Illuminati consider themselves the real-world fraternity, and they were testing me at COMTEK when I thought it was Phi Sig who was testing me.

Another part of this script I wanted to mention (and it's kind of funny) is that Matt Damon is a politician and is elected mayor or some bullshit like that. When I went to my grandpa's funeral in New York, I was dressed like a politician, and a random New York guy came up to me and asked me if I worked for the government. I told him that I did not and that I was just dressed this way for a funeral.

This was pretty ironic, and the first thing I thought about was *The Adjustment Bureau* and how Matt Damon was a politician in this movie. The next part of this script that I wanted to mention is the consequences of our actions. The Illuminati explains to Matt Damon that he cannot be with this girl because there will be consequences bigger than him if he gets with her and that there are millions of other single girls in New York. They also tell him he should just get with one of them. Matt Damon (me) doesn't give a fuck and still goes against their wishes, gets with the girl, and doesn't care how it affects other people negatively. In the real world, I have done the math and know that I can be with so many girls, but there is this one girl on my mind that kind of sticks out from the crowd of all the single ladies in the world. I know that she is the woman I am destined to be with, and everything happens for a reason. She is my perfect match. Too many times they have tried to fuck up this relationship, and I am fucking sick of it. I need them to back off and just let me do my thing so I can finally get with my soulmate because I don't want to be with anybody else. They say I should look around and try to find another lover, but I haven't had sex since 2015, which was with this one call girl after Ava. That was it. Who the fuck else am I looking to get with? As you get older and more mature, you start to realize that it doesn't matter if this person has a kid or if they are a few years older than you; it just matters that you guys are meant to be together.

The next script I wanted to talk about is for *The Heartbreak Kid*. In the Killers' song, he says, "Is there room for one more son?" and this is also how they came up with the script for *Lucifer*. Anyway, in the song, he mentions there is "one more hate and one more heartbreak." In the script, Ben Stiller always has two girls he can't decide between. When he runs into this dilemma, he always says, "Love, love, love" when he knows he can't commit to one girl. In the real world, I started having this problem ever since I was sixteen. My first relationship in my entire life was with Rachel Alt. This relationship lasted two months. A month later, I was able to meet my high school sweetheart, Julia Falk. We fell in love with each other, and she was actually the first girl I ever had sex with. We took a break for about two months when we were eighteen, and I met another girl, Jessica

Arthur. I couldn't decide between these two girls; and Jessica's best friend, Holly, whom Ethan Stewart was dating, said to me, "It seems like you love Julia, but you only like Jessica," and that cleared things up for me.

I ended up breaking it off with Jessica, and Julia and I started dating again. However, Julia got a notice from UVA saying that she was accepted into their program as an athlete. She was a soccer player on my younger sister's travel soccer team, which was always one of the best teams in the nation, and UVA had one of the best soccer programs in the nation. Julia was a year younger than me, and she was going to skip her senior year in high school to go to UVA and play soccer for them. After she left for UVA, I had a party with my high school friends, and some girls from Langley High School came over to my party. There was this one girl, Amy Beck, who was the hottest girl at the party. I ended up hooking up with her, and then we started talking. I broke things off with Julia, but Julia and I kept on talking at the same time. I ended up dating both girls because Julia forgave me for breaking up with her, but I never told her that I had met Amy. I ended up hanging out with Amy until I was twenty-two years old, actually, and then I never saw her ever again. Anyway, I went to UVA one day, and Julia was looking through my text messages and saw that I was texting with Amy. She got really upset, and I just said she was a friend whom I was just talking to. I was only seeing Amy for three weeks at that point in time and then started dating Julia again. Julia and I kept on seeing each other on and off until I was around nineteen or twenty years old.

There was this other girl, Jackie Cook, who went to one of my high school parties, and she attended both my high school and college. I started dating her when I was a freshman in high school. She cheated on me with some guy she met overseas, and I was very angry at her. I started talking to Julia again, and we had sex. I never told Jackie, but because of my anger and attitude and because we were arguing a lot, I ended up breaking up with Jackie after around six months. This was the end of me ever seeing Jackie as a girlfriend again. This pretty much concludes me ever cheating on another girl again. They say once you're a cheater, you're always a cheater.

However, something inside me changed. I still had anger. Maybe my other relationships failed, but it was never because I cheated. I will never cheat again, and my transgressions weren't because I was the devil; it was actually because I found Jesus.

I ended up dating Angie from age twenty to twenty-one, and there weren't any other girls on my radar during our entire relationship. This is actually when my hell story begins. Around six months after I broke up with Angie, I was sent to the hospital at the age of twenty-two because my parents thought I needed help. The doctors at the hospital took me off Adderall and Klonopin and put me on Seroquel and Depakote. Seroquel and Depakote are two of the worst drugs on the market that you can take for mental illness. I ended up being on both of those at the same time. I didn't date any girls for about six or seven years while I was going through that hell and didn't really even hook up with any girls until I started hanging out with Ava. She really transformed my life and helped me out a lot by being my best friend when none of my friends were really talking to me. However, the heartbreak kid was still in action. I had just seen Angie for a visit in New York prior to hanging out with Ava, and at that point in time, I was still in love with Angie. And Ava knew it. Angie found someone else, and then I focused on being with Ava as long as I possibly could while I was still going through this hell.

Ava would watch me on her couch and listen to the songs that Hollywood would put out for me to listen to, and Ava was really annoying me. So I was focusing on Ava and also this girl from Hollywood. Ava knew it and was annoyed by it, but just like me, she was trying to get our relationship steady while we were both going through our own misery and our own hell in our own worlds. I ended up breaking up with Ava in 2015, and the girl from Hollywood paid me two visits near my house. I didn't actually speak to her, but she was walking down my street corner one day and was smiling at me. She was so fucking hot, but nowadays, I have my focus on someone else. There was this brunette girl who also wanted to walk down my street around that time, wanting to see me in person instead of always watching me with those invisible cameras that Hollywood and the CIA supposedly set up around my life to increase my publicity. At that point, I had those two girls in mind, and then there was also Anna Kendrick. One time, I imagined her secret plane was going to land on my property and that we were going to live happily ever after. Timbaland mentioned in his song that Anna Kendrick felt really lonely waiting for me to come to Hollywood and would pretend I was with her so she didn't feel so alone without having anyone close to her to talk to.

Anna Kendrick knew she had to come clean to me about her past relationships, which is kind of what I am doing right now in this section of my book. So she talked about her past relationships in her book. Once she was done, she was like, "Okay, now this is off my chest." She seems like a really cool person, but with all these girls I have talked about so far, it won't work out for the long term. And I am perfectly happy with that.

After all this happened, there were two other girls on my radar. One of them was Ariana, Jack's wife, because when I saw her for the first time, it was like love at first sight. But they are happy, so that won't work out. The other girl is the clever one, the woman of my destiny, and the one with whom I will spend the rest of eternity. Her name will be kept anonymous, and this is how they came up with the script for *The Heartbreak Kid*.

The next script I wanted to talk about is the one for what I am currently watching, *Iron Fist*. It is a Marvel show that aired for two years and was underrated, in my opinion. This script also involved themes that were present in *Ozark*, which I mentioned earlier, and I don't think it was a coincidence that I started watching *Iron Fist* after *Ozark*. Again, in this show, the main character is sent to the hospital against his will. He is sent to the hospital by two people who were his friends before he vanished off the face of the earth, and he is trying to get back the piece of his company that rightfully belongs to him. He has beef with a guy who is extremely rich, and this rich guy reports to his real creator and other assholes who want to bury the guy trying to make things right in his life. This part of the show reminds me a lot of my life. Actually, some of these rich fools died because of the few times I was sent to the hospital against my will back in 2012 and 2013, and even before then, in 2009 and 2010. I had beef with many people in this world and with a certain group, but fortunately for me, I was able to overcome everything that was thrown my way up to this point and am still conquering everything. It kind of reminded me of the situation where I was sent to the hospital those few times, and the third time, they didn't actually admit me because I wasn't suicidal. And it wasn't against my will. There was someone in this world who, along with others, started dying, who wanted to see me in bad condition and dead, and they paid the price. Fortunately, for me, I was able to get back into shape, return to my life, and live normally again.

The next part of the script I wanted to talk about involves the girl named Colleen. She is an Asian girl who didn't know much about the main character and took his side when he was down, and people didn't really care about the struggles he was going through. This character reminds me of my friend Joanna. She is a very good fighter in the show and does her best to defend her friend. In the real world, this is how I view my friend Joanna, who would do anything for my family and is very close to every single person in my family. When my real creator had his heart attack, she was one of the first people to come to my house to make sure everything was okay. She is one of my close friends and has always been there for me, no matter what I was going through. The girl's name, Colleen, always reminds me of my sister's friend Colleen, whom she was friends with in high school. I am talking about two different girls here: my older sister's friend Joanna and my younger sister's friend Colleen. Joanna, the Asian girl, would have my back no matter what I was going through. The other girl, Colleen, Maya's friend, was a good friend to Maya until they stopped talking a little while ago, but I actually just friended her on Facebook. I always thought she was good-looking and fun to talk to, but I never flirted with her or anything. I like all girls who are good-looking and have good personalities. Anyway, Colleen will be important in my life in the future.

The other girl's name in the show is Joy. Her name, Joy, is based on the character that Jennifer Lawrence played in the movie *Joy*. She kind of reminds me of someone else in my life, whom I will keep anonymous.

The next part of *Iron Fist* that I wanted to talk about was that he comes back from the dead after his parents die in a plane crash. He disappears from the planet for fifteen years and just shows up in their lives, and this is kind of why the Joy character doesn't think it's really him. The other rich guy is just an asshole who wants to eliminate him from society. They used this same concept in *Agents of SHIELD*. The main character in *Agents of SHIELD* died and came back to life after he was killed in one of the *Avengers* movies. I wanted to mention this part of the script because in the real world, as Bebe Rexha said in one of her songs, when I was ripped out of my bed and my blood type was taken, people brought me back to life from the dead after I was Tasered by the police and died that day. I remember seeing the afterlife, and it wasn't great. We need to make this life everlasting so that nothing is incomplete. Anyway, I fucking died that day and had so many other Goddamn death experiences throughout my life. My life was crazy back then, and now everything is coming more clearly to me. This is how I am able to live my life normally again, but I am still on another level, which is why I am able to do so much in any given day, help out so many people, and make my life the best life anyone can imagine.

The one problem is that for a long time after that, I couldn't control my anger. The entire time I was dating Ava, I couldn't control my anger; and even before then, I was always an angry person. However, because of all the side effects of all this demon and Jesus crap that I was going through, in addition to all the meds and everything else involved in the shit that I was going through, I was always so fucking angry. They mentioned this part in the last part of the movie that I was watching. The guy had anger problems, and it caused him to lose relationships and make too many mistakes. Fortunately for me, I still have many friends, but the part about losing relationships was mostly meant for Avery because he lost all his friends. Furthermore, when a voice came into our conversation when I was talking to him, saying that nobody befriends the beast just to pay rent and make ends meet, he said to me that he is still going to be friends with me. He didn't have any fucking friends, and when I think about what he said to me that day, I wish terrible things upon him. It is very evident that he was the one who tried to beat me with his Mafia buddies, who try to control everything, and I am fucking sick of them coming into my life and making shit worse for me. Like I said, Hollywood doesn't want Avery anywhere near Hollywood because he doesn't belong in this new society that we are building, and neither do any of his Mafia friends. I am sick of Hollywood respecting me, and after they saw what kind of person Avery was and the great and fabulous person I was becoming, you can't even put the two of us on the same level.

The next part of the script I wanted to talk about was that the company is called Rand, and I thought they were talking about the company in the real world called Randstad. The Rand company is the company the main character is trying to get his rights to when he comes back to life. In the real world, maybe there were some issues going on with this company that they had to work through.

The last part of the show I wanted to talk about was the hand that *Iron Fist* is trying to solve as part of his crime investigation. When they are talking about this part, they are talking about the hand of God. I had issues with the hand of God when I was around twenty-four or twenty-five, and I was sitting on my porch. I told Dr. O'Connor about this—that there was this hand that punched me and spread a disease and cancer in me. I think it was Jack, and that is a very good reason to lose a friend. It was fucking scary, and as I approached the hand, it punched me even harder. My entire skin then felt like it was on fire. I was so fucking scared and didn't know how to explain it to my parents until later in life. The people who had beef with me were some serious people who threatened my life and obviously thought I was the devil, trying to instill the fear of God in me. Honestly, I don't think it was Jack. I believe it was Avery again and the Mafia. I have no proof and would love to get some proof one day because that shit was the scariest, something you only see in movies. However, I have a great story to write about these days, and my legacy lives on while I am still alive. I don't know what else to write about this script, now that I've written over two pages about it so far. My story is great, and it will have a happy ending once we figure out more about the world.

I wanted to add to the *Iron Fist* show. In each of their shows, it includes new people coming to Hollywood, and they write a lot of their songs based on movies and TV shows represented in their scripts. Anyway, the place where the Joanna character would go to work out and improve her fighting skills was called the dojo. Because of this part in the script, Doja Cat was the next best singer to enter Hollywood. For the music award shows, Doja Cat actually won the best new artist award. I thought it was interesting that I was able to figure this out. I think I already talked about how Halsey is my girl from *Hunger Games* and Billie Eilish is my girl from *Legend*, and so on. Lizzo is the girl from *Empire*, and there are more examples. Anyway, Doja Cat was the best new artist, and her entrance to Hollywood had a lot to do with the show *Iron Fist*.

The next script I wanted to talk about was called *The Martian*. It's a Matt Damon movie in which he goes to outer space and saves the world. Hollywood got the idea for this script from Kid Cudi's song "Embrace the Martian." In Kid Cudi's song, he goes, "Look at what I made true God to teach you… Don't be afraid of all y'all." He was talking about me and that I should keep on acting funny, and I am here to change that. They actually talked about making the funniest guy in the movie *Tropic Thunder* start acting more seriously so that he could be a better actor. This is also how they got the idea of putting that part in *Tropic Thunder* based on my life and Kid Cudi's song. In Kid Cudi's song, he said, "You are mean, like it or not." He stated that real recognizes real and that you are mean, like it or not. He was referring to Jack, saying that Jack is really mean and that for those dealing with demon problems, he is to blame. Anyway, Matt Damon ends up saving the world in this movie, which is what Kid Cudi was talking about in his song. The movie is great, and most of the things I am writing about in my book, I didn't know before. I didn't know that Hollywood was going to write all these scripts and songs about my life.

The answers that the rest of the population can figure out depend on how free or fake they are. Many people in this world are free, and many are fake; it just depends on how you were rated before. People can always change for the better and become more real, but you cannot fake being real. You are either real or fake. I know that I have had trust issues with people, and granted, I think a lot of people would love if I came back into their lives. But for the time being, I have to keep on doing what I am doing every day to save the world. Anyway, I think this is all I want to write about this script for the time being.

This is fresh on my mind, and I was just watching this movie called *The King of Staten Island*. There are a few points I wanted to talk about that were mentioned in this movie. One of the points of this movie is that this guy is using people—including girlfriends, his family, and his friends—to get ahead in the world, not caring about how they are doing but only about how he's feeling about himself and his own self-worth. He gets into a fight with his mom's boyfriend because he doesn't trust him and thinks his mom could do better since their real creator passed away in the movie. He goes to his mom's boyfriend's ex-girlfriend's house to try to get information on how to make his mom break up with her new boyfriend, and the boyfriend ends up beating the shit out of him. His mom kicks him out of the house, and he goes to his ex-girlfriend's. Then they have sex. Then she realizes that he's using her because he was kicked out of his parents' house. This reminds me a lot of how Avery was burning bridges with everyone and why his real creator cut him out entirely from his will, and everything bad that was happening to Avery was because all he cared about was himself.

On the positive end of things, even with all the negativity in this movie surrounding Avery's life, I look for happy endings, and I will have a great family life going forward and finally kiss the girl of my dreams after waiting all this time. Everything works out for the character in the movie at the end. I am not sure that everything will work out for Avery, but I know that everything will work out for me. I will have to work hard to make money, and I am perfectly aware of that. I will get rich. I know that people made fun of me for working hard when I wasn't, but it was more of a joking way. In the movie, his mom kicks him out of the house because she doesn't believe him when he says he's working hard, and this reminds me a lot of why Avery's mom disowned him.

The next part of this movie I wanted to talk about was his wait-ing skills. When they show him as a waiter, everyone is complaining about bad service and how he's always serving people late and can't remember the things they're ordering. This is exactly how I would be if I were a waiter, and it would be a disaster. If anyone were watch-ing from the outside, then it would be a comedy, but it wouldn't be a comedy for anyone actually involved. My waiting skills would be fucking terrible, and this is part of the reason I would never be a bus-boy or a waiter. He was doing so bad waiting tables, and my mom and I were laughing pretty hard at this scene.

The next part of the movie I wanted to talk about was the parts about Ava and Mike's relationship. Ava got with Mike pretty soon after we broke up, and people actually felt bad for me because it seemed pretty subtle. And she had a kid pretty soon after that. It was a fucking disaster for me because it seemed like she didn't care about our relationship at all. Anyway, I think this is sort of similar in real life; however, Mike has low self-esteem, and obviously, he isn't on my level in terms of earning respect in this world and how far down the totem pole Ava went from dating the best guy in the world to going to a guy she's known since sixth grade. They had sex in one scene, and they talked about how weird this is because they have known each other since fourth grade. I think Ava has known Mike since sixth grade or something like that. Yeah, it's pretty fucking weird, but then people make stupid decisions sometimes.

The last part of the movie I wanted to mention was the shooting that happened the night I was watching the movie with my mom. It was another shooting in America, and two people died. It occurred in Rochester, New York, and there was a scene in the movie where his friends robbed a grocery store and they were sent to jail, but somehow he gets away. Again, he is burning bridges because he goes to their jail to ask his friend if he could crash at his house. He didn't care how his friend was doing in jail but instead, he was asking him for a favor. These kinds of behaviors were what Avery was doing. I am not saying that Avery would rob a grocery store, but Avery was using people. Anyway, the shooting happened, and I thought something might happen that night because of the scene where they robbed the grocery store. Apparently, the two people were on the list of people who died in real life, and they were hating on me at some point throughout my journey. Anyway, this is all I want to write about this script for the time being.

To add to my thoughts on the script of *The King of Staten Island*, the guy was really into putting tattoos on people's bodies. Based on this script, one of Eminem's biggest fans put on her body sixteen tattoos of Eminem's face, which set a world record.

An Eminem Fan Has Set a New World Record by
Having 16 Tattoos of Eminem's Face on Her Body

Guinness World Records has announced that Nikki Patterson, a nail technician from Aberdeen, now holds the record for having the most portraits of the same musician on her skin. The 35-year-old was 19 when she got her first tattoo of the rapper. "He's been the one constant in my life," Patterson told the BBC. The tattoos appear on her legs, arms, chest, and fingers. "Even I am losing count," she said. Eminem's last album, Music to be Murdered By, reached number one in the UK earlier this year.

The next script I wanted to write about is for *The 100*. There are many key parts I wanted to talk about. The first part I wanted to mention was the population shrinking to make room for the best people in the world. They talk about eliminating these one hundred people, but in the real world, we are eliminating a lot more than one hundred people. This is part of the test for the coronavirus, which is shrinking the population size so that we have more natural resources and more space in the world for the right people instead of those taking up space and not doing shit with their time on the planet. I can deal with fate; and if the Illuminati didn't give me credit when I was at COMTEK, then I just walked away. Hollywood knows there is nothing left to fix in the entire world because of me, but in this particular show, the game testers want to eliminate these one hundred people because they are criminals and don't deserve to live anymore. They also talk about an additional three hundred people who died in the show. Anyway, these game makers made me the center of attention; and if people can't get what they want, then it will be all because of me. I don't see anyone up in the clouds, down below, or on this planet who can help people out the way that I can. I am just saying I do believe in myself and in my own product, and I can really help people out every single day. If people are more patient, then I will find a cure for every single illness in the world. Another part of the script that I wanted to mention was that it kind of reminds me of *The Hunger Games* when everyone is being monitored and the game makers are putting them through all these impossible tests, and they end up going against the game makers in *The Hunger Games*. Right now, in *The 100*, there are a lot of people dying in the group of one hundred, and I just think that it's relevant to compare the two shows to each other.

The next part of the script I wanted to talk about was the radiation exposure they are talking about. I was exposed to radiation when I was twenty-four and still get some radiation exposure inside my body, and hopefully, it goes away soon. The game makers say that hopefully, the radiation is enough to kill the best people in the world, who are being tested every single day. I am very strong and very powerful, so I don't think this radiation is going to kill me; however, in the show, they are trying to kill the one hundred criminals with the radiation. I was so fucking scared when I was working at COMTEK; and hell hit me when I was living with Jack, Aaron, Sanchez, and Khalil. I think it was in 2009. I was working at COMTEK for three months, and then the worst conspiracy known to mankind hit me. The stars were going crazy; there was radiation on the screen in my blinds, and I was just smoking a bowl and watching the Knicks game. I was so fucking scared that I ran outside my house. I was running for my life. I knocked on the door of my neighbor, trying to get him to help me out; and I didn't realize that it was actually Kiki's door, who is now married to Kevin.

If I want to add to the connections part of this book, then I can add Kiki and Kevin. They actually met and got married because of me while I was going through all this hell.

Anyway, the cops came that night, and I had to call my sister before going over to her house. That night, they were still radiating me from the stars and pretty much giving me signals to leave my sister's house after she went to bed. Again, I was so fucking scared. I ended up leaving my sister's place and walked, following the pattern in the stars as if I were in fucking *Star Wars*. The main star, the Death Star, was the star that was following me in the sky. I go crazy when I hear a symbol. And I didn't know it at the time, but every time I was taking a step in the wrong direction, weird sensations were going on in my body. I ended up going into one of the empty condos and got hit by big radiation. I looked at the dot in the sky, and it had eyes on it as if I were in fucking *Eagle Eye*. In this room is where I got hit by the radiation. This is why Hollywood was talking about radiation in the show. The amount of radiation that was in that room would've killed anyone else in this world. I ended up going back to my sister's house, and she was actually living with this girl who I met for the first time, Joanna. I am really close with her now. I didn't really talk with anyone about the things I was going through, but everyone thought I was crazy, just like what people thought about Albert Einstein and Abraham Lincoln before they realized both these guys were geniuses.

The next part of the script I wanted to talk about was that they were talking about the end of the human race. I went through the apocalypse twice before anyone besides Hollywood was even talking about it. The end of the human race happened the second time I went through the apocalypse. I thought that every single person in the world was dead except for my parents and me. I was so fucking scared, and it was kind of like the Will Smith movie *I Am Legend*. After about three days of my mom sleeping in the same room as me, I was able to leave my house and see that more humans existed. I was still scared that the world was going to end, but at least I was able to leave my house and see that more people were still alive. I went through this one more time, and when I was done going through the apocalypse the second time, I was good again. I am still living in fear, but at least I know that the world won't end. They were talking about the end of the human race in this script, and I was able to witness it with my own two eyes during this experience. There are a lot of mixed messages in this script, and the one I wanted to talk about was that the girl's mom in the script is the main woman behind all their miseries. I think this is pretty similar to the girl in the real world who I am interested in, and she actually tried to trip me in Kids R Us one day when I went there with my mom. Anyway, I think that there was a girl in the real world who just had her mom pass away, and she said she still talks to her spirit. The other people around her, though, were like, "What the fuck are you talking about?"

The next part of this script I wanted to talk about was false hope. When I was going through the apocalypse the first time, I was experiencing something called false hope. OneRepublic actually mentioned in one of their songs that hope is a four-letter word, and Obama was big on hope in his book and when he was leaving the presidency. I saw what hell looks like, and it is people curled up in corners, burning to death. It wasn't pretty. Throughout this episode, I kept hearing this voice saying, "False hope." I was scared out of my fucking mind. I actually didn't take a shower for around three weeks straight because of how scared I was. My parents were sleeping in the living room one night, and I was like, *Why the fuck are my parents sleeping in the living room? They should be sleeping in their beds.* Another crazy thing that happened to me throughout this period was that my dog teleported from my dining room into my parents' room. My life has been so fucking crazy, but it turned to blue when Chloe teleported to my parents' upstairs bedroom.

The next part of the script I wanted to talk about was that each of these people is there because they broke the law. In the tests we are all going through in this world by people (*not by God*), they are testing all these criminals. Some of them actually feel like they are chosen for a reason, but they are just simply a part of the entire experiment. Most of my enemies at this point are either in prison or dead, so I don't have to worry about enemies much anymore. Anyway, these one hundred people are chosen to be killed off the planet because they are criminals and wastes of space. In the real world, the one hundred chosen people that Hollywood is talking about are not criminals, and this includes me. But we are going through the toughest tests to make us the best individuals we could possibly be in the future. Some of the tests I have been through were so fucking hard that I couldn't live a normal life anymore, so some of the test makers started dying. I would say about twenty-five test makers have died at this point in time, just like what was directed in these two scripts. The two scripts I am talking about are for *The 100* and *Hunger Games*.

The next part of the script I want to talk about involves the character named Dax. They came out with this character's name because of Dak Prescott. He is the starting quarterback for the Dallas Cowboys and a stud. He is one of the top five quarterbacks in the league. I actually drafted him in two of my fantasy leagues this year, in 2020. They wanted him to be included as a part of this script because Hollywood knew that I was going to draft him, and he was going to produce big numbers for me. It is really important that I step back into the line so that everyone's problems in the world can be fixed. I would really like my problems to be fixed, and I will look after myself first; however, I can help out every single person in the world with more time. I have already helped out each individual in the world who is going to survive the apocalypse at least one time, and everyone is waiting on cue to be helped out from here on out. I just know that people care and want the best for me, and I am so selflessly going out of my way every day to make sure that the world is in the shape it needs to be in by the year 2022.

To go along with the character in this show, the character Avery died, which he should do in real life, considering the things he did to me in the real world. He didn't remember any of it until the Mafia showed him the highlights of the things he did to me. I am the worst person in the world you would want to fuck with, and Avery is facing my devilish karma every single day because he was the one and only Jesus asshole who tried to kill and beat the demon in the world. One lesson in this world that people need to realize is that you *do not* want to be the enemy of the demon. Eminem actually mentioned this in one of his songs, and it's true. He released a song with Juice WRLD called "Godzilla," which states that Godzilla is the bad guy; and in the real world, believe me, you do not want to be my enemy, considering how strong and powerful I am.

The last part of the script I want to mention for the time being involves this beautiful girl with a great personality who helped out this guy who was tied up and about to die. This is another mixed message telling us that we need to help out the needy in the world. I saw this character, and the first thing that came to my mind is that the rich just get stronger, and the poor get poorer. It is fucked up, and people in this world need someone like me to keep the balance in this world safe. I want to make Jeff Bezos money one day to help out every single person in this world. I still can right now, even though I don't have that much money, because of how powerful I am.

Furthermore, in *The 100*, the next storyline in the second season follows the one hundred people facing killers called Reapers who were targeting them. They talk a lot about Reapers in *Supernatural* as people who control who lives and dies in this world and in the afterlife. They are kind of like Death and tell everyone when their time is up. In *The 100*, they are the enemy, and the main girl and the rest of them defeat them with the weapons in the show. I thought this was pretty cool and relevant to talk about. There is a good character in the show called Marcus. They named the character Marcus because of my older sister's friend's husband, Marcus. I got to know him really well, and I am actually in a fantasy basketball league with him and his friends. I think Hollywood names these characters on purpose to keep my relationships with people going strong, and this is one example. I know I talked about the character Avery dying, but he kind of deserves to since he tried to beat me in the past with all these devilish and sinister things he was doing to me. Anyway, Marcus and I are really close, and I would like to hang out with him more often in the future.

There is more that I wanted to add to my thoughts on the script of *The 100*. They talked about one character named Raven, and they got that name from *X-Men*. The character Raven is supposed to be Ariana, and she is the Raven character in *X-Men*. The Raven character is an important character, and she is a part of the Sky People. They got the name Sky People from the script of *Avatar*. The Sky People in real life are the empires that are trying to control the entire population. I can't stand them, and I think they actually took their planes out of the sky. Anyway, these are some of the terms from the script of *The 100*. There are some crazy fight scenes, and the Sky People go against the Reapers, I am pretty sure. The Reapers are the bad people, and the Reapers are actually the people who control who lives and who dies in this world. The Reapers are the Illuminati. They are bad people who need to also stop controlling us. The other term I wanted to discuss was the title of one of the episodes, "Remember Me." They gave title because people keep on forgetting about me, especially my close friends, old friends, and acquaintances, and even my family sometimes. I never got the love I deserved, and that is what Shaggy said in one of his songs. He said I never got the love I needed and that the girl I am meant to be with is a queen and should be treated as one when the time is right, when this is all over.

There is this one kid named Johnny who used to be a part of Jack's clique, and I ran into him one day at Glory Days. He was like, "Hey, Will," and I looked at him confused. Then he was like, "Remember me?"

I was like, "Yeah, of course." It took a little time to register in my brain exactly who that was because I hadn't seen him since college, but then I remembered. Anyway, I know it's going to change in the next few years, but I would really like for people to start remembering who I am.

I can add more to my thoughts on the script for *The 100*, and that is what I am going to do right here. In the script, there were robots creating nuclear warheads. In the real world, the robot problem is an issue with all this technology. Also, the nuclear warheads were an issue in the movie *GI Joe*. When they mention nuclear warheads, it reminds me of Donald Trump and the leaders of North Korea, Iran, and other countries that wanted to involve themselves in a nuclear war. This could be part of the end of mankind; however, I think people have calmed down and don't want to form nuclear warheads as much anymore. I can help with this issue by spreading Jesus inside people's systems, instead of Satan getting in people's ways every single day. This idea in the script is based on the North Korean crisis, which they also talked about in *It's Always Sunny in Philadelphia*. Anyway, the North Korean leader started going through health issues; and last New Year's, despite the previous few years, he didn't talk about threatening the US. Hopefully, he has calmed down; but people like me, Hollywood, and the CIA can fix this problem and make that crazy asshole calm the fuck down. For this part of the script, they are talking about missile launchers and codes for those missile launchers. The bad people developed the robots that created the missile launchers. The good guys, however, stopped the bad guys and won the war. The good guys always win in the real world. I think North Korea, Iran, and Russia will all go against the US; but we need someone like me, who wants to have peace in this world, to take control and make these power-hungry people calm down. We need peace in this world, and I am the only one who can solve this problem once I step back into the line, once karma catches up, or once I am fully healed.

The other part of this script I wanted to talk about was that the nuclear part is self-destructing because of the codes. I want to talk about my own issues with self-destructing. In 2016 (or maybe it was 2017), Avery came over for my younger sister's thirtieth birthday party and went from Fort Minor's song "Remember the Name" to the one that goes, "The devil's got a fresh new place to play," and he said that he really liked that song. Ever since then—and it matters more than he realized at the time—I have been self-destructing a lot. I haven't been self-destructing as much recently, thank goodness, but it's been hell ever since Avery came into my house and played that song. He doesn't even remember playing it because a lot of people's memories are shit in this world. My memory got a lot better, and my mind and brain get fixed every day. I also remember a lot of things that people would never remember unless they saw the highlights. I would go to parties and have to leave early, which had never happened before, because of these athletes and people in Hollywood who made it harder for me because I was simply fucking self-destructing. Before that, I never had any of these issues, and they knew they shouldn't have made it harder. To add to the fact that the athletes shouldn't have made it harder, the coronavirus and the perfect storms in Puerto Rico and Texas wouldn't have happened, and a lot more lives could have been saved if people had never made it harder for me. I know how important it is for me to step back into the line, but I am sick of killing and want all this shit to end. It might take another year or two, but we will get it done. We also need to find a solution for every problem known to mankind. Anyway, this is what I thought about when they mentioned self-destructing in this script.

I wanted to add to my thoughts on the script of *The 100*. They talked about the history of voting in ancient times, and they included this part in the script because the election is coming up soon. I actually just voted today with my parents and voted for Biden. I think it was important, and one guy was like, "I am on the right side and won't go for the team that always loses these games." The right side in this election would be Biden, but I wouldn't be too upset if Trump won because it doesn't matter what any of these guys do; I will save the world in the next year or two. They talked about how they built robots in the show to end the world, and they discussed it more with artificial intelligence that would end the world. The good guys try to stop it, but honestly, people need to understand that robots are not good and that the asshole 1 percent need to stop controlling us and making people think it's okay for humans to build robots. It actually causes humans to lose more jobs, and they will overtake humankind one day unless we stop the production of robots. We don't need to stop the production of man-made things, but we do need to stop the production of robots. The last part of the script I wanted to talk about, for the time being (and I am currently on season 3), is that they are talking about the kill order. They also talked about it in *Divergent* and *The Maze Runner*, but the kill order is when people need to go in this world, and the Illuminati throw it on me so that we can get rid of the flesh. It is what it is, and there are still too many fucking people in the world, most of whom are useless and doing absolutely nothing with their fucking lives. I hate it when people are just doing nothing, merely adding wasted time to this planet. I know that the flesh needs to die, and it doesn't matter how it gets done. I don't think a lot of people in this world are doing much to make the world a better place, and when I receive my kill orders from the Illuminati, I don't hesitate because I know that I am not wasted space and that many people on this planet are wasting time and precious energy that could be used for those who deserve it more. I understand that a lot of people think that we are all getting older, but we will be here forever. It doesn't matter how much older we are all getting. There are people working around the clock to find solutions for the human race, and this is part of the reason I had to conquer everything and am the biggest part of this whole conspiracy—so that we can fix people up and make sure nobody goes through any misery or downfalls ever again. Obviously, not everyone will win all the time because only one team or one person can win every matchup that you ever play in, but we can make the world the best place possible. I think that people need to be patient, just like I was, for when I used to be useless but now am accomplishing so much in this world that it is unreal the number of people I can help out daily. Anyway, like I was saying, when I receive my kill orders, I don't hesitate to pull the trigger and kill the flesh.

I wanted to add even more about the script called "The 100." One line that stuck in my head is that they said in the script, "When you're angry, people die." This goes along the lines of my story. When I get mad, there's usually a reason for my actions, but people always die somehow and someway. In one of B.o.B's songs, he said that we are filled with so much hatred that the kids don't stand a chance, in terms of being forever young. When I get mad and angry, then old people or people younger than me start dying because people in my generation have so much hate inside our systems. I talked about how they picked out one hundred criminals and that there were one hundred special people in the world whom Hollywood and the Illuminati were targeting, but I want to add that they are also talking about the top 1 percent of the population: the richest people in the world. I discuss in the section below how they are, in a sense, controlling things from the top, making the middle and lower classes suffer. This needs to stop. I am sick and tired of all these rich people who complain about life without knowing what it's like to suffer the way I do, along with billions of other people who don't have any money. With shadow play, I can make them realize that they are doing things wrong and make them pay for their mistakes. The next part is about the girl, Raven, who tried to kill herself. It's hard for many people in society to be happy, and for people to reach the point where they consider suicidal actions is terrible. I want everyone to be happy and don't want anybody to be suicidal. I have seen it in person with Ava, and I have seen it on the news and heard stories. People, in general, need to be happier and enjoy life. I know that sometimes things don't go your way, and you feel frustrated and stuck in a rut that seems impossible to escape. But cheer up because there is always a light at the end of the tunnel.

The next part of the script of *The 100* I wanted to talk about was when the guy told Raven to get some sleep if she couldn't focus. We are all connected through technology, so they wrote this part in the script so I can make certain people in this world not wake up from their sleep and die. Whether they were old people or young people, it was part of the population control that was necessary. I thought he was talking about me; however, after watching this episode, I went downstairs to work out, and Wiz Khalifa's song popped up, the one about people not waking up from their sleep. Raven was also brain-dead in the show. Avery talked about being brain-dead at one point, and I have dealt with issues of being brain-dead. But it is a big problem for many people in this world, including former athletes who have dealt with concussions and shit like that. Being brain-dead means that one, on artificial life support, no longer has any brain functions. This means they will not regain consciousness or be able to breathe without support. A person who's brain-dead is legally confirmed as dead. When I told other people that Avery was brain-dead, people didn't believe him, and I would never tell anyone that I am conquering everything because they wouldn't believe me. However, it is a real thing, and people usually don't rebound from being brain-dead. A big part of this script is the elimination of all robotics in the world and the things that cost humans jobs, as well as the robots trying to take control over the human race. There was this humanlike robot in the show *The 100* named ALIE, and the main character found a way to defeat her and save the human race. In the real world, they are discussing Alexa, and they wouldn't have written this into the script if Alexa wasn't a problem for the human race. I always knew that robots were a problem ever since I watched *I, Robot*, but I never thought we would come to a society where so many people rely on that stupid-ass Alexa device to control their lives. We need to find a way for people to not be so dependent, especially when people even use that dumb thing to turn on the lights in their homes and other things of that nature. This is how we need to try to end that story.

The next part I wanted to talk about was the fact that in the show, the human race was going to survive for the next six months based on the enemies and creatures they were up against. They said six months because Blink-182 wrote in "Avery's Song" that he had another six months to live and that the choice was his. The next song I want to mention was written was by Sum 41, and in his song, he says, "Everybody's got their problems. Everybody says the same things to you. It's just a matter how you solve them." He is referring to the forever-young movement. I never chose this path because it was Avery's choice. I know I can save the human race with everything I have talked about up to this point in my books and everything I discuss with my mom, my therapist, and with others in my life. I need about two to three more years to fully save the human race, but every day that we are all still alive is progress. I know I went through the apocalypse twice before anybody, but Hollywood was talking about it. I pretty much know what I am doing these days, though, and with people's help, I can save this life for everybody who survives the apocalypse.

I can add even more about the script for *The 100*. The criminals and bad people in the script, and even the good people who have done some bad things, are hoping for a forgiving god. I am the person in the world who can be seen as a forgiving god. I know that in the Bible, when Jesus was alive for the first time, he forgave everyone, including Judas. I know that Jack is Judas, and sometimes I am reminded every single day that Judas is bad and keeps on getting in my way every day. In the script, the Sky People, who are the good guys in the show because they are actually the one hundred people, are looking for a forgiving god. Also, the people who started this game are looking for a forgiving god. I shouldn't say that the

Sky People are looking for a forgiving god; but the main girl, who is meant to be with the main guy (me), is looking for a forgiving god because she did some bad things in her life and is hoping for forgiveness. I think everyone can look at me and say that I will forgive them because I am always way too nice to ever be too mean. I know that I lose my mind sometimes and have even done a lot of bad things in this life; but you can look to me for guidance, survival, and hope. I know that I forgive people, and many people have done a lot of shitty things to me. But I will always forgive people. One of the main reasons I forgive people is because hating is bad for your brain, and a lot of people don't know about the things and issues I have been through since Peyton Manning put me back into this devilish game the second time. Four years later, I have actually accomplished more than anyone can do in a thousand years. I have gotten so much done, and I believe that I was able to help people out as much as I am now throughout my entire life, though not like the way I am doing now. I have helped out every single person in this world at least one time.

Another point in the show called *The 100* that I wanted to mention was that the character Raven reminds me of different people in this world; but one person she particularly reminds me of, as I mentioned, is Ariana, Jack's wife. Additionally, she also reminds me of my ex-girlfriend Jackie Cook. They both have that Spanish, sexy, not-fucking-around aura. Jackie was really important to me for a while in college. I would love to be friends with her at some point in the future when the time is right; however, Hollywood sends me a lot of mixed messages, and this Raven character reminds me of these two girls, as of now.

I wanted to talk about this Raven character a little bit more. She has a seizure and a near-death experience because of it. When I was dating Angie, I told the doctors that I had a panic attack, but it was more like a seizure. We were on spring break one year, and I was drinking alcohol and taking my Clonazepam. Then I started spasming on the bed, and she called my closest friends, who called an ambulance. I blacked out. I was sent to the hospital. Anyway, I think this seizure serves as mixed messages for people in this world so that we can find a solution for people who go through seizures and try to fix those problems. Some seizures are caused by conditions such as low blood sugar or a change in how the heart is working. Some very young children have febrile convulsions when they have a high temperature. These are not the same as epileptic seizures, which occur often, and approximately fifty thousand people with epilepsy die each year.

The next part about the Raven character I want to talk about is that she has a broken leg. I know that a lot of people break their legs, but I think this was directed toward certain people in this world, as many people can break their legs all the time. My friend Andrew Ke broke his leg once, and then when I was reading one of my books, his name came into my head. He knew that one of the reasons I was born was to free America. When I was reading this book, I think he figured out that I was also born to save and fix the world. If he still remembers this, that would be cool. Anyway, the mixed messages mean that we can fix people who break bones in their bodies and find a solution for these kinds of problems. I've actually been conquering everything over the last several years, and people are going to finish what they started with me, in terms of me being this specific science experiment. So I don't think anyone should panic about anything they are going through.

The next part of the script I wanted to discuss involves a five-year-old kid who is going to die because of the tests the one hundred people are undergoing. This five-year-old kid, who is going to die in the script, is real in the real world because I go through a lot of tests, especially because of my asshole real creator. Anyway, all these tests that I go through always result in people dying every day. I feel bad for the family of the five-year-old that died, but there are still too many people in the world. And maybe you shouldn't have had your kid five years ago. You need to think about the big picture, and when people in my generation are having kids as if it's their fucking job, then more people are going to start dying. It is the circle of life, but sometimes you have to enforce these changes and bring change upon the planet. I am also sick and tired of people being happy that another Goddamn kid was born in this world. I don't feel sorry for any kids or anyone else who fucking dies because too many idiots in this world thought it was cool to pop out as many Goddamn kids as they could. There are already too many fucking people in this world, and I have already been through the apocalypse twice. So I am done fucking around and want people to realize that they are the main reason for bad things happening in this world. *Stop having kids.*

The next part of *The 100* I wanted to talk about was that the guy in the show shows the utmost respect for his sister and says that if anyone fucks with his sister, then bad things will happen to that person. This part of the show reminds me of how I feel about Rebecca. I have threatened people in the past for disrespecting my older sister and said, "I will fuck you up if you mess with my sister." I am very close to my older sister and very similar to her, so I don't like when people disrespect her or say bad things about her. And I can take matters into my own hands when people fuck with my older sister. She was there through my darkest times and through my highest times, and I will always be there for her. Okay, this is all I am going to discuss about *The 100* for the time being.

I can add more on my thoughts about the script of *The 100*. In one part of their script, the guy says that he doesn't trust anyone. He says this because Avery doesn't trust anyone except for his wife and me. Sia and Taylor Swift released songs about this, and I don't blame them for releasing these songs. I am trying to work things out with Avery, and he doesn't really remember the bad things he did to me in the past. I know that everyone wants me to put the past away, but there are certain things I can't forget. Avery was always my go-to person, and once I step back into line, I think he can be a more reliable friend. I know I can't tell Avery any of the negative things that Hollywood has said about him. There were a lot of positive and negative things that Hollywood released about Avery, and that was why they couldn't let him into the gates of Hollywood.

Anyway, the guy also says that I have been quiet for too long. This saying is meant for me. I was quiet for a long time because I didn't really know who I was anymore, but more recently, I have been more outgoing. I don't really talk much when people act fake around me or if they act out of character. I was getting sick and tired of people calling me shy, so I started killing the people who were to blame for calling me shy. Nobody even remembers calling me shy because a lot of people's memories fucking suck. Also, Marshmello released his song "Silence," and Hollywood came out with that movie called *Silence*. In Marshmello's song, he said that I am tired of killing. I am not sure that I am, though. I am still stuck pretty deep, and people still want to play games with me. So I don't think I am sick of killing. Most of the things that have happened to me probably should have never happened, and a lot of people who were involved. Many innocent people died because of the things that happened to me. The last part of *The 100* script that I want to talk about is that they are scared and trying to eliminate the eye in the sky. They also got this part from *Avatar* and *Eagle Eye*. The eye in the sky and the planes in the sky are pretty much fading away, and I am actually going to delete that Clint Eastwood song because it says I am useless. However, I am not useless at all, and when I look around in society, I see a lot of useless people. I am not useless at all, so that song is useless to me and will not be a part of my playlist anymore.

I understand what they are saying about the eye in the sky. It was part of how people were watching me in the past. It was more of a blessing than a curse. Actually, in one of the *Avengers* movies, Hollywood got people to stop watching me as much by making them disappear in the movie, but they were just fading away in my house so that I would have more room to breathe and more time to think about myself. In the script, the eye in the sky is bad, and they are trying to kill it. I think that in the real world, the eye in the sky isn't good either, and I want it to go away.

The next script I wanted to talk about was for the movie *Wonder Woman*. There is one woman in the world who is my Wonder Woman, and I know exactly who that is. But anyway, B.o.B. put in his song that there are so many beautiful girls in the world, but only one is on my mind. They came out with this script knowing that the wars were going to end overseas and that all the individual wars and the hate were going to go away in this world. The one lie about World War II was that it was supposed to be the war to end all wars. One time, I told Dr. O'Connor that this is the war to end all wars. I did not know at the time that World War II was called the

War to End All Wars. If that is the case, then why did all these other wars happen in the world? Anyways, Camila Cabello put in her song "Wonder Will" the line "Can I get a hell no?" disrespecting Jack with all of his "hell yes" stuff. It would be me in heaven when everyone is praying here on planet Earth because I am answering people's prayers from the ground.

The last part of this script I wanted to talk about was that it has a lot to do with the war against ISIS ending. There are a lot of bad things that ISIS is wishing on me, and they kind of made me stuck deeper in ways that will help ISIS destroy America. However, since the military and government are smart, I think they will be able to help me out and not let the light beams and sun get in my way every day. I want peace in this world, and I want the world to form one big family. When ISIS keeps on prolonging the inevitable, it gets annoying. I was able to help out America in this war so many times. Whenever America needed my help throughout this entire time, Hollywood would have me play certain songs from my technology that would help the troops win those individual battles. I didn't pick up on this until recently, but I know exactly what songs can destroy ISIS and help America win these battles. Another example was when America captured ISIS's flag or whatever the fuck happened in Afghanistan. This was a big victory for America. When America was in Iraq, songs such as Katy Perry's song and Rihanna's song helped eliminate the Iraqi troops, and we won those individual battles. This is all I am going to say about this script for the time being.

The next script I want to talk about has Ben Affleck as the main character. The script is about a guy who coaches a high school basketball team and actually dropped out of college and pro basketball because he was addicted to pills, alcohol, and drugs. He tries to turn his life around and ends up coaching this basketball team. The name of this movie is *The Way Back*. The first part of this movie I want to discuss is that Ben Affleck was still a wreck when he was coaching the basketball team, and he accidentally broke into someone's house. The guy took out his baseball bat and then ended up pushing him onto the concrete, where he was found by the cops, and they brought him to the hospital so that he could get cleaned up. Anyway, Joe

Montana, in the real world, had a home intruder, and Joe Montana took care of it and protected his family. They put this part in this script so that I can save Montana and his family. I thought this was interesting because they put these things in the scripts, and they are almost always real-time so that I can interpret them and throw them in the sky or put them in play in the real world while they are happening in people's lives.

The next part of the script I wanted to talk about was the scores of all the basketball games in the movie. They seem real and are based on real-time, just like what I said in the previous paragraph. The scores are sometimes like 58–56 or 65–62 and shit like that. I came up with this number scheme, and I think this was going on this entire time that I just started picking up on recently. The numbers include everybody's credit card numbers, license plate numbers, and other numbers in the world. They all have meaning behind them, and it is important that I dissect the numbers in my solution pit to make everybody's lives better and so that everyone in the world can feel equally important. The scores in the games are really important, and they will have huge impacts on the NCAA tournaments and NCAA games this year and going forward.

The next part of the script I wanted to talk about, which I think I mentioned when discussing the show *The 100*, involves a character named Marcus. He is the center in this movie, makes some mistakes but eventually gets his shit together to become a great asset to the team. I think this is also a preview for when we play two-on-two and three-on-three games across the United States and overseas. Marcus is my Black buddy and my partner in crime from *White Men Can't Jump*, and they also wanted to make him a bigger player in my life. I talked about him in my discussion on *The 100*, but he is also in one of my fantasy basketball leagues.

The last part of this script I wanted to talk about concerns the point guard. The coach, Ben Affleck, sits him down and asks him if he wants to be the captain. He says he needs to be more vocal. This is exactly how I used to be. I was never one to talk too much and was more of a listener, but when I got drunk, I would always talk more. Recently, we kind of fixed people's memories so they wouldn't remember me not talking much because it was screwed up that people thought that about me when it didn't make any sense. I wanted to talk about this because when I achieve perfection and when we do these two-on-two, three-on-three, and five-on-five tournaments within the middle class, I will be the vocal point guard who runs the show and wins all the fucking games because he is the best athlete and person on the planet.

There was something that caught my eye about this script, specifically regarding the point guard in this movie. The coach, Ben Affleck, keeps asking him why he hesitates and passes the ball when he should be taking the last shot because he is the best person on the team. LeBron James was facing the Miami Heat on Friday, October 10, and his team had the last possession in the game. LeBron was carrying the ball to make the game-winning shot; but instead of taking the shot, he passed the ball to his teammate, who missed the final shot. Hollywood and Ben Affleck based this scene and part of the movie on LeBron James passing up this final shot. I know that other people do it too, but it was specifically based on the future and LeBron passing up this particular shot.

The next script I wanted to talk about was for *Ready Player One*. It is a big computer game about good guys beating the bad guys in this world. The bad guys are my enemies, and I actually read this book before the movie came out. The computerized person who is their mentor in this movie is named Halliday. This name was based on Roy Halladay and the lives he touched before he died in that plane crash. It didn't happen by accident, and it seems like one man's pain is another man's gain. So the people who wrote the book and those who were part of this script benefited. They were able to write this script about Roy Halladay, the future of the world, how we are all connected by technology, and how we can all run this world like a computer game. Sometimes life is like a computer game, and we are all connected through the Internet and through the sky, just like I said earlier in my book.

The next part of the script I wanted to mention was that they named the playing field in this script Oasis, which is what people say when the devil interferes in people's lives, and it is supposed to be a cry for help when people want the gods of the world to defeat the devil's wrath. Aaron actually said it once when I was at his house, and the insides of my body started going crazy. Then I realized, and people told me, that the people in the world who believe in God use that word to get rid of the devil's part in this world. Hollywood and the writer of the book actually use this movie in the year 2045 because we are preparing for the future. Obviously, we are not waiting for the year 2045 for the future; we are more likely looking at 2021 and 2022 for my future to begin. However, I am not useless, and people figured I was Satan-bound. But the things I am doing right now, which I explained when discussing Selena Gomez's song, are important. People will see the results in their own lives in the next year or two. If people are real, then they already see the benefits. If people are fake, then they only see narrow-minded stuff, not how beautiful this place really is and all the magical things that I am doing for the world. We need to create this kind of safe space in the world and a thinking pad for me, and we need to create heaven on earth.

In my first book, I explained that heaven is where one second is like one thousand years, and one thousand years is like one second. But we need to find the master pill and the magical pills, including the Limitless one that I have been taking, and put that into play in other people's worlds. People who put me on these drugs and through other experiments are working every single day on a solution for the human race, but we need to work quicker. I understand that people think 2020 is the worst year ever, but it really isn't. You can look at the coronavirus and see the negatives; or you can work out three hours a day, put your body in better shape, spend more time with your family, and make money online. You can view things from a positive perspective or a negative one. I look at the coronavirus as a positive thing because I made the most out of my time and helped bring the planet back to life after more places and the roads were more open for more people to travel. I lost twenty pounds throughout the coronavirus because of working out and actually sixty-five pounds since 2015 up to 2020. I don't really need to lose any more weight, but like they say in *Ready Player One*, you need to understand the future and the direction the world is heading in to grasp the full picture.

Eric Sanchez explained to me his view of the future of the world, which makes complete sense, and it's actually covered in this movie. He talked about how important trees are in the world, and they covered that in *Avatar*. Sanchez also talked about gravity and how we can fix it as humans if we take better care of the planet. Sandra Bullock starred in the movie *Gravity*, which either won or was nominated for some Grammys, and Hollywood is right on the ball. Somehow, I am in the middle of this, and people either understand it or they don't. Eric Sanchez knows a bit about the world, but he doesn't understand that all these scripts have meaning to them, including *Ready Player One*. *Ready Player One* is a computerized game from the future where the good guys try to save the planet. They are stuck in the Oasis and need to break the chains and the wrath of society to escape the hell that they are in. Of course, the good guys always have enemies, so he destroys the enemies that are going against him. The bad guys are those who try to destroy his life. The bad guys could be the Illuminati or the 1 percent. The 1 percent are the richest guys on the planet. Actually, Joe Biden posted on Twitter earlier that he doesn't want to destroy anyone but believes there should be more wealth provided for people who actually need it, not for all the greed in this world. There is a very thin line between all the love and hate in this world, and like it or not, Jack is the leader of all the hate in this world. We need more Will Coakleys who believe in peace to come alive and be leaders in this world. I don't want to be an asshole, but there is too much hate in this world. We don't need any more unnecessary hate that has developed between people and between countries.

The next script I wanted to talk about was for *The Addams Family*. In this script, they are talking about Adam Seaman's family. The first part of this family I wanted to talk about was that his mom was playing games with my mom when I was living in all the fear when I was twenty-four or twenty-five years old. I was about to go pick up my Xanax at the store for a refill, which I really needed because I have always had anxiety and it helps me focus. Actually, nowadays I am on clozapine. Anyway, his mom shone a light at my mom, which scared the shit out of me, then my instincts took over.

I was like, "It's bad enough that these people are fucking with me, but now they are messing with my mom."

The person who was shining this light at my mom was actually Mrs. Seaman. Adams Seaman's family was pretty much normal at that point in time. However, Mrs. Seaman ended up getting in a lot of fights with her husband, and she used all her money on his credit cards. One time, she bought these bags from an expensive store with his credit cards and kept on maxing out his credit cards. She ended up getting mild Alzheimer's because she was facing karma for making that move. She should have never fucked with me that day. Maybe her life would be a little bit more normal right now. Obviously, hating is bad, and I don't hold a grudge against her. But c'mon, she should have known better.

The next person I want to talk about is Avery himself. He is facing karma every single day for looking into my eyes and telling me to die that day when I was twenty-four or twenty-five years old. They even wrote in one of their songs, "I hope you die, all alone at best." That day is one of the worst days that have ever been a part of in my life. I still feel these Goddamn pains, and sometimes they take over my body so much that I cannot live a normal life. He should have never done this to me, and he didn't even fucking remember until his fake-ass empires and his real creator showed him the highlights of what he did in their fake place. Another example is that Avery came to my sister's thirtieth birthday party and disrespected me in front of everyone, and now he is facing even worse karma than anything he has ever experienced before. The Mafia and he were playing games with me and with my mind, and now he is by himself and got into that car accident, which he complains about. Now he has nobody by his side except for his wife.

When I was at the hospital and having all those malfunctions that were destroying my neck and when I was sent to the hospital against my free will for the first time, those were his doing, and that was some of the worst shit that has ever happened to me. They lied to me about my organs failing, and I looked crazy. So my real creator sent me to the hospital against my will. This is all I am going to write about Avery for his part in *The Addams Family*.

I wanted to add some positivity to Avery's story in *The Addams Family*. I know that he feels bad for the shit that he did to me in the past, and I think he is trying to get back into my life. Here is a great example that everything I do is special and that every move I make is magic. I just bought some new clothes from Gap, and the total for my order was $88.61. The number eighty-eight stands for Avery, and I don't want to see that number popping up any more than I want to see fifty-five or forty-four pop up. But it has everything to do with what I am doing at the current period of time and with what Avery is doing in his life. The other number, which was sixty-one, stands for Andy. The only reason I am so close to Andy is because of Andy, and the fact that these two signs are connected with each other means that Avery and Andy can connect in the future when Avery gets his shit together. This is all I am going to write about this for the time being.

The next person I am going to write about is Avery's sister. She was always polite and nice to me, but she is facing karma for fucking with my sisters. She was going to school (college), and everything was going great for her. But then she ended up taking a lot of cocaine and heroin and fucking a lot of Black guys, which pretty much fucked up her entire life. She played as big a part in this devilish game as the person sitting next to anybody in this world. Everyone played their part, and the guy who was on the receiving end of these tricks ended up forgiving everybody in this world. That is what I am going to do. However, I do not want to see anyone having power or a say in this world, especially when their opinions are bullshit and mean-ingless. I feel bad for her; she is like a sister to me. But I thought this was important to write about because they based the script for *The Addams Family* on his family.

The next person I want to talk about is Mr. Seaman. He had developed this persona for people not liking him because he was an asshole to people. I always liked him, and he always liked me in return. But for the sake of this movie, I need to write about this. His life went downhill after the Mafia and he were playing all those games with me. He doesn't have a life; and the book he was trying to write went downhill, especially after he was fucking with the book that I was trying to write, which is this book. This is how they came up with the script for *The Book of Eli*, where Denzel was going through lengths to give the Bible, the book that nobody had heard of, to the right person and killing anybody who was getting in the way. This actually makes sense to me now (I didn't know it at the time), but they try to fuck up your dreams and are all falling all over the Goddamn place because of the karma I am giving them. These people fucked with the wrong dude, and they can all get fucked unless they finally leave me alone. I am having so many issues because of the Mafia. This is all I am going to write about him for the time being.

20 Percent Concentrated Power of Will Coakley

Willpower, motherfuckers!

In this section, I wanted to talk about the economy a little bit.

I wanted to mention this article because there was a man at the grocery store who misplaced one of his items, and I pointed it out to him but said I didn't want to touch it because of the virus. He was very thankful that I was able to help him out. The article headline reads, "How Helping Your Neighbor Could Hurt Your Neighborhood." I also don't wave to some of my neighbors like I used to because of their disrespect in the past, but maybe that'll change one day.

> For more than a week, Clark Hamel has not left his Brooklyn apartment. He cannot risk exposure to the coronavirus; Since he was a teenager, he has been on drugs that suppress his immune system so he will not experience the excruciating symptoms of rheumatoid arthritis. Still, Mr. Hamel, 24, and his partner have not been along. In a gesture of friendship, another young couple in their building has also agreed to go into an even stricter form of quarantine than most in order to protect Mr. Hamel. They venture out only to pick up groceries, leaving the food outside his apartment in bags and disinfecting milk cartons with bleach wipes. The arrival of the coronavirus has led to many similar arrangements in

New York, a city usually famous for neighbors who mind their own business. People who until recently limited their interaction to a nod in the elevator are now knocking on doors, offering to fetch a prescription or an extra C-Town grocery special, or to act as contacts with older neighbors' children in other states.

But in this particular crisis, as New York becomes the country's epicenter of a virus that can be fatal, the danger of spreading infection has added a note of tension to what might otherwise be simple acts of generosity. As offers of help proliferate across WhatsApp, Slack, laundry rooms and lobbies, and college students band together to grab groceries for older people, elected officials and others warn that selfishness might be putting vulnerable people at greater risk. "There's no doubt that New Yorkers want to help their neighbors," said Carlos Menchaca, a Democratic councilman from Brooklyn, who is asking volunteers to wait for guidance from medical experts. "But before we self-activiate, we need to pause and put together guidelines that allow us to do it in a safe way." People are sounding the same warning from London to Minneapolis, as a so-called mutual-aid movement gains momentum around the world. Mutual-aid networks are a community-organizing tool often used after events such as natural disasters, and consist in neighbors serving each other in a building or a block.

Mr. Menchaca said he felt it was necessary to ask people to "pause" as he saw mutual-aid Google documents and intake forms pop up everywhere last week, while witnessing countless offers to help in his own neighborhood of Red Hook. "We are trying to flatten the curve—in the city and the country—but a neighborhood has to think that way, too," Mr. Menchaca said. Mayor Bill De Blasio has applauded the efforts of New Yorkers to help each other. But a sense of alarm has grown in recent days as the number of confirmed cases of coronavirus in New York has increased. As of Tuesday morning, New York State had more than 25,000 cases, with almost 15,000 of those in densely-packed New York City. The city's health department said in a statement to The Times that New Yorkers could help each other most by connecting by phone and video to offer "emotional support." If a sick neighbor needs groceries, the city advised to "leave them on the door step."

Javier Lopez, the chief strategy officer with the Red Hook Initiative, a youth development organization, said the ways of helping that developed after Hurricane Sandy hit the neighborhood in 2012 have had to be "tweaked." Staffers from the initiative have been working through a list of 2,000 phone numbers for residents of the Red Hook Houses, one of the largest public housing projects in the city, to create a map for who might need help. "But throughout the process," he said, "There is hesitancy. This is not Sandy. This is different. It's a different response. They're checking in through social distancing." When it comes time to distribute food and supplies, he added, there will not be central collection spots as there were after Sandy. Large volunteering organizations like New York Cares are also changing, requiring volunteers to meet certain health requirements and community partners to have hand-washing stations and adequate spacing between staff.

The question of how to help can be a complicated calculus. "Having weighed things out, I worry more about our vulnerable population withering in the dark than the slight possibility of transmission," said Kimi Weart, a Brooklyn resident who joined an effort in her building in Lefferts Gardens to help frail or older neighbors. Helpers there are trying to reach such people by phone, said Ms. Weart, a graphic designer. If they can't, they knock on doors with their elbows, she said, then quickly move back six feet. As the city has largely shut down and people have been asked to remain indoors, efforts to help beyond one's own building have been also increased, an expression of the perceived need for assistance in a city with 1.73 million residents over 60, as well as the large numbers of people restlessly stuck at home, wishing they could do something.

Students sent home early from college helped create a website, Invisible Hands, to take groceries to the homebound. No-contact courier services modeled to those in Wuhan, China have also surfaced. And New Yorkers are offering all manner of help on Facebook, Instagram, Nextdoor and on new neighborhood Slack channels like Hastag BedStuyStrong. Some are offering child care, or help navigating Google classrooms. Others have collected monthly MetroCards for workers who still have to commute, and pooled rent money for the newly unemployed. In Manhattan's Inwood neighborhood, one man offered to share his "Inwood Quarantine Sourdough Starter" so others could also bake their own bread. Invisible Hands drew nearly 7,000 volunteers in just over a week, said Liam Elkind, a junior at Yale University and one of its creators. "People need food now, and we are trying to get them food as quickly as possible," he said. By Monday, Invisible Hands volunteers had delivered groceries and other goods to more than 250 homes. Mr. Elkind said recipients slide cash under the door to the volunteers, who sanitize the bags they are delivering. The service asks volunteers to follow guidelines issued by the Centers for Disease Control and Prevention, and to wear gloves and clean their delivery baskets. After Mr. Elkind delivered groceries to one woman in her 70s, he said, she invited him for cookies and tea. "I said, "No, this is the opposite of what this is about!" The whole point is we are minimizing physical contact."

Organizations that bring food to homebound people, such as God's Love We Deliver, City Harvest, and City Meals on Wheels, have said that while demand has increased recently, the volunteer pool has shrunken, in part because volunteers are usually older New Yorkers. Representative Alexandria Ocasio-Cortez, Democrat of New York, has encouraged people to create mutual-aid networks in their buildings or blocks-creating "pods" of neighbors-to bridge the gap. "It's really important because we can choose to share instead of hoard, "Ms. Ocasio-Cortez said on a rent call to promote the idea. Would-be helpers were encouraged to grocery shop during off-peak hours and to avoid public transit and face-to-face exchanges, tips her office said were consistent with the city's public health guidance. A "tool kit" that was distributed after the call also suggests that people avoid touching doorbells with their fingers. In Brooklyn, Emily Claypoole has taken such precautions when she shops for her neighbor, Mr. Hamel. They knew each other in college but ended up in the same Bedford-Stuyvesant building by coincidence last year, she said. Now, they are connected in ways neither could have imagined.

Ms. Claypoole, who just lost her serving job at a Manhattan restaurant, sanitizes her hand often while making grocery runs, and wipes down packages items with Clorox wipes before leaving the bags outside Mr. Hamel's door. She covers her hand with her jacket sleeve or a cloth when opening doors. Helping her neighbor "has been a pleasure, it has not been a burden," she said. "The thing I would caution against is doing it out of guilt," said Ms. Claypoole, 24. "just because you're not symptomatic, doesn't mean you can't pass it along." Mr. Hamel, who described himself as "an extrovert to the heart and core," is hunkering down patiently with his partner, Alex Harwood, and their cat, Basil. He urged well-meaning volunteers to think about the real danger they could pose to people like himself, especially when the medical system is becoming more strained. Ms. Claypoole said that because of Mr. Hamel, she and her boyfriend skip random jaunts to the corner store for a forgotten item, and forego all but the most important outings. "We are even more cautious," she said, "and it even feels like that's helpful for me and my friend, and the community at large."

I wanted to talk about this part of the coronavirus because doctors need to start dying to give more wealth to more important people.

37 Doctors Have Died after
Contracting COVID-19 In Italy

At least 37 doctors have died after contracting coronavirus in Italy. The National Federation of Orders of Surgeons and Dentists has announced further fatalities at the country's death toll from Covid-19 continues to rise. Among the names on a list updated daily are those of GP's, an epidemiologist, a retired doctor, a paediatrician, and specialists. The federation described the list as "a warning, a lesson for everyone." In Italy-where nearly one-tenth of more than 74,000 infections are among medical workers-doctors and nurses have been begging the government to provide more masks, gloves and goggles. Dr. Francesca De Gennaro, who heads up a small private medical clinic in hard-hit Bergamo, where some 90 of 460 workers have tested positive, wrote an open letter asking for equipment. "Please don't leave us alone: Help us help you," she said. Scientists say stopping just one person from getting the virus means scores of others will not become infected down the road. Dr. Hugh Montgomery, professor of intensive care medicine at Unversity College London, explained how one person can infect 59,000 others-compared to 14 with flu. Italy's death toll from the coronavirus outbreak rose by 683 on Wednesday to 7,503. This was a decline in deaths compared to the previous day which saw a spike of 743 deaths following 602 on Monday and 650 on Sunday.

The country recorded 793 cases on Saturday-the highest daily figure since the pandemic began. The Federation of Italian Pharmacist Orders (FOFI) has also announced deaths among pharmacists, prompting its president Andrea Mandaelli to urge the public to stay inside. Mr. Mandelli said: "Italian pharmacists are playing their role as far as possible, but I have to reiterate a message to citizens: the pharmacy is a health centre in which one must go only for important reasons. "I also invite you to strictly respect the safety distance and to follow the indications of the staff for the ordered access to the pharmacy premises. "Basically, I ask citizens to help us assist them in the best way; we can only get out of this emergency with the utmost collaboration of all." The Italian government has imposed strict measures to curb the spread of the virus and harsh punishments for those who ignore them. These include fines and even a up to five years in prison for anyone caught breaking their quarantine after testing positive.

I wanted to talk about this article because it was my doing, with x-ing out people in this world to make the stocks do better. Most people wouldn't understand, but it is true what they say: one man's pain is another man's gain. I know my real creator was trying to downplay the success that the stocks are having, but that's just assholes trying to downplay all the progress that I have made in this world. I don't know who, but I want them to fucking stop. It is crazy because the threes connect, and the threes stand for everything that I and Anna Kendrick do. The article's headline is "Stocks Surge as Washington's Aid Package Advances."

The S&P 500 is up more than 17 percent over the past three days, it's best such run since 1933. Boeing is up nearly 90 percent this week. American Airlines has jumped almost 50 percent. Carnival Corporation has soared nearly that much as well. Wall Street has been in rally mode, as investors bid up shares of companies that were set to receive support from Washington's $2trillion coronavirus aid bill. With the package advancing through the Senate, the gains continued on Thursday. The S&P 500 climbed 6.2 percent, even after the government reported a staggering jump in unemployment claims by workers.

As it has been all week, investors' focus was on companies likely to get help from the spending plan that passed the Senate on Wednesday night. The House of Representatives and President Trump are expected to approve it. Boeing rose nearly 14 percent on Thursday because the specifically sets aside $17 billion for "businesses critical to maintaining national security"-language that was seen as intended at least partly for the aircraft manufacturer and key Pentagon contractor. Other companies that were hit hard in the early days of the coronavirus outbreak continued to soar: American and Delta Air Lines rose nearly 2 percent. Carnival was up about 14 percent. The game on Thursday also spread to Europe, with major benchmarks there reversing their losses to end the day sharply higher. The FTSE 100 in Britain climbed more than 2 percent. The three-day rally has lifted the S&P 500 by more than 17 percent, its best such run since 1933, according to data from Howard Silverblatt, senior index analyst for S&P Dow Jones Indices. Most of the gains came on Tuesday, when stocks rose 9.4 percent, amid growing hope that the large stimulus package would offer support to an economy crippled by the outbreak and efforts to curtail the spread of the virus.

But the economic crisis is perhaps the most daunting since World War II. On Thursday, a government report showed a record rise in weekly applications for unemployment benefits, which jumped to nearly 3.3 million from 282,000 in a week. Until now, the record occurred in the fall of 1982, when 695,000 Americans applied for benefits in one week. At that point, the United States was more than a year into a recession, and the unemployment rate had passed 10 percent. The numbers, released by Labor Department on Thursday, are some of the first hard data on the economic toll of the coronavirus pandemic, which has shut down whole sectors of American life. General Motors said on Thursday it would suspend production at its North American factories indefinitely, lay off 6,500 salaried employees and cut executive pay, signaling that the automaker believes that coronavirus will take a serious toll on its business. "We are actively monitoring the situation and the possible impact of the crisis on consumer demand," a G.M. spokesman, David Barnes, said. "When we can safely resume production, we will."

G.M. and other automakers shut down their North American plants in the last few days in an effort to prevent the spread of the virus. Most had hoped to restart production next week, but have now scaled back those plans. Ford Motor aims to restart production at several plants across the United States on April 14, and a plant in Mexico on April 6. Flat Chrysler said its plants would stay closed until April 14, "dependent upon the various state stay-in-place orders and the readiness of each facility to return to production." Toyota Motor said its North American plants would remain closed until at least April 17. The United Automobile Workers union has been pushing G.M., Ford and Flat Chrysler to keep their plants closed. "The only guideline in a boardroom should be management asking themselves, "Would I send my family—my son or my daughter—into the plant and be 100 percent certain they are safe," Rory Gamble, the union's president, said in a statement. Auto sales have plunged in the past week. ON Wednesday, Group 1 Automotive, a large dealership chain, said it was laying off 3,000 employees in the United States and cutting its chief executive salary by 50 percent.

To cut costs, G.M. said it was suspending development work on some new models. Senior executives will take a pay cut of 5 percent or 10 percent, and defer 20 percent of their salaries to be paid at a later date. The 6,500 salaried put on furlough will receive 75 percent of their normal pay. Ford has taken similar steps, deferring salaries of its top 300 executives. Lawmakers put some restrictions on the compensation of executives whose companies receive government assistance under the bill, in an effort to address one of the criticisms about bailouts of banks and other companies during the 2008 financial crisis. But the limits will not do away with multimillion-dollar paydays for corporate bosses. Executives who made more than $3 million in 2019 could be awarded $3 million, plus half of any sum in excess of $3 million. As a result, a chief executive who earned $20 million in 2019 would be allowed compensation of $11.5 million, or $3 million plus half of $17 million per year. Companies receiving assistance will not be allowed to increase the compensation of executives who earned $425,000 to $3 million in 2019 until a year after government support ends.

The package includes more than $370 billion in much-needed help for small businesses, and those loans will be backed by the Small Business Administration. It could take at least two weeks after the bill is signed into law for the money to begin flowing. Small businesses would not have to repay portions of loans that were spent on paying employees, a mortgage, rent or utilities. The banks lending the money would be reimbursed for those portions by the Treasury Department. The role of banks in the rescue bill is to provide much-needed capital to businesses and taxpayers. "This is all about preserving the incentives for banks to lend," said Mike Mayo, who researches large banks for Wells Fargo. To ensure access in cash is not hampered by a raft of new client demands or market developments, the Fed has encouraged banks to use the so-called discount window, its lending operation for big banks, and at least eight major financial institutions already have. Banks can opt out of observing new federal accounting standards for estimating future credit losses during the period covered by the law, a rule known as Current Expected Credit Losses. The bill revises a crisis-era program to guarantee all bank debt, a move that once again puts taxpayers on the hook if a bank runs into trouble.

The nearly 3.3 million new jobless claims filed last week dwarfed any previous weekly figure. Until now, the record occurred in the fall of 1982, when 695,000 Americans applied for benefits in one week. At that point, the United States was more than a year into a recession, and the unemployment rate had passed 10 percent. In that case, the recession was caused not by a health crisis, but by a decision by political leaders and the Federal Reserve that raging inflation had to be shoved down, despite the cost to workers. The central bank sharply reduced the money supply while benchmark interest rates neared an astounding 20 percent. Industries that relied heavily on borrowing like construction and manufacturing were hit hard. The jobless rate in construction reached 22 percent; among autoworkers, it was 24 percent. Today, the circumstances are markedly different. Despite uneven rewards, the economy had achieved the longest expansion in history. The jobless rate had been below 4 percent for more than a year. A preoccupation of the Fed was raising the persistently low inflation rate toward 2 percent. Interest rates are near zero. Efforts to slow the spread of the coronavirus meant to service industry bore the initial brunt of layoffs—workers at restaurants, bars, hotels, nail salons, gyms and more.

Boeing appeared poised to capitalize on the stimulus bill. The struggling aerospace giant, which had lobbied for government aid, signaling its approval of the bill on Wednesday night, though neither the federal government nor the company detailed exactly what it would receive. Though Boeing was not named in the text of the bill, the inclusion of $17 billion in loans "for businesses critical to maintaining national security" is intended to at least in part for Boeing. Besides being the largest manufacturing exporter in the United States and one of two major commercial airplane makers, Boeing is a major defense and space contractor, making systems for the military and NASA. Boeing may also be eligible for funds from the larger $454 billion pool of loans. What's not clear is exactly how much Boeing might receive, or on what terms. On Tuesday, Boeing's chief executive, David Calhoun, suggested he was not interested in the government taking an equity stake in the company.

How much money will individuals get—and how will it be distributed? How are unemployment benefits changing? Are gig workers included? The Senate unanimously passed a $2 trillion economic stimulus plan on Wednesday that will offer assistance to tens of millions of American households affected by the coronavirus. Its components include payments to individuals, expanded unemployment coverage that includes the self-employed, loans for small businesses and nonprofit organizations, temporary changes to withdrawal rules from retirement accounts, and more. The House of Representatives was expected to quickly take up the bill and pass it, sending it to President Trump for his signature. We collected answers to common questions about what's in the bill.

I wanted to talk about this because they just mentioned it in *Supernatural,* that burgers are affected by old habits as our habits change over time. I am not saying that we won't be forever young; however, they mentioned something about burgers in *Supernatural,* and then I discovered this article. The article headline reads, "Coronavirus-Themed Foods Aim to Raise a Smile During the Crisis."

Among global efforts to offer some light relief to the current crisis, bakers and chefs have been producing coronavirus-related dishes that

are hopefully a lot tastier than the epidemic
which has inspired them. In Hanoi, Vietnam,
a chef at Pizza Home has created a coronavirus-themed burger. Hoang Tung says he dreamed
up the burgers, which feature green-tea stained
buns with tiny "crowns" designed to look like
microscopic images of the virus, to take the fear
out of the infectious disease. "We have this joke
that if you are scared of something, you should
eat it," Tung Reuters. "That's why the coronavirus isn't scary any more after you eat a burger in
the shape of the virus itself. That way of thinking
spreads of joy to other during this pandemic."

According to Reuters, the takeaway shop is
currently selling around 50 of the burger every
day, which is particularly impressive considering
the number of businesses that have been forced
to close down as a result of the pandemic. In
France, pastry chef and chocolatier Jean-Francois
Pre opted to create coronavirus Easter eggs. The
chocolate eggs, which have been painted black,
are dotted with red painted almonds to repli-
cate how the virus looks while viewed under a
microscope. Pre told French language newspaper Le Telegramme he devised the eggs to bring
some humor to the situation after growing "tired
of hearing" about coronavirus. He began selling them at his shop in Landivisiau, which is
located in Brittany, northwestern France, earlier
this month, a few weeks before France went into
lockdown. Meanwhile in western Germany, the
Schuerener Backparadies bakery has added two
different coronavirus-themed creations to its
selection. Not only can customers buy biscuit
versions of the face mask emoji, the establish-
ment, owned by Tim Kortuem, is also offering

toilet roll shaped cakes. A nod to the well-doc-
umented toilet paper shortage that's occurred
across the world as consumers frantically buy up
huge quantities, the marble cakes are wrapped in
white fondant etched with tiny diamond shapes
in the style of quilted toilet role. The novel cakes
were an instant hit with customers, and the team
at the bakery, situated in the city of Dortmund
in Germany's North Rhine-Westphalia region,
are currently making at least 200 a day. In
fact, Kortuem told Reuters Television the toilet
roll cakes are helping to keep the Schuererner
Backparadies in business during these difficult
times.

"The customers are totally crazy about it,"
he says. "Most people just like it as it adds some
fun to these times." Like France, and many countries around the world, Germany has imposed
extensive restrictions and many non-essential
businesses have been forced to close. However,
restaurants and eateries that offer food delivery
and pick-up are allowed to remain open. Over in
the US, a New York doughnut shop has dedicated
its latest offering to infectious disease expert Dr.
Anthony Fauci, a member of President Donald
Trump's coronavirus task force who's won the
public over with his straight-talking approach.
The team at Donuts Delite in Rochester decided
to make Fauci the "Face" of one of its doughnuts
as a way of lifting the mood. "We wanted to find
a way to cheer up the people in our neighborhood," owner Nick Semeraro told CNN. The
team were impressed by Dr. Fauci's handling of
the situation so far. "We loved his message and
how through he was, and how he kept everyone
informed during the crisis...so we wanted to give

back and say thanks." According to Semeraro,
the shop has sold thousands of the butter-
cream-frosted doughnut, which features Fauci's
face printed on edible paper, with customers asking for the treat to be sent to various cities and
states. "We had no idea it was going to blow up
this big," he said. "We didn't know everyone else
felt the same way we did." There's no word on a
coronavirus-themed pizza yet, but we suspect it
won't be far off.

There are so many people dying of the coronavirus, and I
wanted to talk about some of them. The reason many people died
is that I am done with the pairs, and the people that are considered
"flesh" are dying from the coronavirus.

A 33-Year-Old Member of the
Louisiana Governor's Staff Dies of
Coronavirus Complications

A 33-year old member of Louisiana Gov.
John Bel Edwards staff has died due to complications from coronavirus. April Dunn served in the
governor's office of disability affairs. "It is with
heavy hearts that we mourn the loss of our dear
April," Edwards said in a statement Saturday.
"She brightened everyone's day with her smile,
was a tremendous asset to our team and an inspiration to everyone who met her." Dunn served as
the chair of Louisiana Developmental Disabilities
Council was a part of the State as a Model
Employer Taskforce, Edwards said in the statement. "I was proud to have an advocate like April
on the task force and on my staff. She set a great
example for how other businesses could make
their workforce more inclusive," Edwards said.

Edwards announced Dunn's death on the same day as the US total reported coronavirus deaths jumped to more than 2,000. Nationwide, there are over 121,000 confirmed cases. Louisiana currently also more than 3,000 cases, and the numbers are climbing quickly. The state Department of Health says it is monitoring clusters at six nursing homes. The department is working to contain the spread at the facilities, spokeswoman Mindy Faciane said.

I wanted to talk more about the coronavirus because it seems like this is all on everybody's minds, and it is apocalyptic, but I do think that people are blowing it out of perspective.

Spanish Princess Becomes First
Royal to Die from Coronavirus

It was probably written in the script called Game of Thrones. Spain's Princess Maria Teresa of Bourbon-Parma has become the first royal in the world to die from coronavirus, according to a statement from her brother, Prince Sixto Enrique. The princess, a distant cousin of King Felipe VI, was 86 and died in Paris on Thursday, her brother said. Her funeral was help in Madrid on Friday. As of Sunday a total of 2,606 people in France had died from coronavirus, France's director-general of health, Jerome Salomon, said, marking an increase of 292 deaths in 24 hours. France recorded a total of 40,174 confirmed cases of the virus Sunday, according to the French public health website. That's 2,599 more cases than on Saturday, marking a 6.9% increase-a smaller rise than the past several days. Spain has also recorded a smaller percentage increase in case numbers in recent days. The country has recorded more than 80,000 cases and 6,803 deaths, according to figures from John Hopkins University. The British royal family has also been affected by the global pandemic. Prince Charles, first in line to the British throne, tested positive for coronavirus on March 25. Charles, 71, is currently self-isolating.

Here is another person who died of the coronavirus.

CBS Journalist Maria Mercader Dies at 54 of Coronavirus.

CBS News producer and talent executive Maria Mercader died of Covid-19 in New York Sunday, CBS said. She was 54. Mercader worked at CBS for three decades, getting her start in the network's page program, CBS said in a release. She most recently worked as a director of talent strategy. She had medical leave for an unrelated matter since late February, the network said. Mercader "courageously fought cancer and related illnesses for 20 years, enduring numerous treatments and surgeries," CBS said. "To her colleagues and family, she was an inspiration and a symbol of hope each time she returned to work after the latest medical setback threatened to end her life." As a producer on CBS News' foreign and national desks, Mercader helped produce coverage of "some of the biggest breaking news," including the death of Princess of Diana and the 9/11 attacks, the release said. "A hard hit to the heart, news longtime colleague and friend Maria Mercader died from coronavirus," tweeted former CBS News anchor Dan Rather. "A paragon of grit and grace, she embodied the best of the CBSNews mission. Millions of Americans learned of the world through her efforts. Now our world is less with her loss. RIP." In 2004, Mercader won an Emmy for business and financial reporting for her work producing a "CBS Sunday Morning" report on computer spam. As a talent executive, Mercader "helped spearhead" the networks efforts to diversify its workforce, CBS said. "Maria was a friend to all," said Laurie Orlando, senior vice president for talent at CBS News. "It's nearly impossible to be someone EVERYONE loves, but Maria was. She always had a warm hug, a word of advice or support and a big smile for everyone in her life. She was a bright light and will be sorely missed."

Nurses Die, Doctors Fall Sick and Panic Rises on Virus Front Lines

The pandemic has begun to sweep through New York City's medical ranks, and anxiety is growing among normally dispassionate medical professionals. A supervisor urged surgeons at Columbia University Irving Medical Center in Manhattan to volunteer for the front lines because half the intensive-care stuff had already been sickened by coronavirus. "ICU is EXPLODING," she wrote in an email. A doctor at Weill Cornell Medical Center in Manhattan described the unnerving experience of walking daily past an intubated, critically ill colleague in her 30s, wondering who would be next. Another doctor at a major New York City hospital described it as "a petri dish," where more than 200 workers had fallen sick. Two nurses in city hospitals have died.

The coronavirus pandemic, which has infected more than 30,000 people in New York City, is beginning to take a toll on those who are most needed to combat it: the doctors nurses and other workers at hospitals and clinics. In emergency rooms and intensive care units, typically dispassionate medical professionals are feeling panicked as increasing numbers of colleagues get sick. "I feel like we're all just being sent to slaughter," said Thomas Riley, a nurse at Jacobi Medical Center in the Bronx, who has contracted the virus, along with his husband.

Medical workers are still showing up day after day to face overflowing emergency rooms, earning them praise as heroes. Thousands of volunteers have signed up to join their colleagues. But doctors and nurses said they can look overseas for a dark glimpse of the risk they are facing, especially when protective gear has been in short supply. In China, more than 3,000 doctors were infected, nearly half of them in Wuhan, where the pandemic began, according to Chinese government statistics. Li Wenliang, the Chinese doctor who first tried to raise the alarm about Covid-19, eventually died of it. In Italy, the number of infected health care workers is now twice the Chinese total, and the National Federation of Orders of Surgeons and Dentists has compiled a list of 50 who have died. Nearly 14 percent of Spain's confirmed coronavirus cases are medical professionals. New York City's health care system is sprawling and disjointed, making precise infection rates among medical workers difficult to calculate. A spokesman for the Health and Hospitals Corporation, which runs New York City's public hospitals, said the agency would not share data about sick medical workers "at this time."

William P. Jacquis, president of the American College of Emergency Physicians, said the situation across the country was too fluid to begin tracking such data, but he said he expected the danger to intensify. "Doctors are getting sick everywhere," he said. Last week, two nurses in New York, including Kious Kelly, a 48-year old assistant nurse manager at Mount Sinal West, died from the disease; they are believed to be the first known victims among the city's medical workers. Health care workers across the city said they feared many more would follow. Mr. Riley, the nurse at Jacobi, said when he looked at the emergency room recently, he realized he and his colleagues would never avoid being infected. Patients struggling to breathe with lungs that sounded like sandpaper had crowded the hospital. Masks and protective gowns were in short supply. I'm swimming in this," he said he thought. "I'm pretty sure I'm getting this." His symptoms began with a cough, then a fever, then nausea and diarrhea. Days later, his husband became ill. Mr. Riley said both he and his husband appear to be getting better, but are still experiencing symptoms. Like generals steadying their troops before battle, hospital supervisors in New York have had to rally, cajole and sometimes threaten workers. "Our health care systems are at war with a pandemic virus," Craig R. Smith, the surgeon-in-chief at NewYork-Presbyterian Hospital, wrote in an email to staff on March 16, the day after New York City shut down its school system to contain the virus." You are expected to keep fighting with whatever weapons you're capable of working."

"Sick is relative," he wrote, adding that workers would not even be tested for the virus unless they were "unequivocally exposed and symptomatic to the point of needing admission to the hospital." "The means you come to work," he wrote. "Period." Arriving to work each day, doctors and nurses are met with confusion and chaos. At a branch of the Montefiore hospital system in the Bronx, nurses wear the winter coats in an unheated tent set up a triage patients with symptoms, while at Elmhurst Hospital Center in Queens, patients are sometimes dying before they can be moved into beds. The inviolable rules that once gave a sense of rhythm and harmony to even the busiest emergency rooms have in some cases been cast aside. Few things have caused more anxiety than shifting protocols meant to preserve a dwindling supply of protective gear. When the pandemic first hit New York, medical workers changed gowns and masks each time they visited an infected patient. Then, they were told to keep their protective gear on until the end of their shift. As supplies became even more scarce, one doctor working on an intensive care unit said he was asked to turn in his mask and face shield at the end shift to be sterilized for future use. Others are being told to store their masks in a paper bag between shifts.

"It put us in danger, it puts our patients in danger. I can't believe in the United States that's what's happening," said Kelley Cabrera, an emergency room nurse at Jacobi Medical Center. An emergency room doctor at Long Island Jewish Medical Center put it more bluntly: "It's literally,

wash your hands a lot, cross your fingers, pray."
Doctors and nurses fear they could be transmit-
ting the virus to their patients, compounding the
crisis by transforming hospitals into incubators
for the virus. That has happened in Italy, in part
because infected doctors struggle through their
shift, according to an article published by physicians at a hospital in Bergamo, a city in one of
the hardest-hit regions. Frontline hospital workers in New York are now required to take their
temperature every 12 hours, though many doctors and nurses fear they could contract the disease and spread it to patients before they become
symptomatic. They also say it is a challenge to
know when to come back to work after being
sick. All medical workers who show symptoms,
even if they are not tested, must quarantine for
at least seven days and must be asymptomatic for
three days before coming back to work. But some
employers have been more demanding than others, workers said. Lillian Udell, a nurse at Lincoln
Medical Center, another public hospital in the
Bronx, said she was still weak and experiencing
symptoms when she was pressured to return to
work. She powered through a long shift that was
so chaotic she could not remember how many
patients she attended. By the time she returned
home, the chills and the cough had returned. "I
knew it was still in me," she said. "I knew I wasn't
myself."

Christopher Miller, a spokesman for the
Health and Hospitals Corporation, said the
agency could not comment on Ms. Udell's claim,
but said its hospitals had "never asked health
care workers who are sick and have symptoms of
Covid-19 to continue to work or to come back

to work." There is also the fear of bringing the disease home to spouses and children. Some medical workers said they were sleeping in different rooms from their partners and even wearing surgical masks at home. Others have chosen to isolate themselves from their families completely, sending spouses and children to live outside the city, or moving into hotels. "I come home, I strip naked, put clothes in a bag and put them in the washer and take a shower," one New York City doctor at a large public hospital said. Because the pathogen has spread so widely, even medical workers not assigned directly to work with infected patients risk contracting the disease. A gynecologist who works for the Mount Sinai hospital system said she had begun seeing women in labor who were positive for the coronavirus. Because she is not considered a front-line worker, she said, restricting on protective gear are even more stringent than on Covid-19 units. She said she was not aware of any patients who had tested positive after contact with doctors or nurses, but felt it was only a matter of time.

"We're definitely contaminating pregnant mothers that we're assessing and possibly discharging home," said the doctor, who spoke on condition on anonymity because her hospital had not authorized her to speak. Mount Sinai said in a statement that it had faced equipment shortages like other hospitals, but added the issues had been solved in part by large shipment of masks that arrived from China over the weekend. The hospital "moved mountains" to get the shipment, the statement said. This week, the Health and Hospitals Corporation recommended transferring doctors and nurses at higher risk of infection-such as those who are older or with under-lying medical conditions-from jobs interacting with patients to more administrative positions. But Kimberly Marsh, a nurse at Westchester Medical Center outside New York City, said she has no intention of leaving the fight, even though she is a 53-year old smoker with multiple scle-rosis and on medication that warns against get-ting near people with infections. "It almost feels selfish," she said, though she acknowledged that with two years before retirement she could not afford leave if she wanted to. Even so, she said, the fear is palpable each time she steps into the emergency room. A nurse on her unit has already contracted the virus and one doctor is so scared he affixes an N95 mask to his face with tape at the beginning of each shift. Ms. Marsh said she sweats profusely in her protective gear because she is going through menopause and suffer from hot flashes. "We all think we're screwed," she said. "I know without any doubt that I'm going to lose colleagues. There's just no way around it."

I wanted to talk about this article because it is really important that we start addressing issues like this one. The article is talking about erectile dysfunction. I have been conquering everything while everyone's been living their normal lives until this coronavirus thing started happening. When I was going through the apocalyptic things in the past before it became known to the public, I was so fucking scared with certain things. One of those things was when I couldn't get my thing up, and I thought I was going to die alive. I had to have my mom sleep in the same room as me three nights in a row, and Hollywood had to come rescue me. It was how they came out with the script for the *Last Man Standing* and also the Will Smith movie *I Am Legend*. That shit was so scary, and it was because of lack of sleep. It was pretty much the end of time and the world. Now everyone is talking about apocalyptic stuff when I was actually going through all this bullshit before anyone knew anything was wrong with the world.

The article headline reads, "Men with Erectile Dysfunction May Face a Higher Risk of Early Death, Study Says."

Erectile dysfunction isn't just an issue in the bedroom. It could also be an indication of a man's risk for heart disease and early death. And this holds true, a new study says, regardless of a man's testosterone levels. Erectile dysfunction is defined as the inability to get or maintain an erection long enough to have sex, and it's a common condition affecting nearly 30 million American men, according to Harvard Medical School. It occurs more often in older men, and is often attributed to low levels of testosterone-the primary sex hormone that's key in the development of male reproductive tissues and for growing muscles, bone mass, and body hair. Low testosterone levels have previously been linked to a risk of early death for older men compared to those with normal levels of the hormone, but results from previous research has been inconsistent, said Dr. Leen Antonio of KU Leuven-University Hospitals in Belgium, the lead researcher on the new study examining the relationship between hormone levels and sexual function in men. What Antonio's team discovered indicates that a man's testosterone levels may not be as big of a warning sign as having erectile dysfunction, period.

"As both vascular disease and low testosterone levels can influence erectile function, sexual symptoms can be an early sign for increased cardiovascular risk and mortality," Antonio said. Her team's research published Tuesday in the Journal of the Endocrine Society. The researchers examined data from nearly 2,000 men ages 40 to 79 who participated in the European Male Ageing Study that investigated age-related hormonal changes and health outcomes in older men between 2003 and 2005. The participants' sexual symptoms, including erectile dysfunction, morning erections and libido, were measured via questionnaire, and their sex hormones were measured using mass spectrometry, which tells a researcher the presence and concentration level of a hormone. During a follow-up period of 12 years, about 25% of the men died. Antonio's research team found that of the men who died, the participants with normal testosterone levels and erectile dysfunction had a 51% higher risk of death than those without those symptoms. What's more, the men with low total testosterone and sexual symptoms had a greater risk of early death than those with normal testosterone levels and no sexual symptoms. The results indicated that overall, those with sexual symptoms—including erectile dysfunction and poor morning erections—had a higher risk of early death. Low libido was not associated with a higher risk of early death.

In addition to low testosterone levels, there are several potential causes of erectile dysfunction, chiefly by clogged arteries, or cardiovascular disease, which can impede the blood flow necessary to create an erection. That's why erectile dysfunction, regardless of testosterone levels, can flag a risk for heart disease and early death—the blood vessels that provide blood for an erection are smaller than the coronary arteries, Antonio said. "This means that in men with atherosclerosis (build-up plaque in the arteries causing obstruction of blood flow), the blood flow in the penile vessels is compromised earlier than in the coronary arteries," she added. Other possible causes of erectile dysfunction including certain medications; stress and anxiety; sleep disorders; smoking; alcohol consumption; nerve problems from prostate surgery; illnesses; and accidents. Psychological factors such as stress, relationship problems and depression may also contribute. Erectile dysfunction can be both prevented and treated by practicing a healthy lifestyle and, if necessary, treating heart disease risk factors such as smoking, high blood pressure, high cholesterol and obesity, Antonio said. "These things are also beneficial to improve general health and reduce mortality risk in men suffering from sexual dysfunction," Antonio said. "Men dealing with sexual dysfunction," Antonio said. "Men dealing with sexual symptoms should keep in mind that sexual symptoms could be an early warning sign of poor or worsening health status as well as increased risk for cardiovascular disease and mortality. "It is important to discuss sexual symptoms with your doctors, as to identify and treat other cardiovascular risk factors or apparent cardiovascular disease," he added.

I wanted to talk about this guy, and this was one guy I was targeting because he was written in the script for Supernatural that he was going to die.

He Was a "Perfectly Healthy"
44-Year-Old Father of Six
He Died from the Coronavirus

Adolph "TJ." Mendez was still playing basketball with friends earlier this month. He died from complications of COVID-19 on Thursday. "Every Sunday they would give out stickers to the kids in their bibles and the little kindergarteners would give him stickers to put on his name badge," Brenda Johnson, Mendez's daughter, told the Texas newspaper New Braunfels Herald-Zeitung. "He was very loved by all." From the pews of Oakwood Church, where he taught Kindergarteners on Sunday, to the local basketball court where he often played, Mendez was a beloved member of his close-knight community in Texas Hill Country. "He was patient, loving, kind, RIDICULOUSLY smart, and he was so silly," Johnson said in a statement provided to BuzzFeed News. "My dad was the type of person that could strike up a conversation with anyone and would make a friend everywhere he went. In my opinion, that usually describes fake people. He had an unbelievably big heart and loved to share it with everyone around him wherever he went." Mendez died Thursday due to complications stemming from COVID-19, the disease caused by the novel coronavirus. He was 44.

A water technician engineer who traveled often for his job, Mendez was the first member of the Texas community to die of the disease-leaving his town in shock. By all accounts, Mendez, who played college basketball at the University of Texas at San Antonio, was in excellent health. He was still active at his local basketball court earlier this month, playing up until the court was closed March 9, friends told KABB, the Fox affiliate in San Antonio. A kid at heart, Mendez could often be found jumping on the trampoline with his three young boys, the youngest of whom is just 9. After beginning to feel ill earlier this month,

Mendez started treating what he thought was a cold with over-the-counter medication, according to Johnson. When he didn't get any better, he visited his doctor, who gave him steroids in hopes of stopping what the doctor thought was a common virus. On Thursday, March 19, Mendez still didn't feel well and returned to his doctor. This time the doctor sent him to the hospital for a COVID-19 test. After he got the test, Mendez was told to go home and self-quarantine. But on March 23 at 3 am., Mendez was taken to a local hospital by ambulance after his fever spiked. That night, he was transferred to a hospital in Austin for an emergency surgery. The next day, he test results finally came back. He had COVID-19. By then Martinez was fighting for his life, dealing with multiple organ failure.

On Thursday, the family received a call. He had suffered from a massive brain hemorrhage. There was nothing more the doctors could do for him. "Before they unplugged him, they let us speak with him, they put the phone on speakerphone and all of his family were able to say goodbye," said Johnson. "the nurses held his hands the whole time and made sure to tell us that he was never alone throughout his entire stay." "We want people to know that they need to take this pandemic SERIOIUSLY-it is not just something that happens across the world," added Johnson. "This can happen to anyone, just as it did to us." The day after Mendez died, Ray Still, pastor at Oakwood Church, put out a statement on Facebook. Like Johnson, Still used his statement not only to mourn the loss of his parishioners but also to compel other members to take this disease seriously. "He was healthy and strong, and in no fault of his own, was stricken with this dreadful virus. His passing should be sobering to all, that this pandemic must be taken seriously," wrote Still. "God the giver of all good things, has given us a brain and we should use it for the benefit of our family and our communities. Follow what our officials have asked of us and we will endure with God's help."

Mendez is survived by his parents, wife Angela Mendez, and his six children—two of whom were from a previous marriage, according to his obituary. At the time of the obituary's publication, a date for his memorial still hadn't been set. Like so many who have lost loved ones to this virus, the family is mourning in quarantine. On the day her father died, Brenda Johnson changed her Facebook profile photo to one of her and her dad walking down the aisle at her wedding just last year, both with wide smiles on their faces, Johnson talked to the New Braunfels Herald-Zeutung about how she remembers that day. "It was really special to get him to do that for me," she told the newspaper. "I looked at him and told him that he wasn't allowed to look at me or I would start crying." "Before they opened the chapel doors, he looked down on me and I looked at him and we both started crying," she said. "It was the sweetest thing."

I wanted to write about this unemployment update, and I was just talking about it with my friend Rory.

Another 6.6 Million Americans Filed for
Unemployment Benefits Last Week

Another 6.6 million joined the U.S. unemployment rolls last week. More than 6.6 million people filed new claims for unemployment benefits last week, the Labor Department said Thursday, setting a grim record for the second straight week. The latest claims brought the two-week total to nearly 10 million. The speed and scale of the job losses is without precedent. Until last month, the worst week for unemployment filings was 695,000 in 1982. "What usually takes months or quarters to happen in a recession is happening in a matter of weeks," said Michelle Meyer, chief U.S. economist for Bank of America Merrill Lynch. A month ago, most forecasters still thought the United States could avoid a recession. Today, with the pandemic shuttering businesses and forcing vast layoffs, many economists are expecting a decline in gross domestic product that rivals the worst periods of the Great Depression.

The Labor Department's report on Thursday that 6.6 million Americans filed claims for unemployment benefits last week only increases the pressure on President Trump and members of Congress to ready another package to further aid workers and businesses through the coronavirus crisis. The 2.2 trillion package that Mr. Trump signed into law week includes enhanced benefits for unemployed workers for up to four months, along with aid for large and small businesses and direct payments to millions of individuals, as the country struggles through a shutdown of economic activity meant to slow the spread of the virus. Many economists have warned that the $350 billion included in that most recent package for aid to small businesses will not prove sufficient to help all of the companies that might otherwise go under during the shutdowns. R. Glenn

Hubbard, a Columbia University economist and former adviser to President George W. Bush, said in an interview that the necessary assistance was likely to be "closer to $1 trillion," which would require another $650 billion appropriation from Congress.

Democrats, including Speaker Nancy Pelosi of California, have pushed for additional payments to reach more Americans, to help people to continue to pay their bills through the crisis. Senator Sherrod Brown of Ohio has called for federally funded "hazard pay" for doctors, nurses, grocery store clerks, postal carriers and other workers on the front lines of the virus. Mr. Trump and Democratic leaders have also called for a sweeping investment in infrastructure, like broadband expansion and bridge repair, that could put millions of Americans to work once the crisis abates. Republican leaders in the House and Senate have shown less enthusiasm for many of those ideas. The arts-and-crafts chain Hobby Lobby was accused of defying stay-at-home orders in at least four states during the coronavirus outbreak, prompting officials to take action against the retailer. The moves by state and local authorities in Colorado, Indiana, Ohio and Wisconsin to shut the stores down came as governors across much of the United States have signed stay-at-home orders and health authorities have urged Americans to practice social distancing. Still, some haven't heeded the advice, from spring breakers to some megachurches. In Florida, a pastor was arrested after defying virus orders.

W. Eric Kuhn, the senior assistant state attorney general of Colorado, where there are 10 stores, sent a cease-and desist letter to the company after it had reopened its stores in the state this week. The letter said the company's actions violated a March 25 executive orders signed by Gov. Jared Polis directing Coloradans to stay at home and requiring all businesses to close that were not designated by state health officials as critical, Mr. Kuhn wrote that the company had until 5 p.m. on Thursday to comply with the closing order or the state would seek court relief, including a temporary restraining order. Ohio's attorney general, Dave Yost, wrote on Twitter on Wednesday that he had sent a similar cease-and desist letter to Hobby Lobby and that the company had agreed to close stores in his state, where there are 10. With a $350 billion emergency lending program for small businesses supposed to begin on Friday, bank lobbying groups have told the Treasury Department that the structure is unworkable and creates too much risk. The program, created as part of a $2 trillion spending plan passed by lawmakers last week, offers companies and nonprofit organizations with up to 500 workers to low-interest loan to cover up to two months of payroll and other expenses. Most—and in some cases, all-of the loans will be forgiven If the borrower retains workers and does not cut wages.

In letters and telephone calls, the groups have warned the Treasury Department that the program as written will not be workable, and that millions of businesses expecting funds to be approved and released in a matter of hours are likely going to be disappointed if the current government guidance is not updated. The top concern among banks is about their own liability as they try to rush money to borrowers while being required to verify their applications and keep tabs on potential fraud. Banks are concerned that they could be held liable for loans made to borrowers who provide inaccurate or fraudulent information. Remuneration for taking on these risks is also a worry. The Independent Community Bankers of America sent a letter to Treasury Secretary Steven Mnuchin on Wednesday complaining that the existing guidelines that call for loans to be made with 0.5 percent interest rates means that banks will not be able to break even on those loans, creating "unacceptable losses" for lenders. Amazon, which has come under fire from employees and politicians for not taking sufficient steps to protect workers on the job during the pandemic, said it would ramp up safety efforts.

The company said in a blog post on Thursday that temperature checks, which it began at certain facilities last Sunday, were likely to be put in place across all of its U.S. and European facilities and Whole Foods stores by early next week, and that it was already checking the temperatures of more than 100,000 workers each day. Anyone with a fever of more than 100.4 degrees is sent home and asked to stay home until they are freed of fever for three days, the company said. The company also said it was in the process of procuring more hand sanitizer and disinfectant wipes for workers, and that it was beginning to distribute millions of masks to workers. Workers who learned they had contracted the coronavirus or presumed they had but were unable to get tested could receive extra paid time off, and any worker who had contact with a person with the illness would receive 14 days of paid leave, Amazon said. Amazon also said that it had already hired 80,000 of the 100,000 new workers it had pledged to hire in mid-March to keep up with recent demand. Delta Air Lines told employees on Wednesday that it would allow flight attendants, baggage handlers, gate agents and other so-called front-line employees who were concerned about the coronavirus to stay home and still get paid.

Any employee concerned for their safety would be allowed to take voluntary leave and continue to be paid "in some form," according to an internal memo to managers that was viewed by The New York Times. Managers, who are referring to as "leaders" at Delta were also instructed not to question the employees about whether they were personally at higher risk and were told to share guidance from the Centers for Disease Control and Prevention on high-risk factors associated with the virus. "This is the right thing to do for our people who may be part of a high-risk group based on the latest C.D.C. guidance," the airline said in a statement to the Times. Separately, International Airlines Group, which operates British Airways, Iberia and other airlines, said on Thursday it was slashing its schedule by 90 percent in April and May. And British Airways said it had reached an agreement in which ease of its 4,000 pilots would take four weeks of unpaid leave over the next two months.

I thought this article from LinkedIn was cool to write about.

Goldman Sachs CEO: Remote Work
Policies Could "Attract" New Employees
after the Coronavirus Pandemic Is Over

To prevent the spread of COVID-19, cities across the U.S. have enacted social distancing measures, like shelter-in-place orders and bans on large gatherings. In keeping with these order, all non-essential employees have been mandated to work from home, if they are able to. That includes investment book and financial services company Goldman Sachs. A full 98% of the company's employees are working remotely, Goldman Sachs CEO David Soloman said in an interview on CNBC's "Squawk on the Street" on Thursday. To make it work, the company has had to adapt. "When you go through something like this, it forces you to ask questions and think about things differently," Solomon said. But even after the coronavirus pandemic calms down, Soloman believes the company will continue to see an increase in the use of video conferencing and become more comfortable with that type of technology. "It will make us more comfortable in providing more flexibility to employees, which, by the way, makes this a more attractive place for people to work," said Solomon.

The ability to work remotely can be enticing for workers. It can help provide work-life balance, improve job satisfaction and help employees save money. Allowing employees to work from home can pay off for companies as well, in ways including increased productivity, a study from researchers at the Stanford Graduate School of Business found. It's not just Goldman that could change. The coronavirus pandemic could have a lasting impact on companies and remote work policies nationwide, according to consulting organization Global Workplace Analytics. It estimates that within two years, 25% to 30% of the U.S. workforce will work from home on a regular basis. That's due to a number of factors, including increased demand from employees and renewed trust from managers. However, change at Goldman Sachs will not be swift and dramatic, Solomon says. It will be "gradual," as his man focuses right now are the safety and health of his employees, serving clients and helping communities. "There will be lots of time when we get through this to the other side to think about those other things," he said.

I think I have a good handle on this but I think the Spain's deaths from the coronavirus and the U.S.'s deaths will go down and all the other coronavirus deaths will go down. In my opinion Jeff should pay for all this because Jesus isn't going to forgive Judas this time around like he did the first time. The headline reads: Spain's coronavirus death toll shows sign of flattening. A further 809 people have now died from coronavirus in Spain, bringing the total to 11,744 deaths, according to Spanish Health Ministry figures released Saturday. The deaths represent a 7.3% rise but are the lowest increase since March 26. On Thursday, Spain's death toll surpassed 10,000, and the country joined Italy as one of only two to report five figure death tolls. The ministry's most recent data shows there are now 78,733 active cases of Covid-19 in Spain, an increase of 2,511 from Thursday—but also the smallest daily rise since March 20. A total of 6,532 people have been admitted to intensive care units since the pandemic began. The Spanish Health Ministry also reported that 34,219 people have recovered from the virus-which is roughly 4,000 more than the number reported Friday, and a 12% increase. While the number of active cases continues to rise, the rate of increase continues to slow. The latest numbers show the number of active cases recorded has risen 3% since Friday. The peak, on March 19, was a 27% increase in one day.

Spanish Prime Minister Pedro Sanchez has announced that the country's state of alarm, which demands strict limits on people's movements and continues the closure of schools and most businesses, will extend for another two weeks, until April 26. "We are facing the great crisis of our lives," Sanchez said in a nationwide address. The state of alarm had already been extended until April 11. The government will ask the Spanish parliament to approve the extension on Tuesday. Sanchez added: "Weeks of strict restrictions await us. We ask families to stay at home. To young people, to continue to study, to maintain momentum. To the elderly, to protect yourselves." He said that he understood how difficult it is for the nation to continue isolating at home for a further two weeks. These days test our serenity. They are frenetic days. They make us anxious for our friends and family. They are the most difficult days of our lives," Sanchez added. Sanchez also said that the government was preparing a plan for the eventual resumption of economic and social activity, once the curve of the coronavirus pandemic flattened. "Once the curve clearly descends, a new scenario will

open, a second stage, the progressive return to
a new social normality and to a reconstruction
of our economy and the social impact it is having in the form of job losses," Sanchez said. "In
reconstruction we will have to protect the most
vulnerable. In this emergency, no one will be left
behind. Our strength will come from the union
between business, administration and the different regions."

I just read this report, and it is important because we are trying
to fix people's mental illnesses in the world. Apparently, the coronavirus isn't helping this cause. The big difference between the coronavirus and the flu is that the coronavirus is apocalyptic and affecting every single person in the world. The headline reads, "A Crisis
Mental-Health Hotline Has Seen an 891% Spike in Calls."

People all over the nation are trying to cope
with the new normal of life during a pandemic.
Many are dealing with health issues, unemployment, grief and facing uncertainty what the
future holds. The Disaster Distress Helpline,
a federal crisis hotline, has seen a huge spike in
calls of people seeking help recently. The national
helpline, ran by the at the Substance Abuse
and Mental Health Services Administration
(SAMHSA), provides counseling for people
facing emotional distress during times of natural and human-caused disasters. In March, the
helpline saw a 33% increase in call volume compared with February, according to spokesperson
with the agency. And compared to last year for
the month of March, they had an 891% increase
of calls. The pandemic has disrupted normal life
routines and lead people isolation as they stay
home to curb the spread of the virus. During a

recent press briefing, President Donald Trump addressed the mental health crisis stating that it is a big problem and people are struggling.

American workers are suffering from devastating job losses, last week another 6.6 million people filed for unemployment benefits. Over 16,000 Americans have died because of the coronavirus leaving families grieving and unable to gather due to the social-distancing guidelines. "Stress, anxiety, and other depression-like symptoms are common reactions after a disaster," reads the program's website. The helpline is a free resource that is offering counseling and support to anyone in emotional distress due the disaster. They can provide advice on how to cope and offer information on how to spot sign of distress in friends and family members. Crisis counselors can also give callers referrals to local crisis centers for follow up care. The helpline was launched in 2012 and has provided assistance to residents during disasters such as hurricanes, massing shootings, wildfires, and now the coronavirus pandemic. Staff is available 24-hours-a-day, seven-days-a-week. People can call, 1-800-985-5990, or e even text, TALKWITHUS to 66746, to be connected to a trained counselor. People seeking help can remain anonymous and they can call for themselves or on behalf on someone else. Anyone is encouraged to use the helpline including: survivors of disasters; loved ones of victims; first responders; rescue, recovery, and relief workers; clergy; and parents and caregivers, the program's website reads.

Everyone is talking about the dangers of the coronavirus. Many people were worried about overpopulation and traffic. Well, when this is all over, I think many people, as long as they didn't lose loved ones, will be happy that we can live without so many useless people. New Jersey reported its deadliest 24 hours since the coronavirus outbreak began, with 365 more people dying. Another 778 people died in New York State. The one-day death toll in New York State from the coronavirus rose again, to 778, Governor Cuomo said Tuesday, after declining for two days. The state has now recorded 10,834 virus-related deaths. But other indicators that measure the fight to contain the virus continued to more encouraging, Mr. Cuomo said: The number of virus patients in hospitals across the state dropped about 1%, the first time it had declined since the outbreak's early days. The number of intubated patients-most of whom never recover-fell slightly for a second straight day. It has fallen three of the last four days. The total number of people who have tested positive in New York State has increased only a few percent per day in recent days. Another 7,177 tested positive, the state reported on Tuesday, bringing the total to 202,208. In New York City, 110,465 people have tested positive. "We think we are at the apex," Mr. Cuomo said at his morning briefing in Albany.

These New York officers are fighting a killer that can't be seen.

New Role for New York Police: Breaking Up Crowds at Trader Joe's

A message popped up on Sgt. Joseph Rosso's phone. It was not a robbery in progress, or a report of shooting, or a domestic dispute. The message said a small crowd had gathered outside a Trader Joe's grocery store in Lower Manhattan. Ordinarily, a cluster of people in front of a city store would not merit the police's attention. But these are not ordinary times. Shaking his head, Sergeant Rosso stepped on the gas, and the police cruiser lurched forward, its red and blue lights blaring. As the car nearing 14th Street and Second Avenue, about 10 people in front of the grocery store slowly stepped apart. "I've lived in the city my whole life, I've never imagined this," Sergeant Rosso said. "It's very surreal." This is law enforcement in the age of a pandemic, Sergeant Rosso and his partner, Officer Nicholas Contardo, are members of a 708-member task force that has been drawn from other duties to enforce social-distancing rules intended to stem the spread of the coronavirus. The epidemic has affected almost every aspect of policing in the nation's biggest city. Violent crime has dropped precipitously. Patrol officers find themselves reassigned to act as public health police of sorts, warning people not to socialize. Detectives are responding to a growing number of calls to investigate at home and wear Tyvek suits, gloves, masks and face shields to prevent exposure to the virus. Rank and file officers are carrying surgical masks and latex gloves along with their usual pistols, mace and handcuffs. And officers of every rank worry that mundane arrests, interviews and other interactions with people-activities they used to do without a thought-might lead to infection.

Mac P Dawg Murder Update: Single
Suspect Shot Rapper and Female
Companion, LAPD Says

Associate of shoreline Mafia hip-hop group was shot and killed Monday. Los Angeles police are pursuing a single suspect who shot and killed up-and-coming Los Angeles rapper mac P Dawg and injured an unidentified woman in the Koreatown Neighborhood neighborhood of L.A. on Monday night. The 24-year-old rapper, whose real name was Joshua Andrade Galvez, was killed shortly before 8 p.m. PT at the cross streets of Hobart Place and Beverly Blvd., LAPD public information officer Norma Eisenman told TheWrap. The unnamed female victim, approximately 20 years old, was transported to a local hospital and was in stable condition Monday night, Eisenman said. No further information about her or her condition was immediately available. "The suspect approached on foot, fired multiple rounds, striking both Vikings," Eisenman said, adding that Galvez was pronounced dead shortly after 8 p.m. "The suspect fled in a vehicle in an un-known direction." The investigation into the homicide is ongoing, Eisenman said, and no suspect has yet been named. Mac P Dawg was a friend and collaborator of former Shoreline Mafia member Fenix Flexin and current member Ohgeesy. He had just released a new music video last Friday for a song called "Salt Shaker" featuring rapper Doley Bernays. Last month, he released the video for a song called "Same Kid" featuring the rapper Bayline. He had also dropped music videos with both Fenix Flexin and Ohgeesy last year.

I have talked a lot about how Trump commuted sentences for people to get them out of jail. Well, this article heading reads, "California Governor Newsom Commutes Sentences for 21 People, Including Killers."

California Gov. Gavin Newsom on Friday commuted 21 prison sentences and pardoned five people who had already served their time behind bars, citing the coronavirus pandemic as a factor in his decision. Fourteen of the commuted cases involved murder or related charges.

In two of the cases, the victims were children. A pregnant woman was the victim in another case. Among those who had sentences commuted were Suzanne Johnson, 75, of San Diego County, who had served 22 years for assaulting a child who died; 64-year-old Joann Parks of Los Angeles County who served 27 years for the deaths of her three young children who were killed in a house fire, which Parks denies setting; and Rodney McNeal, 50, of San Bernardino County, who served 22 years for fatally stabbing his pregnant wife, a crime he also denies. Newsom's office said the clemency grants were in progress before the coronavirus outbreak, which has sickened more than 4,200 Californians. Attorneys representing inmates this week asked federal judges to free thousands of inmates to help prisons better confront the pandemic, which has sickened one inmate and 12 employees. Newsom said mass inmate releases would further burden strained community health care systems and homelessness programs. But he stopped transfers into the system for 30 days. The crisis affected his clemency decisions, spokeswoman Vicky Waters said in an email. Newsom "also considered the public health impact of each grant, as well as each inmate's individual health status and the suitability of their post-release plans, including housing," the governor's office said in a statement. Two of the pardons were intended to help lawful immigrants who face the possibility of being deported based on crimes they committed years ago. Waters said that would be "an unjust collateral consequence that would harm their families and communities."

I wanted to mention this article, and I think it's important to consider that the coronavirus is apocalyptic and that the flu is just part of the circle of life.

The Coronavirus Death Rate in the US Is Far Higher than That of the Flu—Here's How the Two Compare across Age Ranges

The flu and the new coronavirus have similar symptoms, but the latter is far deadlier. Here's how the two diseases' death rates compare among various age groups in the US. The coronavirus is five to 10 times more deadly than the flu for those between the ages of 0 and 45. It is 12 1/2 times more deadly than the flu for those over 85. Research from the Centers for Disease Control and Prevention shows how much more deadly the coronavirus is than the seasonal flu in the US. Many people have compared the flu to COVID-19, the disease caused by the coronavirus, because both can affect the respiratory system and their symptoms overlap. Even President Donald Trump recently said of the coronavirus: "You can call it a germ, a flu, a virus; you can call it many things." But the most crucial difference between the flu and the coronavirus is that the latter is far deadlier. While about 0.1% of people who get the flu die, the coronavirus' global death rate is about 4.7%, based on the current numbers of cases and deaths. However, the death rate of the coronavirus fluctuates constantly and varies strongly by country—in Italy, it was above 11% as of Monday, while it was 1.8% in the US. Death rates of both the flu and the coronavirus vary widely between age groups—the two seem to be most fatal in people over 65 years old. The comparison above shows that the coronavirus is more fatal than the flu across all age ranges but especially deadly among older people. That aligns with data from nearly every country with high numbers of coronavirus cases. The virus also more seriously affects people who have pre-existing health problems. Outbreaks among elderly populations in the US have proven especially tragic. Because the coronavirus spreads via droplets when people are in close contact and is deadliest for people over 80, nursing homes can be dangerous breeding grounds. An outbreak in the Life Care Center in Kirkland, Washington, killed 37 of the 120 people living there, according to Democracy Now. Many states, including Washington, Mississippi, and New York, have barred visitors from nursing and retirement homes.

The Flu infects millions of people every year and kills thousands. During the 2018–19 flu season, about 35 million people in the US contracted the flu and about 34,000 died, according to the CDC. The agency estimates the total number of flu infections in the US via its influenza-surveillance system, which gathers flu data from state and local partners and projects nationwide totals using infectious-disease models. During the 2018–19 season, about one out of every 1,000 people who got the flu died. However, breaking down the numbers by age range reveals a more complex story. Among children, there was about one death in every 10,000 cases. In adults between 50 and 64, about six out of every 10,000 people who got the flu died. For people 65 and older, the rate rose to about 83 out of 10,000. The flu's death rate varies depending on the strains circulating each year. The flu virus also mutates rapidly, so people can get infected by different strains, which is why the vaccine isn't 100% effective and new vaccines are developed every year.

About 10 percent of US coronavirus patients over 85 have died. In the US, the coronavirus has infected more than 153,000 people since the first case was reported on January 22. But that number likely far undercounts the true scope of patients because it represents only those who have gotten tested, and the US has been slow to expand testing capacity. People with symptoms mild enough to recover at home without seeking medical treatment aren't counted in the official totals. Even in New York, which has done the most testing per capita and has the US's highest case total and death toll, few people with noncritical cases are being tested. "Unless you are hospitalized and a diagnosis will impact your care, you will not be tested," New York City's health department said. The coronavirus' death rate changes as more cases are confirmed. Many health experts believe that the rate could drop if more mild and asymptomatic cases were tested.

Stopping the flu and coronavirus from spreading: The flu and the coronavirus spread in the same way: via viral particles that travel between people in tiny droplets of saliva or mucus. If a sick person sneezes, coughs, or eats within 3 to 5 feet of someone healthy, the particles could land on the healthy person; if the particles enter the person's eyes, nose, or mouth, the person can become infected. An average coronavirus patient infects two to 2 1/2 others. That makes COVID-19 more contagious than the seasonal flu. That's the reason so many countries are restricting residents' movement to encourage social distancing. Three-quarters of the US population has been told to stay at home.

The coronavirus can even affect people in my generation, and there have been several people from my generation who have died from this virus. The article headline reads, "Healthy, Strong Baseball Coach, 30, Dies of COVID-19 After Leaving Hospital."

Ben Luderer, a beloved New Jersey high school baseball coach, died in his home from COVID-19 at the age of 30 on Monday. His death occurred after he had been treated at a hospital and was briefly feeling better. The Cliffside Park School District confirmed the news of Luderer's death in a statement on Monday. In addition to being the head varsity baseball coach, he was a teacher for students with disabilities at the borough's School No. 6, which covers grades five through eight. Greg Butler—who was Luderer's baseball coach at Don Bosco Preparatory High School in Ramsey, New Jersey, when the team ranked number one in the country in 2008— told NJ.com that Luderer was "a healthy, strong, athletic 30-year-old." "Even the invincible aren't invincible," a shocked Butler said. "That was a group of guys who could not be beaten. Then something like this happens and shows just how vulnerable we all are."

Luderer's wife, Brandy Luderer, told BuzzFeed News that she tested positive for COVID-19 on March 19. Soon after, her husband began to show symptoms. Last Friday night, he went to a hospital where he was temporarily put on oxygen, prescribed medication, and then advised to go home lest being at the hospital lead to more severe illness. Brandy Luderer said he was doing better over the weekend and was able to get out of bed and hold conversations. But he took a turn for the worse on Sunday night. His wife, who was self-isolating from him by sleeping on the couch, said she began receiving texts from him that he was feeling sick again. "I went back to see what I could do. I tried as much as I could," she told BuzzFeed. "He was sweating through his clothes. He was scared." When she checked on him early the next morning, he was dead. Ben Luderer's friends, family and colleagues are mourning him online with an outpouring of love. The Cliffside Park School District's Facebook page has a memorial, which recalls Luderer as "a great coach, teacher, friend." Luderer's college baseball team, the Marist Red Foxes, paid tribute to Luderer on Twitter. "Saddened with the news of former student-athlete Ben Luderer's passing. He was tough, smart & a great teammate," the post reads. Ben's father, Bill Luderer, told local station ABC 7 NY that his son was "a gift" and that he had a "great sense of humor, he was kind of sarcastic at times, but he was loving and caring." That caring nature extended to his parents: Even as he was ailing, he felt guilty about having exposed them to the coronavirus before he knew his diagnosis. "My son would text or call literally every 15 minutes," Bill Luderer told ABC 7. "'How are you feeling? Are you doing OK? Have you taken your temperature?'" "It's not just the old, it's the young," the grieving father warned. "It's not just the sick, it's the healthy, and it can affect absolutely everyone."

This article is important, and it shows that Trump cares about people because he is a one-of-a-kind president. We needed a change at the front office, and I thought Trump brought a lot of positive changes during his presidency.

Trump Says It Doesn't Seem Fair That 30 Million Americans Are Uninsured and Suggests He May Expand Medicare or Medicaid

President Donald Trump suggested on Wednesday that he would consider opening up Medicare and Medicaid to more uninsured Americans as the coronavirus spreads across the US. Trump has long slammed Democratic proposals to expand government insurance and decided this week not to temporarily reopen the Obamacare marketplace to allow nearly 30 million uninsured Americans to purchase coverage during the pandemic. It's something we're really going to look at, because it doesn't seem fair," Trump said at Wednesday's White House briefing. "If you have it, you have a big advantage. And at certain income level you do." The exchanges are still open to those who recently lost their jobs, including the millions of Americans who've recently become unemployed as a result of the pandemic.

President Donald Trump suggested on Wednesday that he would consider opening up Medicare and Medicaid to nearly 30 million uninsured Americans as the coronavirus spreads across the US. It was a remarkable concession from a president who supports striking down the Affordable Care Act, also known as Obamacare—a move that would strip health insurance away from tens of millions of Americans. During Wednesday's coronavirus briefing, the Fox News White House correspondent John Roberts asked Vice President Mike Pence a series of pointed questions about the administration's decision this week not to temporarily reopen the Obamacare marketplace to allow uninsured Americans to purchase coverage during the pandemic. "There will be people who don't have insurance who get sick before any of these mitigation efforts are put into place," Roberts said. "And without opening the health-care exchanges, where can they find insurance? People who aren't insured by these companies that are covering the cost of the copays, where can people go, now, to get health insurance if they get—before they get sick?" Pence did not answer the question but argued that Medicaid and some American health insurance companies were making "inspiring" decisions to waive copays on coronavirus testing and treatment.

Trump stepped in and conceded that Roberts' question was "fair" and said Pence had skillfully dodged it. He said it "doesn't seem fair" that so many Americans can't afford to purchase insurance but don't qualify for Medicare or Medicaid—appearing to suggest those programs could be expanded to include more people. "John, I think it's a very fair question though, and it's something we're really going to look at, because it doesn't seem fair," Trump said. "If you have it, you have a big advantage. And at a certain income level you do." He continued: "I think it's one of the greatest answers I've ever heard, because Mike was able to speak for five minutes and not even touch your question. I said that's what you call a great professional." Trump said he believed he would "get to" addressing the problem and accused "the other group," presumably Democrats, of ignoring it, though Democrats have long made healthcare a critical policy issue. Sen. Bernie Sanders has aggressively pushed "Medicare for All," while former Vice President Joe Biden has advocated a public option, also known as "Medicare for all who want it."

"I think we're going to get to it," Trump said. "I don't think the other group will get to it. They haven't even spoken about it." But Trump said he wasn't "committing" to doing anything. "I can't commit," he said. "I have to get approval from it. I have thing called 'Congress.' But it's something we're going to look at, and we have been looking at it." Many Democrats and health insurance companies have pushed the White House to temporarily reopen the exchanges and criticized Trump's decision not to do so. "This callous decision will cost lives. Period," Biden tweeted on Wednesday. The exchanges will still be open to those who recently lost their jobs, including the millions of Americans who have recently become unemployed as a result of the pandemic.

I play four songs that can eliminate old people from this world. The songs I was listening to the other day led to this article headline: "Famed Restaurateur and Founder of Le Cirque Has Passed Away at 88."

Famed restaurateur and founder of LE Cirque, Sirio Maccioni, has passed away at the age of 88, according to his son. Le Cirque was a hot spot for the likes of Ronald and Nancy Reagan and Frank Sinatra, according to Marco Maccioni. Maccioni passed away in his hometown of Montecatini, Italy, on Monday morning in his sleep. This was actually because of Wiz Kalif's song I don't want to wake up from my sleep. After his working as a "maître d'hotel" in New York City's Colony Club, Maccioni opened Le Cirque in 1974, which was relocated a few times, until finding a home on Manhattan's East side in the Bloomberg Building in 2006. Le Cirque's lease ran out the end of 2018 and Maccioni's sons are looking to reopen Le Cirque on Manhattan's East Side once again in honor of their father when the coronavirus allows for it. "He was so proud of his work and he loved New York," Marco told CNN. "But no matter what, his greatest accomplishment wasn't the restaurants, it was being a father and I'm so lucky to have been his son." Maccioni is survived by his three sons, Mario, Marco, and Mauro as well as his wife, Egidiana, and his five grandchildren.

While Le Cirque and Sirio Maccioni were known to host many famous faces, they also helped launch the careers of many chefs, such as Daniel Boulud, David Bouley, Jacques Torres, and Geoffrey Zakarian. In an Instagram post, Boulud—who served as a chef at Le Cirque from 1986 to 1992—called Maccioni a "true legend." "I owe him all the respect and admiration for all that he did for me and my career as a chef. No one in the business was more elegant, savvy, and confident in running the dining room of #lecirque," Boulud captioned a picture of Maccioni. There was actually a part in Supernatural where Zacharian was the bad guy and he was killed in the script and I guess that's what they were talking about when they knew this old guy was going to die. Geoffrey Zakarian, who served as a line cook at Le Cirque, posted a picture with Maccioni to his Instagram to remember the late restaurateur. "Sirio Maccioni on the far left in the suit ran the most sophisticated and notable restaurant for over 30 years, the caption reads. "Those that passed away through his doors learned about food, hospitality and family directed from him, the one and only."

I want to write about this story because it talks about the Mafia, and God did shadow play so that I could end their regime and their empires. The headline reads, "Mafia Is Poised to Exploit Coronavirus, and Not Just in Italy."

Earlier this month, there was a funeral procession in the Sicilian town of Messina, in defiance of a nationwide lockdown in Italy. It was no ordinary procession. The couple of dozen people walking behind the hearse were paying their respects to a 70-year-old scion of one of the most notorious Mafia Famiglie. Claudio Fava, president of the regional anti-Mafia committee, described it as a "real scandal, an insult to those who lost their relatives in the pandemic." Funerals have been banned in Italy since early March as part of a broader set of restrictions aimed at curbing the Covid-19 outbreak that has killed nearly 23,000 people as of Friday.

That the procession took place at all speaks to the power—and the impunity—wielded by the Mafia in parts of Italy. Senior anti-mafia officials and researchers have told CNN that Mafia clans are already taking advantage of the coronavirus pandemic, especially in southern Italy. They are providing everyday necessities in poor neighborhoods, offering credit to businesses on the verge of bankruptcy and planning to siphon off a chunk of the billions of euros being lined up in stimulus funds. The most powerful branch of the Mafia—the "Ndrangheta, based in Calabria—is thought to control 80% of the European cocaine market. Evan as the pandemic made distribution more difficult, it took advantage of the lock-down. Journalist Roberto Saviano—author of "Gomorrah: Italy's other Mafia' an expose of the Camorra mafia in Naples—told CNN that "the traffickers took advantage of the lack of oversight of law enforcement in the ports, in the airports." "Who was checking any more?" he asked.

But Mafia groups are far more than traffick-ing cocaine. They are deeply embedded in the economy. While traditional Mafia activities such as extortion may suffer during the pandemic, there will also be fresh opportunities, said Anna Sergi, senior lecturer in criminology at the University of Essex. Frano Gabrielli, head of the Italian police, said that Mafia organizations are already deeply enmeshed in parts of the economy "that have not been blocked by the restrictions of Covid-19: the agriculture-food chain, the supply of medicines and medical equipment, road transport." It's a view shared by Saviano. "Funeral homes they invest in, hospital laundries. Cleaning companies they've always invested in. Good delivery compa-nies, gas stations, this is the portfolio they've had for the past 10 years," he told CNN. Such is the financial muscle of the 'Ndrangheta, Gabrielli said last week, that it could exploit a desperate need for cash faced by businesses it doesn't cur-rently control. "At the end of the emergency, the criminal associations could have polluted the economy, controlling companies previously not infiltrated," he said.

Sergi says past crisis have shown that the Mafia can move money quickly outside the banking system and demand fewer guarantees than book. Lending money to distressed companies and then gradually taking control of them is a well-oiled mafia tactic. Nicola Gratteri, an anti-Mafia investigator and head of the public prosecutor's office in Catanzaro, told CNN that businesses like restaurants and hotels are especially vulnerable. The last great recession, in 20008, offers a sobering comparison. Anti-Mafia groups like SOS impresa said that crisis turned the Mafia into Italy's largest bank. This also has to do with the bank job in Italy with Jason Statham. The Palermo-based group estimated in 2012 that the Mafia had 65 billion euros ($72 billion) in liquidity and described extortionate lending as "a national emergency." At the same time, many Italian banks were struggling to stay afloat and borrowing heavily from the European Central Bank. Saviano believed liquidy will be "the center of everything" in the aftermath of the coronavirus crisis.

"the organization will come to a company in crisis and say: "We don't buy everything, but we will give you cash in exchange for shares—to become part of your company," he said. "this is what they will do with everyone." At the end of last month, video footage of a couple hammering at the doors of a bank in the southern city of Bari went viral. "You suck, the state sucks. How are we going to manage?" the woman shouts. These exactly the sort of circumstances the Mafia exploits. The "Ngrandheta and other clans don't simply live off societies where they are strong. They build loyalty by supplying necessities to poorer neighborhoods and cash to struggling businesses. To Gratteri, this is "a method to create allegiance. If we—the state—don't show ourselves to be efficient, what could happen is that the Mafia presents itself as a winning a model, and maybe asks for a return favor at the elections."

Zora Hauser, a researcher into organized crime at Oxford University, said that "what we are seeing—and will see more and more as the economic and social crisis unfolds—is Mafia groups returning to their core businesses of protection and governance." Salvo Palazzolo, a journalist with La Repubblica newspaper, receiving threats after reporting on food handouts by someone with Mafia connections in the poor "ZEN" district of Palermo in Sicily. "At this moment, Mafia families of Palermo (The Cosa Nostra_ are very strong, especially in drugs and online gambling. They have a lot of liquidity, "Palazzolo told CNN. "I would say the Cosa Nostra are strengthening their control through welfare assistance to families who are in jail, and now this is spreading to all poor families. They want to show themselves as an alternative to the state." In another district of Palermo, a local Mafia boss tried to organize a Good Friday church service in defiance of the lockdown before police intervened.

Criminologist Anna Sergi says the Mafia want the community both to like and need them. The government is aware of the danger CNN obtained a letter written by Interior Minister Luciana Lamorgese to regional leaders warning that criminal organizations would try to use "forms of support" to gain popularity. As Zora

Hauser puts it: "This can be cashed by the organization in different ways, the most worrying one being votes." The government has established a 400 million-euro ($435 million) food voucher fund and allotted another 4.3 billion euros ($4.8 billion) to local mayors. As Prime Minister Giuseppe Conte promised on March 28: "We know that many suffer, but the state is there." But it's a daunting challenge. Saviano says that during this crisis, the mafia will try to hire the "new unemployed" as its foot soldiers. As many as three million Italians work "off the books," according to multiple surveys. One survey by the Organisation for Economic Co-operation and Development in 2017 estimated that a quarter of Italians in their early 20s were neither in employment, nor in education or training.

Getting Italy back to work is the government's priority. It's injecting 750 billion euros ($815 billion) into the economy. Part of the investigation is to guarantee loans to businesses—covering more than three-quarters of a large company's borrowing. But given the massive sums being dispersed, anti-Mafia investigators worry that some of those loans, as well as other support, will go to Mafia-run businesses. Italy also wants Europe-wide "coronabonds," basically a pooling of debt among EU member states. One German commentator, Christoph Schiltz, urged German Chancellor Angela Merkel to reject the idea, writing in Die Welt newspaper that "the mafia is just waiting for a new shower of money from Brussels." Italian Foreign Minister Luigi Di Maio described Schiltz' comments as "shameful and unacceptable." Saviano said: "European funds today help the Italian economy that is on its knees. And an Italian economy that is on its knees. And an Italian economy on its knees means Italy is at the mercy of organized crime." It's not just Italy's problem. The Mafia's tentacles spread across Europe and far beyond. The "Ngrandheta has a Europe-wide network for distributing drugs, often using pizza restaurants at fronts. It has also invested in property.

For now, reinforced border controls and nationwide lockdowns are choking distribution networks for drugs. But like the coronavirus, the mafia groups are no respecter of border. "The Mafia is very powerful also in Germany," said Roberto Saviano. "they shoot less, but they are very powerful." Earlier this month, Pope Francis prayed for "people who during this time of the pandemic, trade at the expense of the needy and profit from the needs of others, like the Mafia, usurers and others." "May the Lord touch their hears and convert them," the Pope said. History, as well as current evidence, suggests he may be disappointed.

I wanted to talk about this story because when people stay in the same home with the same people for an extended period, bad things can happen.

A Teen Was Allegedly Killed by His
Stepfather after He Refused to Stay
Home and Shelter in Place, Police Say

It began as a fight over a stay-at-home directive. By the end, a teenage boy was dead. Atlanta police say they responded to a call of a person shot just after 8 p.m. Wednesday. When they arrived, they found 16-year-old De'onte Roberts gravely wounded. He had been shot in the chest during a domestic dispute with his stepfather, 42-year-old Bernie Hargrove, Atlanta Police Department spokesman Steve Avery told CNN. Roberts was taken to Grady Memorial Hospital, where he died from his injuries. According to a statement police shared with CNN, the dispute began earlier in the day, when Roberts refused his parents' order to remain at home and comply with recent shelter-in-place directives, his mother told detectives.

When Roberts returned home and kicked in the door to the house, a physical fight began between Roberts and Hargrove, the mother told detectives. Roberts was shot during that alter-cation, the statement said. Homicide detectives interviewed Hargrove and charged him with felony murder, according to a police statement. Tracy Flanagan, public affairs officer with the Fulton County Sheriff's Office, told CNN that Hargrove had a first appearance hearing Thursday morning and bond was denied. He is being held in the Fulton County jail. CNN's attempts to contact Hargrove's attorney were unsuccessful. Georgia was one of the later states to implement shelter-in-place order due to the ongoing spread of the coronavirus. Monday, Gov. Brian Kemp announced his plans to allow certain businesses such as fitness centers, bowling alleys and hair salons to reopen on Friday. Fulton County, which includes Atlanta, has recorded 2,436 cases of the virus with 88 deaths as of Thursday, according to the Georgia Department of Public Health.

"Wall Street Powers through Waves of Bad Economic News to One of Its Best Months in Decades" is how the headline of the next article reads. I wanted to write about this because the 1 percent are working on a solution for the world every day, and they are helping me fix the issues that are at hand for the time being. They are good people who want to fix humanity.

Investors looked past weeks of grim economic news to power Wall Street to its best month in decades, even as the three major indexes ended the day in the red. The Standard & Poor 500 index posted its strongest one-month returns since 1987, at a time when the nation saw its economy shrivel and lose 30 million jobs amid the coronavirus outbreak. The gains came even as covid-19 deaths accelerated, surpassing 60,000 on Thursday. The broad S&P 500 index closed April more than 12 percent higher than it started. The blue-chip Dow Jones industrial average closed out its best month since October 2002 with a 10 percent gain. The tech-heavy Nasdaq composite surged 14 percent for the month. Investors have gotten reassurances from the federal government and central bank, which flooded Wall Street and Main Street with trillions in rescue programs. The government pledged to backstop businesses, provide for the unemployed, rescue a grounded commercial air fleet and "The bottom line is don't fight the Red and don't fight the government," said Kenny Polcari of Slatestone Wealth. "We are where we are because of the massive unconditional programs the government has implemented and has promised to implement. There will be a re-pricing of stocks down the road, so enjoy this while it lasts." For the day, the Dow shed 239 points, nearly 1 percent, to close to 24,394.72. The S&P 500 fell 27 points, or 0.9 percent, to 2,912.43.

The Nasdaq slipped 25 points, or 0.3 percent, to finish at 8,889.55.

This article seemed interesting to me, so I wanted to write about it.

De Blasio Says It Was Unacceptable That Bodies Were Stored in U-Haul Trucks

Mayor Bill de Blasio on Thursday said it was "absolutely unacceptable" that dozens of bodies were being stored in unrefrigerated trucks outside a Brooklyn funeral home amid a surge in deaths due to the coronavirus pandemic. "This horrible situation that occurred with the funeral home in Brooklyn is absolutely unacceptable—let's be clear about that," de Blasio told reporters during a conference call. The Andrew T. Cleckley Funeral Services in Flatlands "shouldn't have let it happen," de Blasio said. "Funeral homes are private organizations. They have an obligation to the people they serve to treat them with dignity," the mayor said, adding, "I have no idea how they would let that happen." The NYPD responded to a 911 call around 11:30 a.m. Wednesday for a report of human bodies inside two vehicles near the funeral home on Utica Avenue near Avenue L. Police determined the vehicles belonged to the funeral home, an NYPD spokesperson said. The state Department of Health was notified of the gruesome situation and an investigation is ongoing, according to the spokesperson.

Sources previously told the Post that between 40 and 60 bodies were discovered either stacked in U-Haul trucks outside the funeral home or on the building's floor after neighbors reported a foul odor. The funeral home had two refrigerated trucks stored bodies in addition to the two U-hauls holding corpses, sources have said. Outside the funeral home Thursday, at least one body was seen being taken out of a refrigerated truck. Hizzoner questioned why the funeral home did not contact the state or the NYPD for help with the body situation. "It is unconscionable to me," de Blasio said. "You're talking about the deceased loved ones of family. I'm sorry, it's not hard to figure out if nothing else is working, call the NYPD," said the mayor. "it was an emergency situation." De Blasio added, "I'm very disappointed they didn't do that...They do bear responsibility, they should have figured it out." On Wednesday, Brooklyn Borough President Eric Adams descended on the score outside the funeral home and said the city needed a "bereavement committee" to deal with the uptick of deaths due to the coronavirus crisis. De Blasio called Adams' proposal "a good idea." "We'll find some way to create something like that," the mayor said.

I wanted to write about this because I think it's awesome when I can own something I did, especially when I get into those mindsets where anything goes in this world. The headline of this article reads, "Brian Howe, Singer and Former Bad Company Frontman, Dies at 66."

Brian Howe, former frontman for the British rock group Bad Company, died at Tuesday at age 66, his friend and longtime manager Paul Easton told CNN. Howe was found in his home suffering from cardiac arrest. While Howe was able to briefly speak to EMTs, he died in his home after they were unable to revive him, Easton said in a statement. "Finding the appropriate words to express the pain in our hearts over losing my brother has been difficult," Howe's sister Sandie said in a statement. "Our family would like to thank you for your compassion and the outpouring of love we are receiving." Born in Portsmouth, England, Howe got his career started singing on Ted Nugent's "Penetrator" album. Years later, Howe was chosen to take over as the lead singer for Bad Company after the departure of singer Paul Rodgers. The singer and songwriter was the frontman for Bad Company for eight years. "I feel we are all put in this world for a reason" Howe's son Michael said in a statement. "The passion for music was my father's and I am so happy that his legacy will live on." Howe is also survived by his daughters Victoria and Ella.

I wanted to talk about this article because I am conquering everything, and I am the only person in the world who falls under all the categories in the world, which includes bringing us out of debt and this great depression. The headline reads, "US Unemployment Rate Soars to 14.7 Percent, the Worst since the Depression Era."

The U.S. unemployment rate jumped to 14.7 percent in April, the highest level since the Great Depression, as most businesses shut down or severely curtailed operations to try and limit the spread of the deadly coronavirus. The jobless rate was pushed higher because 20.5 million people lost their jobs last month, the Labor Department said Friday, wiping out a decade of job gains in a single month. The staggering losses are roughly double what the nation experienced during the 2007–09 crisis, which used to be described as the harshest economic contraction most people ever endured. Now that has been quickly dwarfed by the fallout from the global pandemic. During March and April, President Trump and numerous state and local leaders moved to put the economy in a deep freeze in an effort to minimize exposure to the virus. This led businesses to suddenly shed millions of workers at a rapid rate. Analysts warn it could take many years to return to the 3.5 percent unemployment rate the nation experienced in February. Trump, though, claimed in a Fox News interview Friday that there would be a quick rebound. "Those jobs will all be back, and they'll be back very spoon," Trump said.

Governors are now debating when to re-open parts of their state economies. They are weighing the health costs and the economic toll, a harrowing choice, analysts say. There's hope that re-opening quickly will get people back to work, but the job losses are so large that it's unlikely many will be able to return, especially when many businesses operating at partial capacity. "This is pretty scary," said Lindsey Piegza, chief economist at Stifel. "I'm fearful many of these jobs are not going to come back and we are going to have an unemployment rate well into 2021 of near 10 percent. The sudden economic contraction has forced millions of Americans to turn to food banks and seek government aid for the first time or stop paying rent and other bills. As they go without paychecks for weeks, some have also lost health insurance and even put their homes up for sale. Job losses began in the hospitality sector, which shed 7.7 million jobs in April, but other industries were also heavily impacted.

Retail lost 2.1 million jobs and manufacturing lost 1.3 million jobs that typically prove resilient during downturns were also slashed, with firms shedding 2.1 million jobs, and state and local governments losing nearly a million. More slashed in the coming weeks as officials deal with severe budget shortfalls.

There was even 1.4 million layoffs in health care last month, as patients have been putting off things beyond emergency care. Even though the April unemployment figure was horrific by most accounts, economists say the official government rate almost certainly underestimates the extent of the job losses. The Labor Department said the unemployment rate would have been about 20 percent if workers who said they were absent from work for "other reasons" had been classified as unemployed or furloughed. What's clear so far is that Hispanics, African-Americans and low-wage workers in restaurants and retail have been the hardest hit by the job crisis. Many of these workers were already living paycheck-to-paycheck and had the least cushion before the pandemic hit. "Low-wage workers are experiencing their own Great Depression right now," said Ahu Yildirmaz, co-head of the ADP Research Institute, which focuses on the job and wage trends. The unemployment rate in April jumped to a record 18.9 percent for Hispanics, 16.7 percent for African-Americans and 14.2 percent for whites. Women's unemployment was nearly three points higher than men's unemployment, another disparity that largely reflects the prevalence of women in hard hit hospitality and retail jobs. While many highly educated white collar workers have been able to do their jobs from home, low-wage workers don't have that luxury. In April, the unemployment rate soared to 21.2 percent for people with less than a high school degree, surpassing the previous all-time high set in the aftermath of the Great Recession.

While Congress has approved nearly $3 trillion in aid, it's been slow to arrive for many. Millions are still battling outdated websites and jammed phone lines to try to get unemployment aid and a relief check. Economists are urging Congress to act now to ensure aid does not end this summer when the unemployment rate is still likely to be at historic levels. "This unemployment rate should be a real kick in the pants—and maybe even the face," said economist Claudia Sahm, a former Federal Reserve staffer and expert on recessions. "Congress has to stay the course on aid until more people are back at work." There's a growing consensus that the economy is not going to bounce back quickly like Trump wants, even as more businesses re-open this month. Many restaurants, gyms, and other firms are only able to operate at limited capacities, and customers are proving to be slow to return as they are fearful of venturing out. Many businesses also won't survive. All of this means the economy is going to need far fewer workers for months—or possibly years—to come. "We're not going to go sharply down the sharply up. We went sharply down and we'll go gradually up," Thomas Barkin, president of the Federal Reserve Bank of Richmond, said Thursday.

Many businesses initially did temporary layoffs because executives believed the shutdowns would be short-lived. About 18 million of the unemployed in April said their layoff was temporary, according to the Labor Department data, versus only about 2 million who said their job loss was permanent. But the permanent layoffs are expected to escalate as time goes on. The Labor Department surveyed workers in mid-April. "This is a catastrophe. When things go over a cliff, they usually they don't recover quickly," said Danny Blanchflower, an economics professor at Dartmouth.

I have dealt with these problems, so I wanted to write about them in my book. The headline reads, "Doctors Keep Discovering New Ways the Coronavirus Attacks the Body."

Damage to the kidneys, heart, brain-even COVID toes prompts reassessment of the disease and how to treat it. Deborah Coughlin was neither short of breath nor coughing. In those first days after she became infected by the novel coronavirus, her fever never spiked about 100 degrees. It was vomiting and diarrhea that brought her to a Hartford, Conn., and emergency room in May 1. "You would have thought it was a stomach virus," said her daughter, Catherina Coleman. "She was talking and walking and completely coherent." But even as Coughlin, 67, chatted with her daughters on her cellphone, the oxygen level in her blood dropped so low that most patients would be near death. She is on a ventilator and in critical condition at St. Francis Hospital, one more patient with a strange constellation of symptoms that physicians are racing to recognize, explain and treat. "At the beginning, we didn't know what we were dealing with," said Valentin Fuster, physician-in-chief at Mount Sinai Hospital in New York City, the epicenter of the U.S. outbreak. "We were seeing patients dying in front of us. It was all of a sudden, you're in a different ballgame, and you don't know why."

Today, there is widespread recognition the novel coronavirus is far more unpredictable than a simple respiratory virus. Often it attacks the lungs, but it can also strike anywhere from the brain to the toes. Many doctors are focused on treating the inflammatory reactions it triggers and its capacity to cause blood clots, even as they struggle to help patients breathe. Learning about a new disease on the fly, with more than 78,000 U.S. deaths attributed to the pandemic, they have little solid research to guide them. The World Health Organization's database already lists more than 14,600 papers on covid-19. Even the world's premier public health agencies, including the Centers for Disease Control and Prevention, have constantly altered their advice to keep pace with new developments. "We don't know why there are so many disease presentations," said Angela Rasmussen, a virologist at the Center for Infection and Immunity at Columbia University's Mailman School of Public Health. "Bottom line, this is just so new that there's a lot we don't know about."

More than four months of clinical experience across Asia, Europe and North America has shown the pathogen does much more than invade the lungs. "No one was expecting a disease that would not fit the pattern of pneumonia and respiratory illness," said David Reich, a cardiac anesthesiologist and president of Mount Sinai Hospital in New York City. It attacks the heart, weakening its muscles and disrupting its critical rhythm. It savages kidneys so badly some hospitals have run short of dialysis equipment. It crawls along the nervous system, destroying taste and smell and occasionally reaching the brain. It creates blood clots that can kill with sudden efficiency and inflames blood vessels throughout the body. It can begin with a few symptoms or none at all, then days later, squeeze the air out of the lungs without warning. It picks on the elderly, people weakened by previous disease, and disproportionately, the obese. It harms men more than woman, but there are also signs it complicates pregnancies. It mostly spares the young. Until it doesn't: Last week, doctors warned of a rare inflammatory reaction with cardiac compilations among children that may be connected to the virus. On Friday, New York Gov. Andrew M. Cuomo announced 73 children had fallen severely ill in the state and a 5-year old boy in New York City had become the first child to die of the syndrome. Two more children had succumbed as of Saturday.

That news has shaken many doctors, who felt they were finally grasping the full dimensions of the disease in adults. "We were all thinking this is a disease that kills old people, not kids,' Reich said. Mount Sinai has treated five children with the condition. Reich said each started with gastrointestinal symptoms, which turned into inflammatory complications that caused very low blood pressure and expanded their blood vessels. This led to a heart failure in the case of the first child who died. "The pattern of disease was different than anything else with COVID," he said. Of the millions, perhaps billions, of coronavirus, six were previously known to infect humans. Four cause colds that spread easily each winter, barely noticed. Another was responsible for the outbreak of severe acute respiratory syndrome that killed 774 people in 2003. Yet another sparked the outbreak of Middle East respiratory syndrome in 2012, which kills 34 percent of the people who contract it. But few do. SARS-Cov-2, the bad seed of the coronavirus family, is the seventh. It has managed to combine the infectiousness of its cold-causing cousins with some of the lethality of SARS and MERS. It can spread before people show symptoms of disease, making it difficult to control, especially without widespread and accurate testing. At the moment, social distancing is the only effective countermeasure.

It has infected 4 million people around the globe, killing more than 280,000, according to the Johns Hopkins University Coronavirus Resource Center. In the United States, 1–3 million have been infected and more than 78,000 have died. Had SARS or MERS spread as widely as this virus, Rasmussen, they might have shown the same capacity to attack beyond the lungs. But they were snuffed out quickly, leaving only a small sample of disease and death. Trying to define a pathogen in the midst of an ever-spreading epidemic is fraught with difficulties. Experts say it will be years until it is understood how the disease damages organs and how medications, genetics, diets, lifestyles and distancing impact its course. "This is a virus that literally did not exist in humans six months ago," said Geoffrey Barnes, an assistant professor at the University of Michigan who works in cardiovascular medicine. "We had to rapidly learn how this virus impacts the human body and identify ways to treat it literally in a time-scale of weeks. With many other diseases, we have had decades." In the initial days of the outbreak, most efforts focused on the lungs. SARS-COV-2 infects both the upper and lower respiratory tracts, eventually working its way deep into the lungs, filling tiny air sacs with cells and fluid that choke off the flow of oxygen.

But many scientists have come to believe that much of the disease's devastation comes from two intertwined causes. The first is the harm the virus wreaks on blood vessels, leading to clots that can range from microscopic to sizable. Patients have suffered strokes and pulmonary emboli as clots break loose and travel to the brain and lungs. A study in the Lancet, a British medical journal, showed this may be because the virus directly targets the endothelial cells that line blood vessels. The second is an exaggerated response from the body's own immune system, a storm of killer "cytokines" that attack the body's own cells along with the virus as it seems to defend the body from the invader. Research and therapies are focused on these phenomena. Blood thinners are being more widely used in some hospitals. A review of record for 2,733 patients, published Wednesday in the Journal of the American College of Cardiology, indicates they may help the most seriously ill.

"Things change in science all the time. Theories are made and thrown out. Hypothesis are tweaked. It doesn't mean we don't know what we are doing. It means we are learning," said Deepak Bhatt, executive director of interventional cardiology at Brigham and Women's Hospital in Boston. Inflammation of those endothelial cells lining blood vessels may help explain why the virus harms so many parts of the body, said Mandeep Mehra, a professor of medicine at Harvard Medical School and one of the authors of the Lancet study on how covid-19 attacks blood vessels. That means defeating covid-19 will require more than antiviral therapy, he said. "What the virus does is it starts as a viral infection and becomes a more global disturbance to the immune system and blood vessels—and what kills is exactly that," Mehra said. "Our hypothesis is that covvid-19 begins as a respiratory virus and kills as a cardiovascular virus." The thinking of kidney specialists has evolved along similar lines. Initially, they attributed widespread and severe kidney disease to the damage caused by ventilators and certain medications given to intensive-care patients, said Daniel Batlle, a professor of medicine at Northwestern University Feinberg School of Medicine.

Then they noticed damage to the waste-filtering kidney cells of patients even before they needed intensive care. And studies out of Wuhan found the pathogen in the kidneys themselves, leading to speculation the virus is harming the organ. "There was nothing unique at first," Batlle said. But the new information "shows this is beyond the regular bread-and-butter acute kidney injury that we normally see." Like other coronaviruses, SARS-COv-2 infiltrates the body by attaching to a receptor, ACE2, found on some cells. But the makeup of the spikes that protrude from this virus is somewhat different, allowing the virus to bind more tightly. As a result, fewer virus particles are required to infect the host. This also may help explain why this virus is so much more infections than SARS, Rasmussen said. Other factors can't be ruled out in transmission, she said, including the amount of virus people shed and how strictly they observe social distancing rules. Once inside a cell, the virus replicates, causing chaos, ACE2 receptors, which help regulate blood pressure, are plentiful in the lungs, kidneys and intestines—organs hit hard by the pathogen in many patients. That also may be why high blood pressure has emerged as one of the most common preexisting conditions in people who become severely ill with covid-19.

The receptors differ from person to person, leading to speculation that genetics may explain some of the variability in symptoms and how sick some people become. Those cells "are almost everywhere, so it makes sense that the virus would cause damage throughout the body," said Mitchell Elkind, a professor of neurology at Columbia University's College of Physicians and Surgeons and president-elect of the American Heart Association. Inflammation spurs clotting as white blood cells fight off infection. They interact with platelets and activate them in a way that increases the likelihood of clotting, Elkind said. Such reactions have been seen in severe infections, such as sepsis. But for covid-19, he said "we are seeing this in a large number of people in a very short time, so it really stands out." "The virus can attack a lot of different parts of the body, and we don't understand why it causes some problems for some people, different problems for others—and no problems at all for a large proportion," Elkind said. Coughlin, in critical condition at a hospital in Connecticut, deteriorated quickly after she reached the emergency room. Her fever shot up to 105 and pneumonia developed in her lungs. On Wednesday, she called her six daughters on FaceTime, telling them doctors advised she go on a ventilator. "If something happens to me, and I don't make it, I'm at peace with it," she told them. The conversation broke daughter Coleman's heart. "I am deciding to help her go on a ventilator, and she may never come off," she said. "That could have been my last phone conversation with her."

It's been a while since I've written in my book, but I have the motivation to write now. I wanted to write about this positive story. The headline reads, "US Jobless Rate Unexpectedly Declined to 13.3 Percent in May amid Pandemic."

The federal unemployment rate declined to 13.3. percent in May from 14.7 percent in April, the Labor Department said Friday, a surprising turnaround after months of job losses that was hailed as a sign that the economy is recovering more quickly than projected. The economy gained 2.5 million jobs in May as many states and counties began to reopen with the slowing of coronavirus cases nationwide. Yet the 30 million workers who are still collecting unemployment benefits show how significantly the labor market has been upended. The unemployment rate remains the worse since World War II. "The idea you would see job gains and the unemployment rate falling was not something really that people were expecting," said Jay Shambaugh, an economist at the Brookings Institution. "But a 13.3 percent unemployment rate is higher than any point in the Great Recession. It represents massive joblessness and economic pain. You need a lot of months of gains around this level to get back to the kind of jobs totals we used to have."

Some of the sectors that have been hit hardest by the crisis saw the biggest gains in May. The upswing in restaurants, bars and other food service employment accounted for about half the gains, after steep declines the previous two months. Employment in leisure and hospitality increased by 1.2 million. Construction employment increased by 464,000. And the health-care industry also recovered 312,000 jobs between April and May. Kate Bahn, an economist at the Washington center for Equitable Growth, said that the numbers were a sign that the recession would not be as severe as some forecasts had projected, but she cautioned against assuming economy had turned the corner. "Even if it is unexpected, we still have a really high unemployment rate," she said. "We're certainly not in a recovery yet." Even while the impact to businesses most effected by the coronavirus begins to lessen, other economic pain has begun to filter through other sectors of the economy, Bahn said. "We're starting to see the spillover effects of the recession-broader more evenly distributed impacts," she said. A substantial portion of the growth in May-about two-fifths—was driven by part-time jobs, an indication of how fragile and uneven the recovery could be. Economists agree that getting back to normal will take longer and be more challenging than recessions of the past.

Of particular concern to economists as the country has seen an outburst of anti-racism protests is that black Americans saw their unemployment rate, already higher than that of white people, increase. Whereas the unemployment rate for whites went down from 14.2 percent to 12.4 percent, the unemployment rate for blacks ticked up, from 16.7 percent to 16.8 percent. Asian Americans saw their unemployment rate rise too, from 14.5 percent to 15 percent. Hispanic unemployment dropped from 18.9 to 17.6 percent. "One thing we've talked about this week with police protests is that we've left African Americans behind in lot of things. The jobs day numbers reflect that," said Olugbenga Ajilore, a senior economist at the left-leaning Center for American Progress. "Whenever we have a recovery, blacks are always left behind." The crisis has touched nearly every part of the economy. Nearly half of commercial rents went unpaid in May. Oil and gas drillers Whiting Petroleum and Diamond Offshore have filed for bankruptcy protection, as have brands such as J. Crew and J.C. Penney. American Airlines said travel was down 80 percent in May. And concerns are bubbling about another wave of layoffs as state and municipal governments are forced to drastically pare down their budgets.

The layoffs have led to long lines at food banks, with efforts complicated by lack of manpower and supply shortages. And with expanded unemployment benefits set to expire July 31, unemployed workers could struggle even more to pay bills, triggering a wave of defaults on credit card balances, car payments and mortgages. The unexpectedly optimistic jobs numbers are likely to slow the push on Capitol Hill for an additional round of stimulus spending. Congressional Republicans and the White House have expressed skepticism about the need to approve or extend emergency economic aid, saying policymakers should wait to evaluate the impact of easing public health restrictions on the economy. Many economists and congressional Democrats have said additional government funding is urgently needed to avert an even worse economic downturn, with trillions in new spending expected to expire in the coming months. Labor Secretary Eugene Scalia said in a statement that the report signaled that "the worst of the coronavirus's impact on the nation's job markets is behind us."

"Millions of Americans are still out of work, and the Department remains focused on bringing Americans safely back to work and helping States deliver unemployment benefits to those who need them," he said. President Trump called the report "amazing" on Twitter and touted them at a White House news conference. There are more indications that the pain is not being shared equally in the United States. Hispanic workers are nearly twice as likely as whites to have lost their jobs amid the coronavirus shutdowns, according to a Washington Post-Ipsos poll, underlying the pandemic's disproportionate toll on some racial and ethnic groups. The poll found that 20 percent of Hispanic adults and 16 percent of blacks report being laid off or furloughed since the outbreak began in the United States, compared with 11 percent of whites and 12 percent of workers of other races. Complicating the path to economic recovery is the unusual nature of this public health pandemic. Without a cure or vaccine, the virus could deliver more suffering and economic destruction, and public health officials have warned about another wave of infections later this year. "We're not in a normal recession situation where a key priority is getting the unemployment rate down," said Damon Jones, an economist at the University of Chicago. "We're intentionally keeping the economy in a coma to try to treat it."

The path to recovery will be particularly difficult. The nonpartisan Congressional Budget Office expects the economic effects of the novel coronavirus to exceed $8 trillion and projects the economy will not fully recover until 2030. The CBO forecasts unemployment levels continuing at above 10 percent into 2021-meaning the county's recovery could resemble the worst of the Great Recession, at least in terms of employment. Other analysts are more bullish. Moody's Investor Services forecast that unemployment will sink to 8.5 percent by the end of the year as the country reopens and people get back to work. The unemployment rate does not fully capture the profound depth of joblessness right now. It is only a snapshot of those actively looking for work—not college graduates who enter a world with few job prospects or others who are out of work and have made similar decisions about sitting out until the country opens back up. It does not include people like Jennifer Bui, 28, a freelance content creator in Long Beach, Calif., who has lost most of her income from work online since the crisis began and has not paid rent since April. Bui said she didn't she qualified for unemployment payments and has been making do with a dwindling bank account and occasional grocery drops from her mother. "The Stimulus check was the only reason I could finish paying off April rent," she said. That money is long gone now, she said. Bui, who studied English in college, has since applied to work at gas stations, grocery stores-anywhere where she might be able to easily land a job. But she gotten only one interview out of 60 or

so applications, she said, and was told she didn't
have the relevant skills. "They don't call back, or
they say we hired someone else," she said.

I wanted to talk about this article because I pay close attention to the stock market since I play Xzibit's song "X" to make the
world progress with all these people dying. The article headline reads,
"Dow Soars More than 800 Points as US Stocks Close in on Pre-
Pandemic Levels."

Wall Street is in the midst of a stunning
three-month rally that is close to putting investors back where they were in January, before
the coronavirus pandemic obliterated trillions
in wealth. A surprisingly positive jobs report on
Friday helped stock markets extend an already
strong week, pushing the Standard & Poor's
500 index—which has soared 9 percent in three
weeks-within 1 percent of turning positive for
2020, according to Howard Silverblatt of S&P
Dow Jones Indices. The S&P was more than 30
percent in the hole less than three months ago.
It jumped 81 percent or 2.6 percent, to close
Friday at 3,193.93. The Nasdaq-already ahead
more than 9 percent this year-added 198 points,
or nearly 2.1 percent, to settle at 9,814.08. The
tech-centric index is within a hair of its all-time
high. The Nasdaq 100, a collection of the largest nonfinancial Nasdaq companies, set a record
high, led in part by recoveries in airline and hotel
stocks. The Dow Jones industrial average rock-
eted more than 1,000 points after the release
of May unemployment numbers, then cut its
gains to 829 points, or 3.2 percent, to end at
27,110.98—its first close above 27,000 in three
months. The advance put the blue-chip index

within 5 percentage points of turning positive for the year.

The Labor Department said Friday that the nation's jobless rate fell to 13.3 percent-a far cry from the 19.5 percent analysts had forecast and a significant improvement from the 14.7 percent recorded in April-as states incrementally reopened after months of pandemic-fueled shutdowns and some Americans were able to get back to work. More than 2.5 million jobs were created in May. "We have been given today the surprise of our investor lives," said Bryce Doty, senior Portfolio manager at Sit Investment Associates, a Minneapolis money management firm. "The timing of the economy recovery just moved up. Markets had been telling us economic activity was picking up, and today bears that out." Markets thrived this week as investors loaded up on stocks from companies with the most to gain in a reopened economy: Aerospace giant Boeing boomed more than 40 percent, while Coca-Cola, Chevron, ExxonMobil, Walt Disney and Caterpillar soared on the presumption of more dining out, greater travel, increased driving and summer vacations. Apple shares hit a record high Friday, closing at $331.50, up nearly 2.9 percent. The iPhone-maker has seen its stock advance 50 percent since March.

Much of the employment gains were among sectors the pandemic hurt the most, including leisure and hospitality, education, construction and retail. The rebound may be a sign the market may have appropriately anticipated a quick revival-in part because of massive interventions by the federal government and the Federal Reserve. "Some of the economic data already looks V-shaped," said Liz Ann Sonders, chief investment strategist at Charles Schwab & Co. "We saw complete reversals in the industries that lost the most in the shutdown. The persistence of the strength of this recovery is the question." European markets closed their second consecutive day of big gains following the European Central bank's announcement on Thursday that it would add $676 billion (600 billion euros) to its coronavirus rescue plan, making the total package worth more than $1.5 trillion. "The policy stimulus globally has been nothing short of breathtaking," said David Rosenberg of Rosenberg Research. Germany, one of Europe's most powerful economic engines, also announced a fresh stimulus package Thursday amid rising unemployment.

"There are a number of reasons to be cautious in this market but none are clearly as compelling as the grand economic reopening and authorities everywhere pumping out cash like it's going out of fashion," Craig Erlam, an analyst with OANDA, wrote in commentary Friday. "This is purely a stimulus and momentum trade and it's not running shy of either." Despite ongoing protests nationwide since George Floyd died in police custody last week and the U.S. grappling with its worst economic crisis since the Great Depression, investor optimism has been steadily gaining as numbers improve. On Thursday, weekly unemployment claims came in below estimates and appear to have started leveling off—though at 1.9 million the losses are still staggering. The number of people off their mortgage has ticked up, marking the first net decline in active forbearance plans since the Cares Act was enacted. Personal incomes have risen 10.5

percent, thanks largely to federal stimulus checks. Home sales are on the rise, helped by record-low interest rates. Private payrolls shed 2.76 million jobs in May, ADP reported Wednesday, well below the 8.75 million forecasts by economists. Oil prices soared to their highest levels in three months ahead of this weekend's meeting of OPEC and its allies, where the organization is expected to agree to more production cuts while the world gets back in motion. Brent crude, the international benchmark, rose 5 percent to $42 per barrel. West Texas Intermediate crude, the U.S. benchmark, climbed more than 4 percent to $39.17 per barrel.

Analyst caution that recovery could take years, given the magnitude of the economic damage. A Monday report from the Congressional Budget Office estimated that fallout from the coronavirus crisis will shrink the size of the U.S. economy by roughly $8 trillion over the next decade. That amounts to a 3 percent decline of U.S. gross domestic product compared with its initial estimate. Sustained stock gains through June could have a big impact on the American consumer come July, when people open their quarterly retirement statements. "There is a going be a huge change in the number between the end of the first and second quarters," said Ivan Feinseth of Tigress Financial Partners. "When people look at their 401(K) and retirement statements, they are going to be happy. That will help drive the second half other year."

Civil Rights Law Protects Gay and
Transgender Workers, Supreme Court Rules

The court said the language of the Civil
Rights Act of 1964, which prohibits sex discrimination, applied to discrimination based on sexual
orientation and gender identity. The Supreme
Court Ruled Monday, that a landmark civil rights
law protects gay and transgender workers from
workplace discrimination, handing the movement for L.G.B.T. equality a stunning victory.
"An employer who fires an individual merely for
being gay or transgender defies the law," Justice
Neil M. Gorsuch wrote for the majority in the
6–3 ruling. Until Monday's decision, it was legal
in more than half the states to fire workers for
being gay, bisexual or transgender. The vastly
consequential decision extended workplace protections to millions of people across the nation,
continuing a series of Supreme Court victories
for gay right even after President Trump transformed the court with two appointments. The
lopsided ruling, coming a fundamentally conservative court, was a surprise. Justice Gorsuch, who
was Mr. Trump's first appointment to the court,
was joined by Chief Justice John G. Roberts Jr.
and Justices Ruth Bader Ginsburg, Stephen G.
Breyer, Sonia Sotomayor and Elena Kagan.

The decision, covering two sets of cases,
was the court's first on lesbian, gay, bisexual and
transgender rights since the retirement in 2018
of Justice Anthony M. Kennedy, who wrote the
majority opinions in all four of the court's major
gay rights decisions. Proponents of these rights
had worried that his departure would halt the
progress of the movement toward equality. "This

is a simple and profound victory for L.G.B.T. civil rights," said Suzanne B. Goldberg, a law professor at Columbia. "Many of us feared that the court was poised to gut sex discrimination protections and allow employers to discriminate based on sexual orientation and gender identity, yet it declined the federal government's invitation to take that damaged path." The case concerned Title VII of the Civil Rights Act of 1964, which bars employment discrimination based on race, religion, national origin and sex. The question for the justices was whether that last prohibition—discrimination "because of sex"—applies to many millions of gay and transgender workers.

Justice Gorsuch wrote that it did. "An employer who fires an individual for being homosexual and transgender fires that person for traits or actions it would not have questioned in members of a different sex," he wrote. "It is impossible," Justice Gorsuch wrote," to discriminate against a person for being homosexual or transgender without discriminating against that individual based on sex." Justice Samuel A. Alito Jr., in a dissent joined by Justice Clarence Thomas, wrote that the majority had abandoned its judicial role. "There is only one word for what the court has done today: legislation," Justice Alito wrote. "The document that the court releases is in the form of a judicial opinion interpreting a statute, but that is deceptive." "A more brazen abuse of our authority to interpret statutes is hard to recall," he wrote. "The court tries to convince readers that it is merely enforcing the terms of the statute, but that is preposterous." The common understanding of sex discrimination in 1964, Justice Alito wrote, was bias against women or men and did not encompass discrimination based on sexual orientation and gender identity. If Congress wanted to protect gay and transgender workers, he wrote, it could pass a new law. "Discrimination" because of sex" was not understood as having anything to do with discrimination because of sexual orientation or transgender "status" in 1964, he wrote. "Any such notion would have clashed in spectacular fashion with the societal norms of the day." Justice Alito added that the majority's decision would have pernicious consequences. He said the majority left open for instance, questions about access to restroom and locker rooms. "For women who have been victimized by sexual assault or abuse," he wrote, "the experience of seeing an unclothed person with the anatomy of a male in a confined and sensitive location such as a bathroom or locker room can cause serious psychological harm."

Nor did the majority address, he said, how its ruling would affect sports, college housing, religious employers, health care or free speech. "After today's decision," Justice Alito wrote, "plaintiffs may claim that the failure to use their preferred pronoun violates one of the federal laws prohibiting sex discrimination." "Although he court does not want to think about the consequences of its decision, we will not be able to avoid those issues for long," he concluded "The entire federal judiciary will be mired for years in disputes about the reach of the court's reasoning." Justice Gorsuch responded that the court's ruling was narrow. "We do not purport to address bathrooms, locker rooms or anything else of the kind," he wrote. "Whether other policies and practices might or might not qualify as unlawful discrimination or find justifications under other provisions of Title VII are questions for future cases, not these." He added that Title VII itself included protections for religious employers and that a separate federal law and the First Amendment also allow religious groups latitude in their employment decisions. Justice Brett M. Kavanaugh, Mr. Trump's other appointment to the court, issued a separate dissent making a point about statutory interpretation. "Courts must follow ordinary meaning, not literal meaning," he wrote, adding that the ordinary meaning of "because of sex" does not cover discrimination based on sexual orientation or gender identity.

"Seneca Falls was not Stonewall," he wrote. "The women's rights movement was not (And is not) the gay rights movement, although many people obviously support or participate in both. So to think that sexual orientation discrimination is just a form of sex discrimination is not just a mistake of language and psychology, but also a mistake of history and sociology." The court considered two sets of cases. The first concerned a pair of lawsuits from gay men who said they were fired because of their sexual orientation: Bostock v Blayton County Ga., No. 17-1618, and Altitude Express Inc. v. Zarda, No. 17-1623. The first case was filed by Gerald Bostock, a gay man who was fired from a government program that helped neglected and abused children in Clayotn County, Ga., just south of Atlanta, after he joined a gay softball league. The second was brought by a skydiving instructor, Donald Zarda, who also said he was fired because he was gay. His dismissal followed a complaint from a female customer who had expressed concerns about being strapped to Mr. Zarda during a tandem dive. Mr. Zarda, hoping to reassure the customer, told her that he was "100 percent gay."

The case of gender identity, R.G. & G.R. Harris Funeral Homes Inc v Equal Employment Opportunity Commission, No. 18-107 was brought by transgender woman, Aimee Stephens, who was fired from a Michigan funeral home after she announced in 2013 that she was a transgender woman and would start working in women's clothing. Mr. Zarda died in a 2014 skydiving accident, and Ms. Stephens died on May 12. Their estates pursued their cases. Critics sometimes say that the Congress does not hide elephants in mouse holes, Justice Gorsuch wrote on Monday, meaning that lawmakers do not take enormous steps with vague terms or in asides. "We can't deny that today's holding—that employers are prohibited from firing employees on the basis of homosexuality or transgender status—is an elephant," he wrote. "But where's the mouse hole? Title VII's prohibition of sex discrimination in employment is a major piece of federal civil rights legislation. It is written in starkly broad terms. It has repeatedly produced unexpected applications, at least in the view of those on the receiving end of them." "This elephant," he wrote, "Has never hidden in a mouse hole; it has been standing before us all along."

I thought that the DACA ruling was very cool, and I wanted to write about it. Here is one article about it:

"My Mind Was Blown"
Dreamers React to the Supreme Court Ruling

Emanuel Diaz was shocked when he saw the news flash onto his cell phone screen. A text from a friend told him the Supreme Court decision he'd been waiting to hear for months had finally come in. Justices had blocked the Trump administration's attempt to end the program that protects him and hundreds of thousands of other so-called Dreamers from deportation. And Diaz couldn't believe it. The 25-year-old in Savannah, Georgia, responded with an emoji of a brain exploding. "My mind was blown when I found out," he said. "IT's a giant relief." Across the country, the young undocumented immigrants protected by the Deferred Action for Childhood Arrivals (DACA) program are reacting to the news with a mix of emotions-relishing their legal victory, but also bracing themselves for the possibility that officials could find a new way to put the Obama-era program back on the chopping block. "We're not in the clear yet," said Leeia Dhalla, a Daca recipient and press director for the FWD.us advocacy group. "The Trump administration can still try to terminate the DACA program. Are they going to do that in an election year? That's a big question." Here's a look at what several DACA recipients told CNN about how they're feeling and what's next:

She feels like her journey was worth it. The last time CNN spoke with Caroline Fund Feng, she was in the middle of 230-mile march from New York to Washington so she could be in the nation's capital for the Supreme Court arguments last November. When she heard of the justices' decision on Thursday, Fund Feng says she thought of that journey and years of advocacy efforts she and other DACA recipients have been involved in. "It was worth it," said Fung Feng, 31, who'd feared the court would deliver a different result. "At first it took a while to sink in—is this real?…I can't put into words how happy I am and how relieved I feel about the whole thing," she said. If the Trump administration does try again to end DACA, Fung Feng says she and other advocates will be prepared. "They'll try to find a different way, but we will be ready for it. We will be ready to stop him and his anti-immigrant, white supremacist agenda. We'll stop him," she said. "We know that when we organize, we win. And this victory that we have today is proof of that."

He says a lot of major life decisions are still on hold. Angel Oaxca-Rivas, an admissions counselor in Denver, Colorado, also described Thursday's news as a relief. The 25-year-old said many things in his life have been in limbo since the Trump administration's 2017 announcement that it was ending the program. "If my life is on a rotating two-year basis, I can't commit to so many things," he said. "That's where there's relief, in the sense that I feel like there's going to have to be due process if anything is to change," Oaxaca-Rivas said. "That in and of itself makes me feel safer." But Oacada-Rivas said some of the major life decisions he's been putting off-like buying a house and pursuing a master's degree-will have to remain on hold until the outcome of the 2020 presidential election. "We'll figure that out come November," he said.

She's celebrating, and ready to keep fighting. Dhalla, 30, described the Supreme Court ruling as an important step. "This is a victory that has truly changed my life…There's so much more work that needs to be done. But today is a victory," Dhalla said. "I'm going to take today as a day of celebration." Dhalla, who came to the United States from Canada when she was 6 years old and grew up in San Antonio, Texas, said she plans to keep pushing for Congress to take action. "I came to the US a quarter century ago," she said. "I never imaged I would still be fighting for the opportunity to become an American citizen 25 years later."

She was on the steps of the Supreme Court when the decision came down. Luz Chavez, 22, was with a group of demonstrators standing on the Supreme Court steps when the decision came down Thursday. "It's exhilarating," she said. A student at Trinity Washington University who came to the US from La Paz, Bolivia, Chavez said DACA provided her with a lifeline after she learned she was undocumented as a teenager. And federal court decisions over the past few years keeping the program alive gave her hope. But waiting for the Supreme Court's decision was nerve-wracking, she said. "Now I can sleep," she said," knowing I'll still have my job, I'll still be able to provide for my family. But this is the beginning of the long run."

He's training to become a doctor but still worries he could be departed. Jin Park, a second-year student at Harvard Medical School, said Thursday's decision provided some relief but didn't give him the permanence he's hoping for. Park said he had to strike a difficult balance as a medical student with DACA. On the one hand, he said, he wants to uphold his oath to his patients and be committed to them, but he's struggled with the possibility he could be deported and forced to leave his patients behind. In the end, Park said, that's a problem Congress has to help solve. "That question still remains. As a country we'll have to reckon what legislative solution we'll need to apply for me and other DACA recipients," he said. "This is one small advance."

He's excited to tell his mom. Diaz, who's working as an apprentice for a financial planner, said he's been on edge waiting for word of the court's decision. "It's been crazy, just been glued to a screen and always having something set up to where I get an alert if anything happens (with DACA), always looking on the internet. Especially now that the time was closing in on whether they were going to say something on it," he said. Now he hopes the Supreme Court decision will help his career, even though he's worried the administration could try to rescind DACA again. "When I started my apprenticeship with the financial planner, he mentioned he had some concerns about how long I'd be able to stay in the country because of the way DACA was going," Diaz said. "Now that I know it's going to hold up, I feel like I have a more secure future." But first things first. Diaz told CNN he was getting ready to do one important thing: Call his mom and celebrate.

Appeals Court Orders Judge to Dismiss
Criminal Case against Michael Flynn

U.S. District Judge Emmet G. Sullivan
must immediately dismiss the criminal case
against President Trump's former national security adviser Michael Flynn and cannot scrutinize
the Justice Department's decision to drop the
long-running prosecution, a federal appeals court
ruled Wednesday. In a 2–1 decision, the court
said it is not within the judge's power to prolong a
prosecution or examine the government's motives
in the politically charged case. Flynn twice
pleaded guilty to lying to federal agents about his
pre-inauguration contacts with Russia's ambassa-
dor before the Justice Department moved in May
to dismiss the charges. "This is not the unusual
case where a more searching inquiry is justified,"
wrote Judge Neomi Rao, a recent nominee of
the president, in a decision that can be reviewed
by the full U.S. Court of Appeals for the D.C.
Circuit. In a victory for Flynn and the Trump
administration, the panel majority said Sullivan
overstepped his role and committed a "clear legal
error" by refusing to immediately close the case
and instead appointing a former judge to argue
against the Justice Department's position.

The judge's "demonstrated intent to scrutinize the reasoning and motives of the Department
of Justice constitute irreparable harms that cannot be remedied on appeal," Rao wrote in the
19-page opinion that was joined by Judge Karen
LeCraft Henderson, a nominee of President
George H.W. Bush. Soon after the opinion was
published, Trump tweeted: Great! Appeals Court
Upholds Justice Departments Request to Drop

Criminal Case Against General Michael Flynn!"
He later told reporters in the Oval Office, "I'm
very happy about General Flynn. He was treated
horribly." In his dissent, the third judge on the
panel, Robert L. Wilkins, said the majority had
"grievously" overstepped its own authority by
taking the "unprecedented" step to intervene
midstream and force Sullivan's hand before he
had an opportunity to rule. Sullivan "must be
given a reasonable opportunity to consider and
hold a hearing on the Government's request to
ensure that it is not clearly contrary to the public
interest," wrote Wilkins, a nominee of President
Barack Obama. The ruling from the three-judge
panel means that at least for now Sullivan cannot
hold a hearing set for July 16 to formally consider the government's request to dismiss Flynn's
case. Sullivan could ask for a rehearing, or the full
court could decide on its own to revisit the decision from the three-judge panel, whose members
are selected at random.

Attorney Beth Wilkinson, who represents
Sullivan, said Wednesday, "We have no comment
at this time." In May, Sullivan refused to sign off
on the Justice Department's plans and instead
appointed John Gleeson, a former federal judge
and mob prosecutor, to help him decide how to
proceed. Gleeson argued that the government's
move was "highly irregular conduct to benefit a
political ally of the President." Nothing about the
case testing the powers of the judiciary to check
the executive branch has followed a typical path.
Flynn's lawyers took the rare step of asking the
appeals court to step in and order Sullivan to
close the case. Sullivan then hired Wilkinson, a
high-profile trial attorney, to represent him. At

oral argument in June, Wilkinson told the court it was premature to cut off Sullivan's review. The ruling Wednesday was surprising because at least two of the judges at oral argument seemed to agree and repeatedly expressed concern that the judge would be a "rubber stamp" for the government. Federal criminal rules require prosecutors to obtain permission from the presiding judge to drop charges against a defendant. But legal experts and former judges disagree about the limits of that judicial authority. "Courts have said he's not a mere rubber stamp." Henderson said at oral argument of Sullivan's independent rule. "There's no authority I know of that says he can't hold a hearing."

Wilkins cited past cases in which the Supreme Court upheld the power of judges "to perform an independent evaluation" of the government's action. In his dissent Wednesday, Wilkins said the majority had eviscerated the court's role by preventing any review. "Today the majority declares that nevertheless—in spite of the Government's abrupt reversal of the facts and the law, and although the Government declares itself entitled not to be forthcoming with the District Court—these circumstances merit no further examination to determine whether there may be additional reasons for the prosecutor's actions, and if so, if any such reasons are impermissible." Lawyers for Flynn had accused Sullivan of bias and asked the appeals court to reassign the case to a different judge, a request the court denied Wednesday. In a sign of the high-level interest in the matter that could reach the Supreme Court, the Justice Department was represented by Deputy Solicitor General

Jeffrey B. Wall. He referred to Gleeson's report as a "polemic" and had urged the court not to get pulled into a "political spectacle." Flynn was the highest-ranking Trump advisor charged in Mueller's investigation into Russian interference in the 2016 presidential election. Before its reversal, the government had recommended a prison term of up to six months for Flynn.

Instead of moving to sentencing, Attorney General William P. Barr ordered a review of Flynn's case. The review found that the FBI agents who questioned Flynn had no valid investigative basis to do so and that, therefore, any lies he told were irrelevant to any crime. The president and Flynn's defenders have long argued that the retired three-star general was a victim of FBI overreach. But the government's decision to undo a guilty plea prompted criticism that the department was bending to political pressure. The court ruling came the same day of a House hearing in which a former member of Mueller's team testified that Barr and top deputies pressured prosecutors to give Trump's friend Roger Stone" a break" by requesting a lighter prison sentence. Elizabeth Wydra, president of the Constitutional Accountability Center, which filed a brief backing Sullivan, said allowing the court's ruling to stand would erase a vital check on the executive branch. Federal rules, she said in a statement, give the judge" a say in whether Attorney General Barr should be allowed to simply drop the matter, an act that would aid one of the President Trump's stalwart allies by essentially giving him a "Get out of jail free card."

In reviewing the government's actions Sullivan had also asked Gleeson to consider whether Flynn may have committed perjury while pleading guilty to a crime that he and the Justice Department now say is no longer a crime. Gleeson advised Sullivan in his initial report not to impose contempt of court penalties on Flynn but to continue to the sentencing phase of the case. The court majority took issue with the appointment of Gleeson in part because of his public advocacy for an adversarial process and his initial filing with Sullivan. "These actions foretell not only that the scrutiny will continue but that it may intensify. Among other things, the government may be required to justify its charging decisions, not only in this case, but also in the past or pending cases cited in Gleeson's brief," Rao wrote. When new evidence surfaces, she continued, "the Executive Branch must have the authority to decide that further prosecution is not in the interest."

The Top 1% of Americans Have Taken $50 Trillion from the Bottom 90 Percent— and That's Made the U.S. Less Secure

Like many of the virus's hardest hit victims, the United States went into the COVID 19 pandemic wracked by preexisting conditions. A fraying public health infrastructure, inadequate medical supplies, an employer-based health insurance system perversely unsuited for the moment—these and other afflictions are surely contributing to the death toll. But in addressing the causes and consequences of this pandemic— and its cruelly uneven impact—the elephant in the room is extreme income inequality. How big is this elephant? A staggering 50 trillion. That is how much the upward redistribution of income has cost American workers over the past several decades.

This is not some back-of-the napkin approximation. According to a groundbreaking new working paper by Carter C. Price and Kathryn Edwards of the RAND Corporation (Which I was just talking about from Iron Fists), had the more equitable income distributions of the three decades following World War II (1945–1974) merely held steady, the aggregate annual income of Americans earning below the 90th percentile would have been 2.5 trillion higher in the year 2018 alone. This is an amount equal to nearly 12 percent of GDP—enough to more than double median income—enough to pay every single working American in the bottom nine deciles an additional $1,144 a month. Every single year. Price and Edwards calculate that the cumulative tab for our four-decade-long experiment in radical inequality had grown to over $47 trillion from 1975 through 2018. At a recent pace of about $2.5 trillion a year, that number we estimate crossed the $50 trillion mark by early 2020. That's $50 trillion that would have gone to paychecks of working Americans had inequality held constant—$50 trillion that would have built a far larger and more prosperous economy—$50 trillion that would have enabled the vast majority of Americans to enter this pandemic far more healthy, resilient, and financially secure.

As the RAND report (whose research was funded by the Fair Work Center which co-author David Rolf is a board member of) demonstrates, a rising tide most definitely did not lift all boats. It didn't even lift most of them, as nearly all of the benefits of growth these past 45 years were captured by those at the very top. And as the American economy grows radically unequal it is holding back economic growth itself. Even inequality is meted out unequally. Low-wage workers and their families, disproportionately people of color, suffer from far higher rates of asthma, hypertension, diabetes, and other COVID-19 comorbidities; yet they are also far less likely to have health insurance, and far more likely to work in "essential" industries with the highest rates of coronavirus exposure and transmission. It is no surprise then, according to the CDC, that COVID-19 inflicts "a disproportionate burden of illness and death among racial and ethnic minority groups." But imagine how much safer, healthier, and empowered all American workers might be if that $50 trillion had been paid out in wages instead of being funneled into corporate profits and the offshore accounts of the super-rich. Imagine how much richer and more resilient the American people would be. Imagine how many more lives would have been saved had our people been more resilient.

It is easy to see how such a deadly virus, and the draconian measures required to contain it, might spark an economic depression. But look straight into the eyes of the elephant in the room, and it is impossible to deny the many ways in which our extreme inequality—an exceptionally American affliction—has made the virus more deadly and its economic consequences more dire than in any other advanced nation. Why is our death toll so high and our unemployment rate so staggeringly off the charts? Why was our nation so unprepared, and our economy so fragile? Why have we lacked the stamina and the will to contain the virus like most other advanced nations? The reason is staring us in the face: a stampede of rising inequality that has been trampling our lives and livelihoods of the vast majority of Americans, year after year after year.

Of course, America's chronic case of extreme inequality is old news. Many other studies have documented this trend, chronicled its impact, and analyzed its causes. But where others have painted the picture in terms of aggregate shares of GDP, productivity growth, or other cold, hard statistics, the RAND report brings the inequality price tag directly home by denominating it in dollars—not just the aggregate $50 trillion figure, but in granular demographic detail. For example, are you a typical Black man earning $35,000 a year? You are being paid at least $26,000 a year less than you would have had income distributions held constant. Are you a college-educated, prime-aged, full-time worker earning $72,000? Depending on the inflation index used (PCE or CPI, respectively) rising inequality is costing you between $48,000 and $63,000 a year. But whatever your race, gender, educational attainment, urbanicity, or income, the data show, if you earn below the 90th percentile, the relentlessly upward redistribution of income since 1975 is coming out of your pocket.

As Price and Edwards explain, from 1947 through 1974, real incomes grew close to the rate of per capita economic growth across all income levels. That means that for three decades, those at the bottom and middle of the distribution saw their incomes grow at about the same rate as those at the top. This was the era in which

America built the world's largest and most prosperous middle class, an era in which inequality
between income groups steadily shrank (even as
shocking inequalities between the sexes and races
largely remained). But around 1975, this extraor-
dinary era of broadly shared prosperity came to
an end. Since then, the wealthiest Americans,
particularly those in the top 1 percent and 0.1
percent, have managed to capture an ever-larger
share of our nation's economic growth—in fact,
almost all of it—their real incomes skyrocketing
as the vast majority of Americans saw little if any
gains.

What if American prosperity had continued
to be broadly shared—*how much more would a
typical worker be earning today?* Once the data
are compiled, answering these questions is fairly
straightforward. Price and Edwards look at real
taxable income from 1975 to 2018. They then
compare actual income distributions in 2018 to a
counterfactual that assumes incomes had continued to keep pace with growth in per capita Gross
Domestic Product (GDP)—a 118% increase over
the 1975 income numbers. Whether measuring
inflation using the more conservative Personal
Consumption Expenditures Price Index (PCE)
or the more commonly cited Consumer Price
Index for all Urban Consumers (CPI-U-RS), the
results are striking.

At every income level up to the 90th percentile, wage earners are now being paid a frac-
tion of what they would have had inequality held
constant. For example, at the median individual
income of $36,000, workers are being short-
changed by $21,000 a year—$28,000 when using
the CPI—an amount equivalent to an *additional*

$10.10 to $13.50 an hour. But according to Price and Edwards, this actually understates the impact of rising inequality on low- and middle-income workers, because much of the gains at the bottom of the distribution were largely "driven by an increase in hours not an increase in wages." To adjust for this, along with changing patterns of workforce participation, the researchers repeat their analysis for full-year, full-time, prime-aged workers (age 25 to 54). These results are even more stark: "Unlike the growth patterns in the 1950s and 60s," write Price and Edwards, "the majority of full-time workers did not share in the economic growth of the last forty years."

On average, extreme inequality is costing the median income full-time worker about $42,000 a year. Adjusted for inflation using the CPI, the numbers are even worse: half of all full-time workers (those at or below the median income of $50,000 a year) now earn *less than half* what they would have had incomes across the distribution continued to keep pace with economic growth. And that's per worker, not per household. At both the 25th and 50th percentiles, households comprised of a married couple with one full-time worker earned thousands of dollars less in 2018 dollars than a comparable household in 1975—and $50,000 and $66,000 less respectively than if inequality had held constant—a predicament compounded by the rising costs of maintaining a dignified middle-class life. According to Oren Cass, executive director of the conservative think tank American Compass, the median male worker needed 30 weeks of income in 1985 to pay for housing, healthcare, transportation, and education for his family. By 2018, that "Cost of

Thriving Index" had increased to 53 weeks (more weeks than in an actual year). But the counterfactual reveals an even starker picture: In 2018, the combined income of married households with *two* full-time workers was barely more than what the income of a single-earner household would have earned had inequality held constant. Two-income families are now working twice the hours to maintain a shrinking share of the pie, while struggling to pay housing, healthcare, education, childcare, and transportations costs that have grown at two to three times the rate of inflation.

This dramatic redistribution of income from the majority of workers to those at the very top is so complete that even at the 95th percentile, most workers are still earning less than they would have had inequality held constant. It is only at the 99th percentile that we see incomes growing faster than economic growth: at 171 percent of the rate of per capita GDP. But even this understates the disparity. "The *average* income growth for the top one percent was substantially higher," write Price and Edwards, "at more than 300 percent of the real per capita GDP rate." The higher your income, the larger your percentage gains. As a result, the top 1 percent's share of total taxable income has more than doubled, from 9 percent in 1975, to 22 percent in 2018, while the bottom 90 percent have seen their income share fall, from 67 percent to 50 percent. This represents a direct transfer of income—and over time, wealth—from the vast majority of working Americans to a handful at the very top.

But given the changing demographic composition of the U.S. workforce, these topline numbers can only tell part of the story. The

U.S. workforce is now better educated and more urban than it was in 1975. It is also far less white and male—with white men falling from over 60 percent of the prime-aged workforce in 1974 to less than 45 percent by 2018. These changes are important, because while there was far more equality between the income distributions in 1975, there was also more inequality *within* them—notably in regard to gender and race.

For example, in 1975, the median income of white women was only 31 percent of that of white men; by 2018 white women were earning 68 percent as much. Likewise, the median income of Black men as a share of their white counterparts' earnings rose from 74 percent in 1975, to 80 percent in 2018. Clearly, income disparities between races, and especially between men and women, have narrowed since 1975, and that is a good thing. But unfortunately, much of the narrowing we see is more an artifact of four decades of flat or declining wages for low- and middle-income white men than it is of substantial gains for women and nonwhites.

Much has been made about white male grievance in the age of Trump, and given their falling or stagnant real incomes, one can understand why some white men might feel aggrieved. White, non-urban, non-college educated men have the slowest wage growth in every demographic category. But to blame their woes on competition from women or minorities would be to completely miss the target. In fact, *white men still earn more* than white women at all income distributions, and substantially more than most non-white men and women. Only Asian-American men earn higher. Yet there is no moral or practical justification for the persistence of any income disparity based on race or gender.

The counterfactuals in the table above appear vastly unequal because they extrapolate from the indefensible 1975-levels of race and gender inequality; they assume that inequality remained constant both between income distributions and *within* them—that women and nonwhites had not narrowed the income gap with white men. But surely, this cannot be our goal. In an economy freed from race and gender bias, and that shares the fruits of growth broadly across all income distributions, the most appropriate counterfactual for all the groups in this table would be the aggregate counterfactual for "All Groups": a median income of $57,000 a year for all adults with positive earnings ($92,000 for full-time prime-age workers). That would be the income for all workers at the 50th percentile, regardless of race or gender, had race and gender inequality within distributions been eliminated, and inequality between distributions not grown. By this measure we can see that in real dollars, women and nonwhites have actually lost *more* income to rising inequality than white men, because starting from their disadvantaged positions in 1975, they had far more to potentially gain. Per capita GDP grew by 118 percent over the following four decades, so there was plenty of new income to spread around. That the majority of white men have benefited from almost none of this growth isn't because they have lost income to women or minorities; it's because they've lost it to their largely white male counterparts in the top 1 percent who have captured nearly all of the income growth for themselves. According to economist Thomas Piketty, men accounted for 85 percent of the top income centile in the mid-2010s—and while he doesn't specify, these men are overwhelmingly *white*.

The data on income distribution by educational attainment is equally revealing, in that it calls the lie on the notion of a "skills gap"—a dominant narrative that has argued that rising inequality is largely a consequence of a majority of American workers failing to acquire the higher skills necessary to compete in our modern global economy. If workers were better educated, this narrative argues, they would earn more money. Problem solved.

Indeed, at every income distribution, the education premium has increased since 1975, with the income of college graduates rising faster than their less educated counterparts. But this growing gap is more a consequence of falling incomes for workers without a college degree than it is of rising real incomes for most workers with one—for not only have workers without a degree secured none of the gains from four decades of economic growth, below the 50th percentile they've actually seen their real incomes *decline*. College educated workers are doing better. The median real income for full-time workers with a four-year degree has grown from $55,000 a year in 1975 to $72,000 in 2018. But that still falls far short of the $120,000 they'd be earning had incomes grown with per capita GDP. Even at the 90th percentile, a college educated full-time worker making $191,000 a year is earning less than 78 percent what they would have had inequality held constant.

The reality is that American workers have never been more highly educated. In 1975, only 67 percent of the adult US workforce had a high school education or better, while just 15 percent had earned a four-year college degree. By 2018, 91 percent of adult workers had completed high school, while the percentage of college graduates in the workforce had more than doubled to 34 percent. In raw numbers, the population of adult workers with a high school education or less has fallen since 1975, while the number of workers with a four-year degree has more than quadrupled.

It is impossible to argue that a "skills gap" is responsible for rising income inequality when the rate of educational attainment is rising faster than the rate of growth in productivity or per capita GDP. Yes, workers with college degrees are doing better than those without; the economy we've built over the past 45 years has been more unequal to some than to others. But below the 90th percentile, even college graduates are falling victim to a decades-long trend of radical inequality that is robbing them of most of the benefits of economic growth.

The iron rule of market economies is that we all do better when we all do better: when workers have more money, businesses have more customers, and hire more workers. Seventy percent of our economy is dependent on consumer spending; the faster and broader real incomes grow, the stronger the demand for the products and services American businesses produce. This is the virtuous cycle through which workers and businesses prospered together in the decades immediately following World War II. But as wages stagnated after 1975, so too did consumer demand; and as demand slowed, so did the economy. A 2014 report from the OECD estimated that rising income inequality knocked as much 9 points off U.S. GDP growth over the previous two decades—a deficit that has surely grown over the past six years as inequality continued to climb. That's about $2 trillion worth of GDP that's being frittered away, year after year, through policy choices that intentionally constrain the earning power of American workers.

COVID-19 may have triggered our current crisis, but it wasn't its only cause. For even had our political leaders done everything right in the moment, our response to the pandemic would still have been mired in the footprint of extreme inequality: a $50 trillion upward redistribution of wealth and income—$297,000 per household—that has left our families, our economy, and our democracy far less capable of fighting this virus than in other advanced nations. This is the America that stumbled into the COVID-19 pandemic and the economic catastrophe it unleashed: An America with an economy $2 trillion smaller and a workforce $2.5 trillion a year poorer than they otherwise would be had inequality held constant since 1975. This is an America in which 47 percent of renters are cost burdened, in which 40 percent of households can't cover a $400 emergency expense, in which half of Americans over age 55 have no retirement savings at all. This is an America in which 28 million have no health insurance, and in which 44 million underinsured Americans can't afford the deductibles or copays to use the insurance they have. This is an America that recklessly rushed to reopen its economy in the midst of a deadly pandemic because businesses were too fragile to survive an extended closure and workers too powerless and impoverished to defy the call back to work.

There are some who blame the current plight of working Americans on structural changes in the underlying economy—on automation, and especially on globalization. According to this popular narrative, the lower wages of the past 40 years were the unfortunate but necessary price of keeping American businesses competitive in an increasingly cutthroat global market. But in fact, the $50 trillion transfer of wealth the RAND report documents has occurred entirely *within* the American economy, not between it and its trading partners. No, this upward redistribution of income, wealth, and power wasn't inevitable; *it was a choice*—a direct result of the trickle-down policies *we chose* to implement since 1975.

We chose to cut taxes on billionaires and to deregulate the financial industry. *We chose* to allow CEOs to manipulate share prices through stock buybacks, and to lavishly reward themselves with the proceeds. *We chose* to permit giant corporations, through mergers and acquisitions, to accumulate the vast monopoly power necessary to dictate both prices charged and wages paid. *We chose* to erode the minimum wage and the overtime threshold and the bargaining power of labor. For four decades, we chose to elect political leaders who put the material interests of the rich and powerful above those of the American people.

Other nations are suffering less from COVID-19 because they made better choices, and the good news is that America can, too. Economics is a choice. We could choose to raise the federal minimum wage to $15 or $20 an hour and peg it to productivity growth like in the decades before 1975. We could choose to revalue work so that the majority of Americans once again earn time-and-a-half pay for every hour worked over 40 hours a week. We could choose to provide affordable high-quality healthcare, childcare, and education to all Americans, while modernizing our social insurance and retirement systems so that contract and gig workers aren't left out and left behind. We could choose to make it easier for workers to organize, and to defend the rights and interests of those who can't. We could choose to build a more equitable, resilient, and prosperous America—an America that grows its economy by intentionally including every American in it. But given our nation's radical redistribution of wealth and power these past 40 years, it won't be easy.

What American workers need are multiple simultaneous experiments in rebuilding worker power, from tweaking existing labor laws to sectoral bargaining to the creation of whole new trade associations and broad-based not-for-profit organizations. For example, imagine an AARP for all working Americans, relentlessly dedicated to both raising wages and reducing the cost of thriving—a mass membership organization so large and so powerful that our political leaders won't dare to look the other way. Only then, by matching power with power, can we clear a path to enacting the laws and policies necessary to ensure that that trickle-down economics never threatens our health, safety, and welfare again.

There is little evidence that the current administration has any interest in dealing with this crisis. Our hope is that a Biden administration would be historically bold. But make no mistake that both our political and economic systems will collapse absent solutions that scale to the enormous size of the problem. The central goal of our nation's economic policy must be nothing less than the *doubling of median income*. We must dramatically narrow inequality between distributions while eliminating racial and gender inequalities within them. This is the standard to which we should hold leaders from both parties. To advocate for anything less would be cowardly or dishonest or both.

Here is another article that I thought was interesting:

The Big Picture
A Quiet American Apocalypse

Gregory Crewdson's photographs understood social distancing before it became reality. His landscapes, which have a broken-down, apocalyptic cast, usually include a few figures, set adrift in different ways, apparently unable to connect with one another, or with the place in which they find themselves. Redemption Center is the first of a series of 16 taken between 2018 and 2019 on the edge of a town called Pittsfield, about 20 miles from Crewdson's home in rural Massachusetts. He calls the series—huge pictures, seven feet across—An Eclipse of Moths after the effect of a swarm of insects around an outside lamp, that causes the light to dim.

Crewdson, 57, who is director of graduate studies in photography at Yale University, spends a long time scouting locations, then embellishing them, painting billboards, towing in car wrecks. He will contact businesses and authorities and ask them not to mow the verges or collect the rubbish for a while. Fog machines provide a dispiriting miasma; the puddles come from water trucks. Lighting on 40-foot cranes casts an otherworldly, even-handed light over the scene—nothing is out of focus; the list of credits that accompanies the pictures is like the roll call at the end of a movie, a legion of best boys and gaffers and key grips.

Despite the resulting exaggerated blight, the deprivation in Pittsfield is real enough, and the people who inhabit Crewdson's photographs are mostly living it. General Electric dominated employment in Pittsfield, until its vast plant closed in 1987; the area has high levels of opioid addiction. When Crewdson took these pictures he was coming out of a difficult divorce and unable to sleep for nights on end. His intention was like that of any landscape artist, he suggests: "To find that tension between something very intimate and something very removed."

Twitter went crazy when they were talking about this six-foot-two football player. When I saw this report, it reminded me of the Sandra Bullock movie *The Blind Side*, based on the real guy who was an offensive lineman for the Ravens. I can't remember his name off the top of my head, but this is part of why Hollywood wrote this script: because of this kid who was six feet and two inches tall and was ten years old. The online databases went crazy when they saw the potential in this kid. Here is how the article goes:

Twitter Reacts to 6' 2" 10-Year-Old
Football Player Steamrolling Opponents

At the age of ten, how tall were you? Four feet? Maybe even 5 feet if you are lucky? Well, according to Twitter, this ten-year-old football player is 6'2". For reference, the average height for a ten-year-old male is 54.5 inches, so roughly four feet, six and a half inches. That would make this kid nearly two feet taller than his teammates. When the tweet went viral of the tall boy, people on social media were calling for his birth-certificate in disbelief, referencing the 2006 movie, The Benchwarmers. People can reference Benchwarmers, but I think Blindspot is better. The Ravens player is named Michael Oher.

In the video, you see the quarterback throw the ball to the sizable boy as soon as it is snapped. Very predictable. Number 71 then takes the ball all the way to the end zone as the smaller kids are no match for his size, and they bounce off him with ease. You even see the tall boy stiff-arm one unfortunate peewee opponent. The tweet, posted by 'Football Is Life,' has already received more than 80 retweets, 62 quote tweets, and 321 likes. In addition, a boy in Texas dealt with a similar reaction when fans saw him dominating his youth football team. Nearly two weeks ago, another video went viral of a 5'1", 130-pound six-year-old. Yes, you read that correct, six years old.

This article is pretty cool to talk about, but the article says that outer space is becoming too overcrowded:

Space Is Becoming Too Crowded,
Rocket Lab CEO Warns

In 1978, NASA scientist Donald Kessler
warned of a potential catastrophic, cascading
chain reaction in outer space. Today known as
"Kessler Syndrome," the theory posited that
space above Earth could one day become so
crowded, so polluted with both active satellites
and the detritus of space explorations past, that
it could render future space endeavors more difficult, if not impossible. Last week, the CEO of
Rocket Lab, a launch startup, said the company
is already beginning to experience the effect of
growing congestion in outer space. Rocket Lab
CEO Peter Beck said that the sheer number of
objects in space right now—a number that is
growing quickly thanks in part to SpaceX's satellite internet constellation, Starlink—is making it
more difficult to find a clear path for rockets to
launch new satellites. "This has a massive impact
on the launch side," he told CNN Business.
Rockets "have to try and weave their way up in
between these [satellite] constellations."

Part of the problem is that outer space
remains largely unregulated. The last widely
agreed upon international treaty hasn't been
updated in five decades, and that's mostly left the
commercial space industry to police itself. Rocket
Lab set out to create lightweight rockets—far
smaller than SpaceX's 230-foot-tall Falcon rockets—that can deliver batches of small satellites to
space on a monthly or even weekly basis. Since
2018, Rocket Lab has launched 12 successful
missions and a total of 55 satellites to space for
a variety of research and commercial purposes.

Beck said the in-orbit traffic issues took a turn for the worst over the past 12 months. It was over that time that SpaceX has rapidly built up its Starlink constellation, growing it to include more than 700 internet-beaming satellites. It's already the largest satellite constellation by far, and the company plans to grow it to include between 12,000 and 40,000 total satellites. That's five times the total number of satellites humans have launched since the dawn of spaceflight in the late 1950s. It's not clear if traffic from its own satellites has also caused frustrations for SpaceX. The company did not respond to a request for comment.

Researchers have warned for decades that congestion in outer space could have devastating consequences. Kessler's warning said that if space traffic becomes too dense, a single collision between two objects could set off a disastrous chain reaction that effectively turns the space around Earth into an extraterrestrial wasteland. One piece of debris would hit a satellite, and that impact—much like a car crash, except at orbital speeds upwards of 17,000 miles an hour—could generate hundreds, if not thousands, of new pieces of debris in its own right. Those new pieces could hit other objects in orbit, which would hit other objects, and on and on, until low Earth orbit would be saturated with an increasing amount of uncontrollable projectiles. And any one of them could knock out a satellite, a launching rocket, or even an orbiting space station with humans inside.

Kessler Syndrome was central to the plot of 2013's "Gravity," in which satellite shrapnel caused a cascade of disastrous satellite collisions.

The question is whether it will remain fiction. Some experts warn areas of low-Earth orbit have already reached a critical mass of congestion.

SpaceX has said that it is determined to be a responsible steward of outer space. The company says it has equipped its Starlink satellites with the ability to automatically maneuver out of the way of other objects in orbit. SpaceX's constellation also orbits at lower altitudes than the most crowded areas, which NASA and international partners estimate is about 400 to 650 miles high. That's an ideal area for observation satellites that monitor the environment and is also home to swarms of debris. But Moriba Jah, an astrodynamicist at the University of Texas at Austin and a leading expert in space traffic, said most of Earth's orbit below about 750 miles is becoming a danger zone. Jah created a database to help track potential collisions in space, and an online chart uses dots to show how many objects are expected to pass within six miles of each other every 20 minutes. Over the past year, the dots have grown too dense to count. Jah hopes that more satellite operators and rocket companies, including SpaceX and Rocket Lab, will share real-time location data of their rockets and satellites to make the predictions more precise.

Neither company has done so.

Though there haven't been any collisions this year, Jah warns, it could be only a matter of time. Even if SpaceX can manage to keep its area in space clean, there's a line of other companies waiting to build their own giant constellations. Amazon and UK-based OneWeb plan to build their own telecom ventures also using hundreds of their own satellites. Adding to the problem are swarms of junk currently whizzing through space, including defunct rocket parts, dead satellites and debris from prior collisions and anti-satellite tests. That junk is practically impossible to clean up on a large scale. And it will take years, if not centuries, for it to naturally fall out of orbit.

The odds of avoiding disaster only become slimmer with each new satellite launch, Jah added. He remains optimistic that we can avoid Kessler Syndrome, even with swarms of satellites in orbit—but only if the SpaceXs and Amazons of the world agree to abide by certain rules and norms of behavior. "Absent that the answer is no," he said. Beck, the Rocket Lab CEO, said he is frustrated that so much of the conversation about space junk revolves around the risk of in-orbit collisions, and there's not as much conversation about how space traffic is already impacting the launch business. Satellite constellations can be particularly problematic, he said, because the satellites can fly fairly close together, forming a sort of blockade that can prevent rockets from squeezing through. In Rocket Lab's early days, Beck said, the company could pick a 30-minute timeframe on a given day and expect to reach orbit safely. Lately, the company has had to pick "half a dozen separate launch windows because we've got to shoot up in between a train of" satellites, Beck said. Still, Beck said that he's not opposed to SpaceX's plans or massive satellite constellations in general. Starlink, once operational, could provide huge benefits to life on Earth by making internet access available to the billions of people who still lack sufficient connectivity, he noted. But Beck said he is concerned about how rapidly he's seen traffic in space impact his own business. And he's worried that new players in the space industry could be reckless. "It's just a race to orbit, and there's just zero consideration for what environment we'll leave behind," he said. "Anyone flying a launch vehicle now needs to be really cognizant of their responsibilities."

Rocket Lab recently launched its own internal investigation into the traffic issue, hoping to determine how problematic it could be for the company as satellite constellations grow. But for now, Beck said, Rocket Lab would benefit from more precise tracking of in-space objects. The US military serves as the world's de-facto traffic cop because it operates an extensive databases of active satellites and space junk, but the military no longer wants that duty. NASA and military officials are pressing for the US government to hand traffic management duties over to the Department of Commerce, which could work to establish a more comprehensive and internationally collaborative tracking and management system.

NASA chief Jim Bridenstine pressed senators at a hearing last week to fund that effort, noting that even the International Space Station has had to dodge orbital debris three times so far this year, an unprecedented rate.

"We're providing global space situational awareness and space traffic management to the world for free," Bridenstine said at the hearing. "We need to take that data, combine it with commercial and international data to create a single integrated space picture that can be shared with the world. And—by the way—the world needs to support us in that effort." Congress last year chose to commission a study of the issue rather than greenlight the reform. Beck is also troubled by the fact that global regulation of space traffic has lagged far behind technology. The 1967 Outer Space Treaty, which remains the primary international document regulating activity in outer space, was agreed to at a time when only two governments were going to space. Now that more countries and commercial companies are also in the business of spaceflight, regulators are faced with a Catch-22: They don't want to create a lawless environment, but they're reticent to impose new rules for fear that other countries may become more dominant in space. Recent attempts to update rules on the international stage have been "incredibly inspiring, but also incredibly depressing," Beck said. Because even though countries were willing to come to the table, nothing has actually been agreed upon since the 1970s. "We are very pro-democratizing space," Beck said. "But it has to be done in a way that is responsible for each generation."

This article reminded me of *Ozark* and the drug deals that go on in that show:

Cocaine-Filled Plane Crashes in Mexico after High-Speed Airborne Chase

A light aircraft carrying almost half a ton of cocaine crashed in central Mexico after a high-speed airborne chase with authorities, and two people aboard died, the defense ministry said on Wednesday. Mexican military helicopters intercepted the plane in Mexican airspace and pursued it for hundreds of miles until it ran out of fuel and crashed in Botija, Queretaro on Monday, the ministry said in a statement. The plane was loaded with about 400 kilograms (880 pounds) of cocaine, the ministry added. In recent months a number of business jets have crashed or been abandoned in Central America and southern Mexico in an apparent uptick in aerial smuggling. Monday's crash came less than two weeks after a business jet reported stolen in Mexico crashed in a Guatemalan jungle near a hidden airstrip, leaving two men dead near an onboard stash of drugs and weapons. It had made a mysterious trip to Venezuela.

Here is an article that I thought was interesting:

Mcdonald's Is Paying Out 26 Million to Thousands of Workers after Settling a Wage Theft Lawsuit

McDonald's is paying out $26 million to workers after settling a wage-theft lawsuit. On Wednesday, a California Supreme Court judge approved a $26 million settlement, ending a yearlong battle over wage theft allegations. Roughly 34,000 McDonald's employees at corporate-owned locations across California will receive checks as part of the settlement. Workers will receive checks for an average of $333.52, with some receiving as much as $3,927.91, according to a representative for the plaintiffs. The original lawsuit was filed in 2013, on behalf of McDonald's employees in corporate locations in California. Workers alleged that McDonald's committed wage theft in various ways, including failing to pay all wages when due, failing to provide meal and rest breaks for workers, and failing to pay overtime wages or minimum wage.

McDonald's agreed to the $26 million settlement—which required the approval of a Los Angeles County Superior Court judge—last November. The settlement required the company to rework some policies related to overtime, rest breaks, and uniform practices, as well as provide training to inform employees of the correct practices. McDonald's said in a statement to Business Insider that the company is "committed to always doing right by our employees." "While we continue to believe our employment practices comply with the California Labor Code, we also believe resolving this lawsuit—filed back in January 2013—now, instead of engaging in further protracted litigation, is in the best interests of McDonald's, our company-owned restaurants and our employees," McDonald's statement continued. "This mutual agreement aligns with our ongoing commitment to providing employees with resources and training that continue to promote positive employee experiences."

People's new responsibilities that have been taken over by Will Coakley

Aaron Judge	Takes care of all the people who judge in the world with every home run he hits.
Cory Carlton	The Black God.
Adam Seaman	• A guy from the Bible. Many things he does have an impact on the world. (I know exactly who he was from the book in the past, but I will add that in this section when the time is right.)

Aaron Scott	• Moses. • Every time the word *awesome* is said, something great or good happens. Mac in *It's Always Sunny in Philadelphia*.
Steph Bortz	• Helped me get through my fear of the sun. Dee in *It's Always Sunny in Philadelphia*.
Sandra Correa	Addresses sun problems worldwide, especially in Spain.
Jacob Stewart and Jeff Veltri	The two guys who have helped me make this happen
Jeff Veltri	Joey from *Friends*.
Ava Arobo	My soul sister and my *Avatar* sister.
Rory Kadir and Ray Zayas	Business minds making sure we make progress in business daily, weekly, monthly, and yearly and that others learn from us.
Darren Bahn	Dictionary.
Dean Stewart	Dictionary.
Gino Marin	• Technology usage is starting to help us out everywhere with anything related to the word *gym*. • George from Seinfeld (his personality is perfect). All the signs led me to the fact that is first name starts with *G*, and so does *gym* and George.
Chris Zayas	Kramer.

Will Coakley	<ul><li>Chandler from *Friends*.</li><li>Jerry (he uses his first name, just like half the world knows my first name). Charlie in *It's Always Sunny in Philadelphia*.</li></ul>
Rodrigo	Ross from *Friends*.
Maya	<ul><li>Minds. Monica from *Friends*.</li></ul>
Rodrigo (sisters husband)	Can help me monitor the roads, lessening casualties, among other things. I have already been using him for this, and I think the roads are cleaner now. If it does not appear that way to people now, then wait for two or three more years.
Rebecca	<ul><li>Rachel from *Friends*. Elaine from *Seinfeld* (Rebecca Elsie), the white storm</li></ul>
Lauren Copp	Lisa Kudrow, Phoebe from *Friends*.
Francisco	Facebook.
Eric Sanchez	<ul><li>Stars—*Star Wars*—battles between sinners and saints. Every single star in the universe is instrumental to this cause, and Eric Sanchez's technology will put the good guys ahead by a long shot. Dennis in *Its Always Sunny in Philadelphia*.</li></ul>
Real creator	Dembe from *The Blacklist*.
Uncle John	Acts as God in England.
Frieda	Symbolizes freedom for America.
Marcus Walker	Change of seasons.
Tim Cogswell	Time.

Trevor Story	All of our stories, by his production on the field, especially since he is coming back from a rookie year when he was derailed by an injury.
Christian Yelich	Gets rid of all the hellish things in our society.
Dustin Pedroia	Going to help me control the periods so that many people aren't having kids.
Denard Span	Going to help me get rid of all the spam in the world.
Brett Donnelly	Stock market.
Silvia Fowles	• WNBA player. Going to help me get the foul situation corrected in sports.
Ryan Eggold	• Tom Keen from *The Blacklist*. Helping me keep relationships between girlfriends and boyfriends or husbands and wives intact for the long haul.
Christian Press	Helping me organize the press a little better so the athletes actually benefit from press conferences instead of feeling hate and disrespect.
Megan Koster	Fixes all the foster problems in the world.
Jackie Cook	The problems in Japanese.
Kim Le	The problems in North Korea.
Jaime Hoang	The problems in South Korea.
Mike Fiers	Gets rid of everything that makes us live in fear in the world.
Lagarette Blount	Helps me legalize marijuana in the US by his production on the field.

This is so we have all the teams covered for the cities in the United States, by their technology usage:

Aaron Scott	Philadelphia (everything except Phillies and Eagles)
Bradley Cooper	Philadelphia Eagles
Kevin Hart	Phillies
Kevin Kim	Philadelphia Phillies
Jeff Veltri	Everything from Washington except the Wizards
Andy Lee	Washington Wizards (joint effort)
Chris Lewis	Washington Wizards (joint effort)
Heather Fitchel	West Virginia
Olaide Olabanji	Canada (joint effort)
Fefe Dobson	Canada (joint effort)
Drake	Toronto
Jon Doveala	Ohio
Rory Kadir	Half of Florida teams
Frank Dinello	Half of Florida teams
Adam Seaman	New York Rangers
Jacob Stewart	New York Jets and Mets
Bill Coakley	New York Yankees
Chris Zayas	New York Giants
Mike Coppinger	New York Knicks
Will Coakley	Everything else in New York
Paul xxx	Upstate New York (joint effort)
George Gavagan	Upstate New York (joint effort)
Adam Burdell	Everything Pittsburgh except the Penguins

Reid Derco	Pittsburgh Penguins
Jennifer Lawrence	Kentucky
Angie Bell	New England except sports
Spose (rapper)	New England except sports
Eric Sanchez	New England except the Red Sox
John Goodman	Boston Red Sox
Carli Lloyd	New Jersey
Eminem	Detroit
Kevin Pearson	Tennessee
Sandra Bullock	Mississippi
Selena Gomez	Texas
Don Dixon	Arkansas
Ethan Stewart	Missouri
Chris Lewis	South Carolina
Reggie Bennett	North Carolina, VCU
Amy (Dr. Goldstein)	Arizona
Lauren Copp	Illinois (Chicago)
Sarah Wayne Callies (*Prison Break*)	Chicago (joint effort)
Ryan Austin Owens	Dallas
Kara Killmer (*Chicago Fire*)	Everything from Texas except the Dallas Cowboys
Brett Cameron	UCLA
Tracy Purdue	Purdue University
Ava Arobo	Baltimore
Michelle Beadle	San Antonio
Ronda Rousey	Vegas
Rachel (Meg's friend)	San Francisco (joint effort)

Matt McKulsky	San Francisco (joint effort)
Lela Loren (*Power*)	Sacramento and its surrounding areas
G-Eazy (rapper)	Oakland
Lewis Boore	San Diego
Jacob Latimore (*Collateral Beauty*)	Milwaukee, Wisconsin
Atmosphere (rapper)	Minnesota (joint effort)
Adam Young (Owl City)	Minnesota (joint effort)
Omari Hardwick (*Power*)	Georgia
Dyme Def (rapper)	Washington (joint effort)
Ray Zayas	Washington (joint effort)
Jenn Jiron	Hawaii
Tinie Tempah (rapper)	United Kingdom
Dominic Purcell (*Prison Break*)	United Kingdom
Lily James (*Baby Driver*)	United Kingdom
Kate Moss (model)	United Kingdom
Jesse Spencer (*Chicago Fire*)	Australia
Miranda Kerr (model)	Australia
Amaury Nolasco (*Prison Break*)	Puerto Rico (joint effort)
Rico Plumb	Puerto Rico (joint effort)
Joan Smalls (model)	Puerto Rico (joint effort)

Priena	Portugal
Sandra Correa	Spain
Rodrigo	Spain
Shakira	Spain
Barbara Palvin (model)	Hungary
Jackie Cook	Columbia and Ecuador
Alessandra Ambrosio (model)	Brazil (joint effort)
Paola (Sanchez's girl)	Brazil (joint effort)
Natalia Vodianova (model)	Russia
Lara Stone (model)	Netherlands
Liu Wen (model)	China
Rose Bertrand (model)	Belgium
Cardi B	Twins
Kameron Langley (college basketball player)	Fixing the issues at Langley High School
Roman Penn (college basketball player)	Going to fix the problems at the University of Pennsylvania
Xavier Johnson (college basketball player)	Helping the issues at Xavier University

Printed in the USA
CPSIA information can be obtained
at www.ICGtesting.com
CBHW031604150824
13252CB00010B/118